Volume 4
By Ako Yutenji

TOKYOPOP®

HAMBURG // LOS ANGELES // TOKYO

Liling-Po Vol. 4
created by Ako Yutenji

Translation - Takae Brewer
English Adaptation - Michele Ashamalla
Retouch and Lettering - Alyson Stetz
Production Artist - Fawn Lau
Cover Design - Al-Insan Lashley
Editor - Julie Taylor

Digital Imaging Manager - Chris Buford
Production Manager - Jennifer Miller
Managing Editor - Lindsey Johnston
VP of Production - Ron Klamert
Publisher and E.I.C. - Mike Kiley
President and C.O.O. - John Parker
C.E.O. and Chief Creative Officer - Stuart Levy

A  Manga

TOKYOPOP Inc.
5900 Wilshire Blvd. Suite 2000
Los Angeles, CA 90036

E-mail: info@TOKYOPOP.com
Come visit us online at www.TOKYOPOP.com

ISBN: 1-59532-522-0

First TOKYOPOP printing: April 2006
10 9 8 7 6 5 4 3 2 1
Printed in the USA

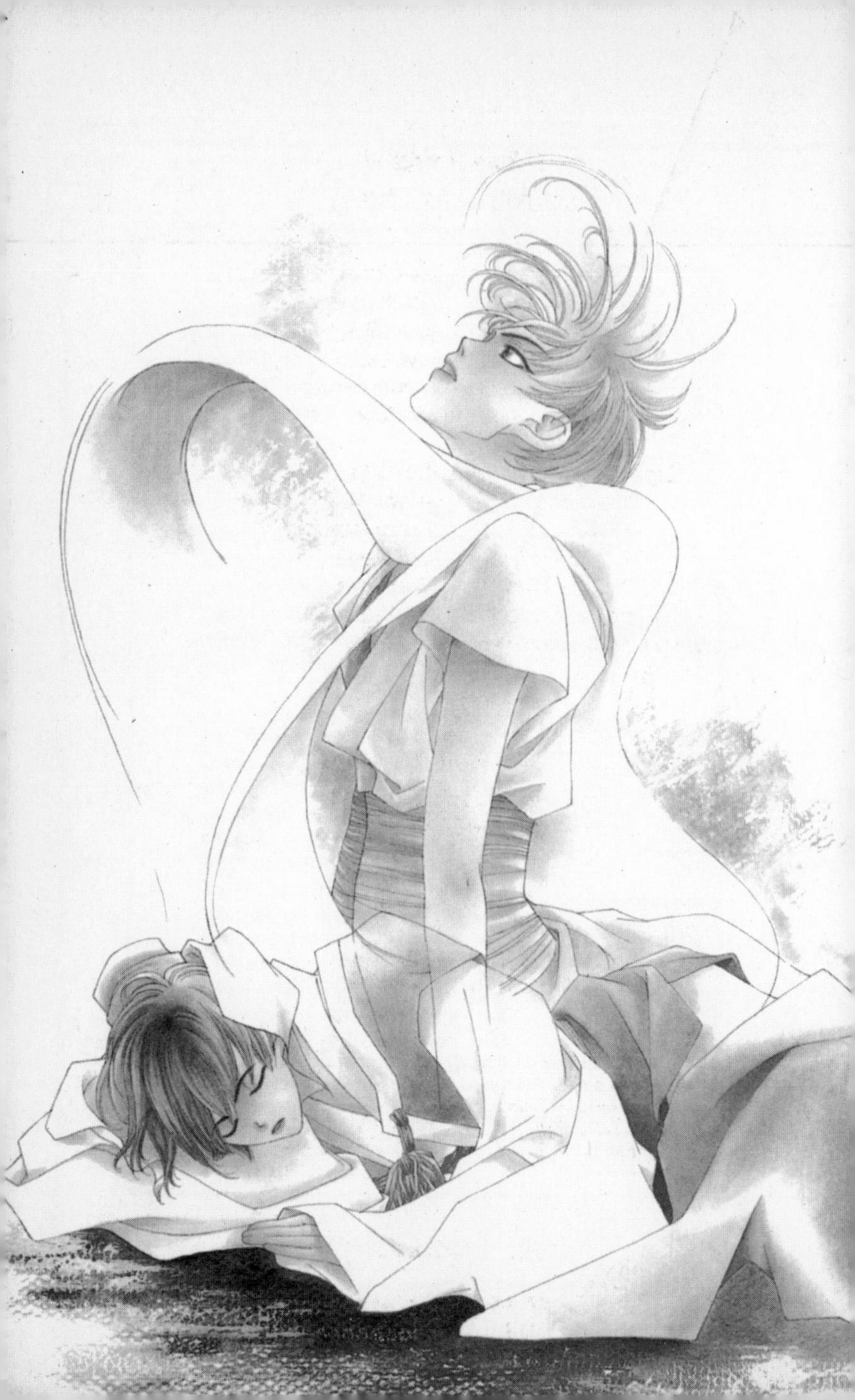

STORY

Liling-Po
Liling-Po is a boy who later becomes a master thief. He steals all Eight Great Treasures and becomes known throughout China.

Riko
Riko is Liling-Po's father, a weaver, and one of the ten great artists.

Ria-hu
Ria-hu is Liling-Po's mother, a textile-dyeing artist, and one of the ten great artists.

Liling-Po is a master thief who stole the Eight Great Treasures from the palace. He is known all over China. When young, he lived in the palace of Emperor Koku-ryo-ko with his parents and other imperial artists who all loved Liling-Po dearly. One day, Liling-Po's parents incured the emperor's wrath and were brutally murdered in front of Liling-Po. Some of the other artists escaped from the palace with Liling-Po and found refuge at a local temple.

Liling-Po gradually recovered from the death of his parents. One day, Toyo, one of imperial artists who remained at the palace, found his way to the temple where Liling-Po and the others were hiding. Toyo stayed with them to spy on Liling-Po and the artists and report back to the emperor.

Then a man who was sent by the emperor came to the temple and kidnapped Liling-Po. Liling-Po is now a hostage at the palace and waits for Shagen and the others to rescue him...

CHARACTER PROFILE

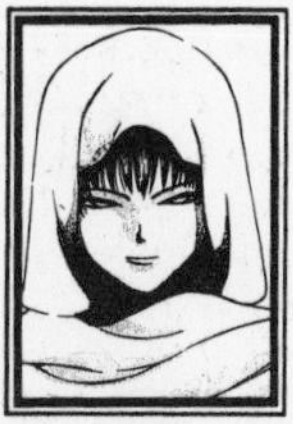

Toyo

Toyo is a painter and one of the ten great artists.

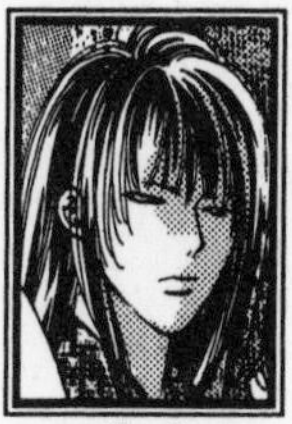

Fu-I

Fu-I is a ceramics artist and one of the ten great artists.

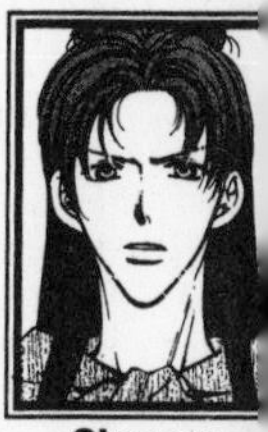

Shagen

Shagen is a swor making master an leader of the te great artists.

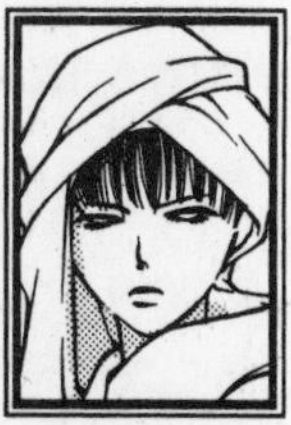

Yoko

Yoko is a sculptor and one of the ten great artists.

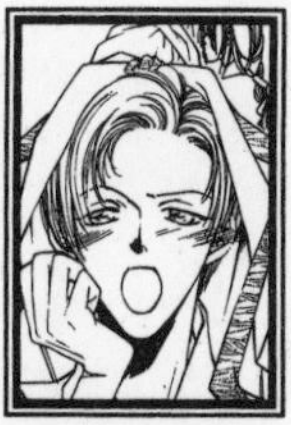

Oh-haku-to

Oh-haku-to is a gyokki artist and one of the ten great artists.

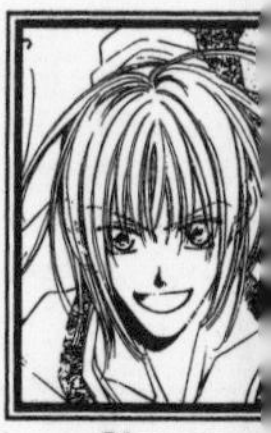

Shu-yu

Shu-yu is a cloison artist and one of t ten great artists.

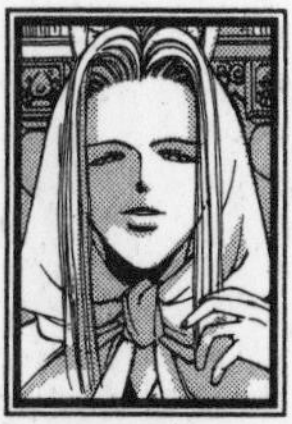

Koku-ryo-ko

Koku-ryo-ko is the cruel and oppressive emperor.

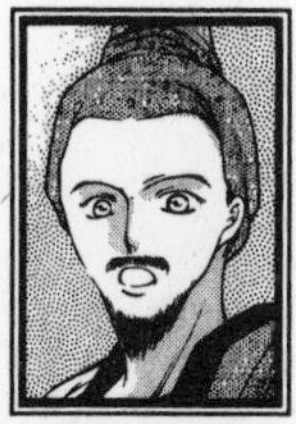

Zen-yu-shin

Zen-yu-shin is a metalsmith and one of the ten great artists.

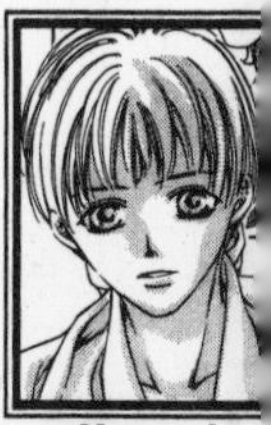

Han-rei

Han-rei is a lacqu ware artist and o of the ten gre artists.

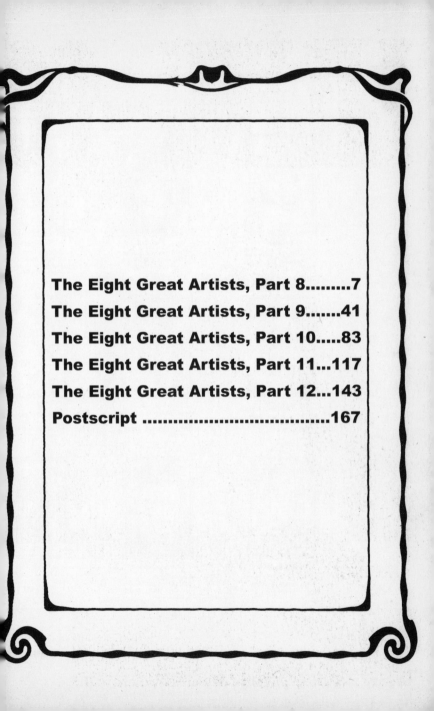

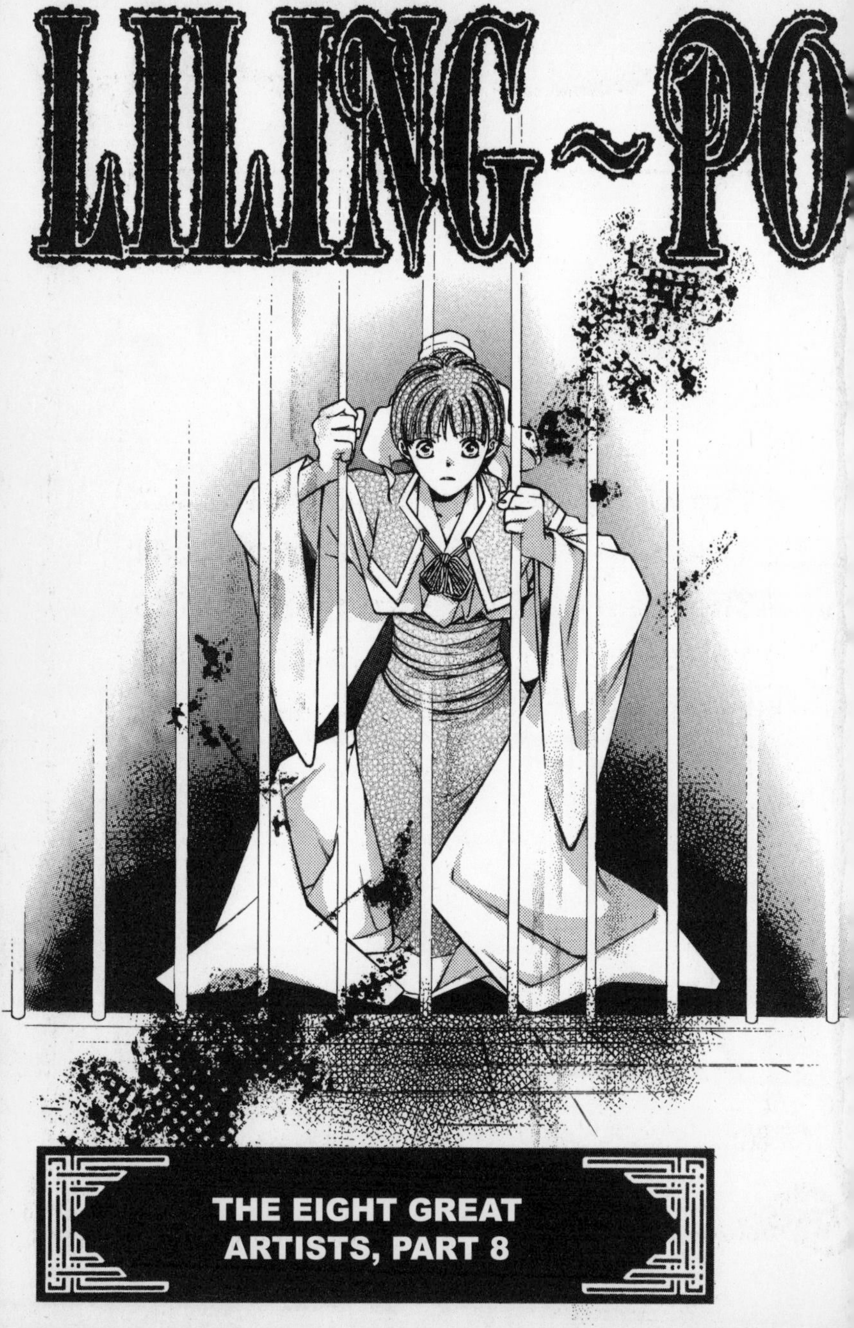
LILING~PO
THE EIGHT GREAT ARTISTS, PART 8

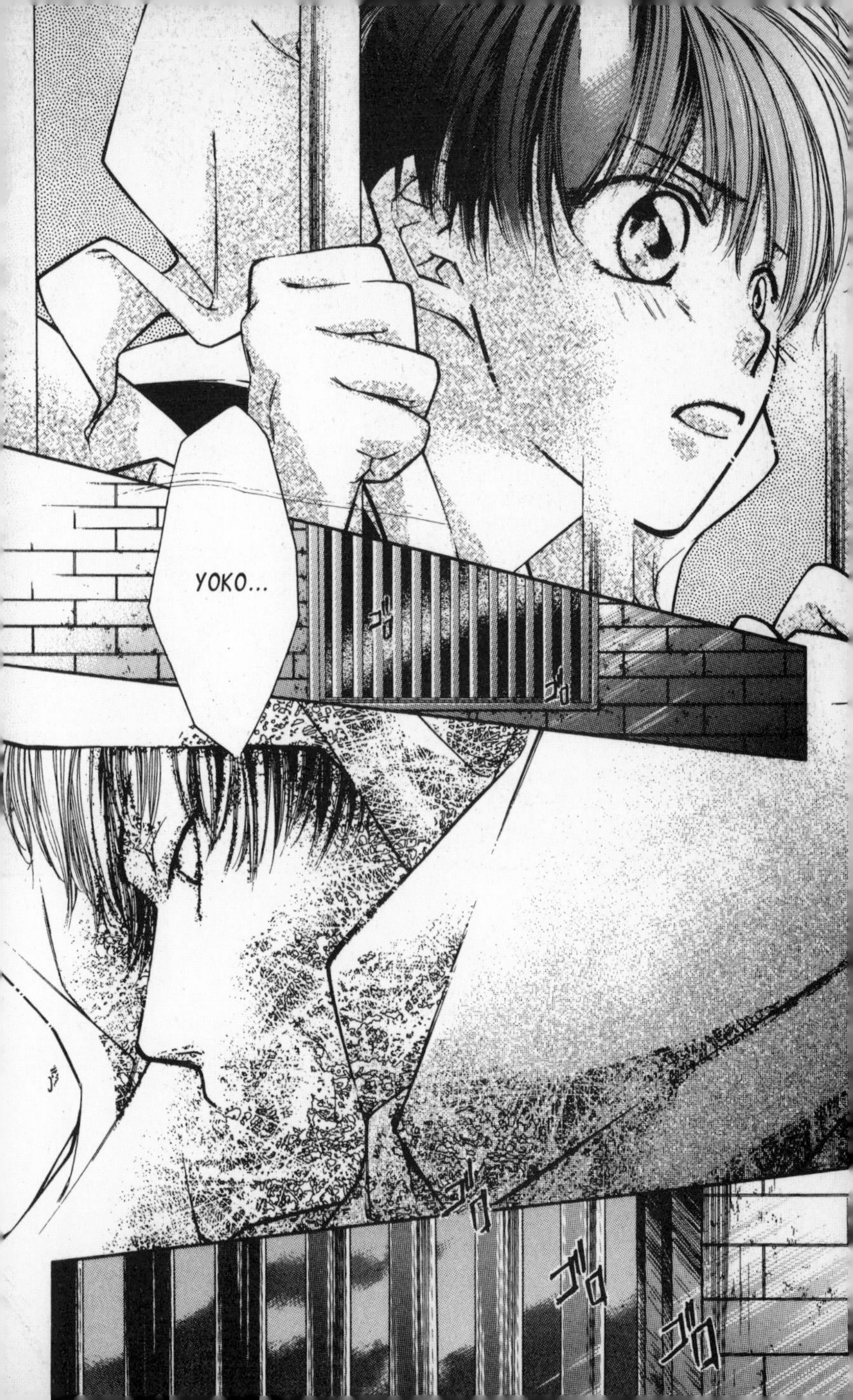
YOKO...
ゴロ
ゴロ
ゴロ

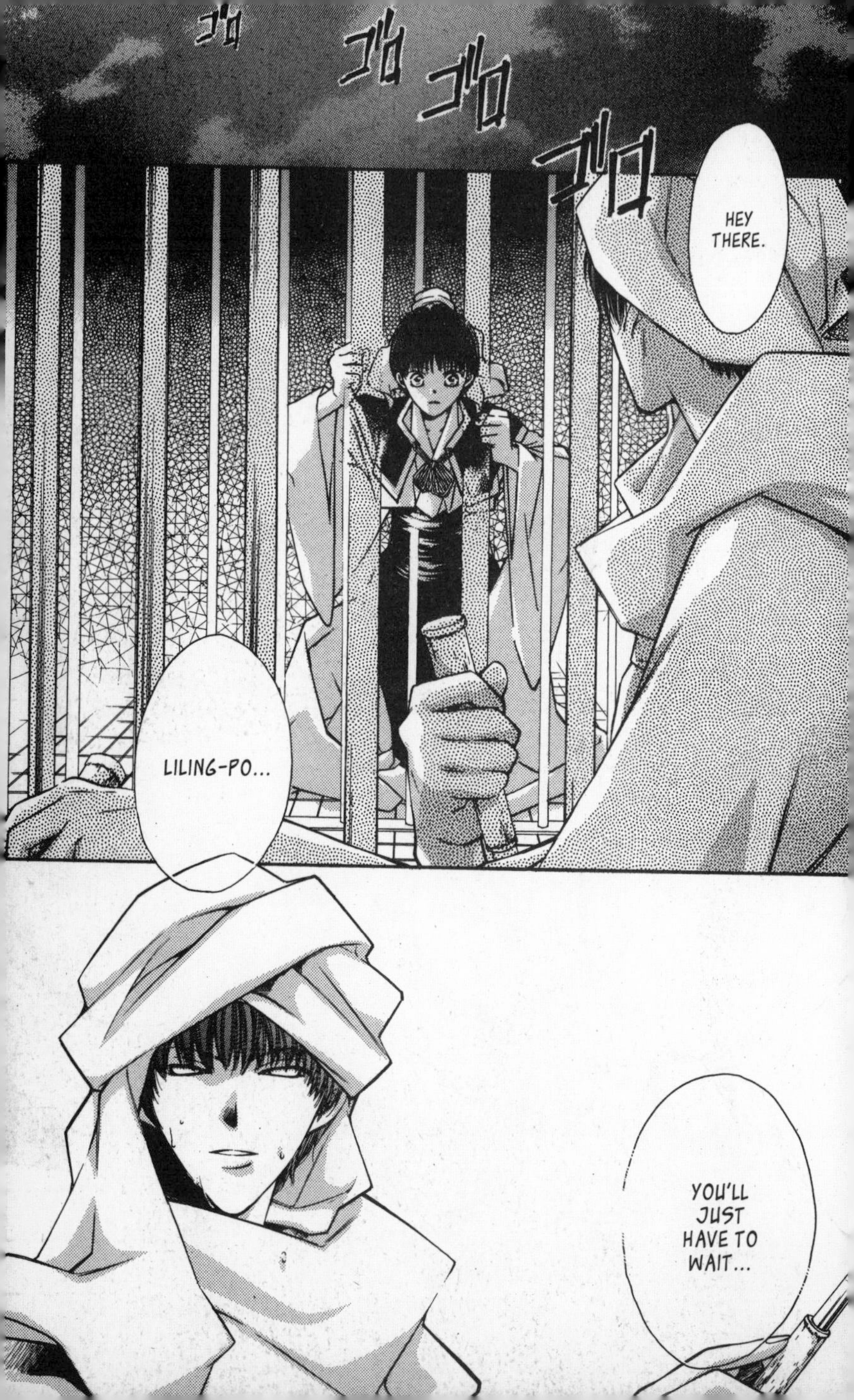
ゴロ ゴロ ゴロ ゴロ
HEY THERE.
LILING-PO...
YOU'LL JUST HAVE TO WAIT...

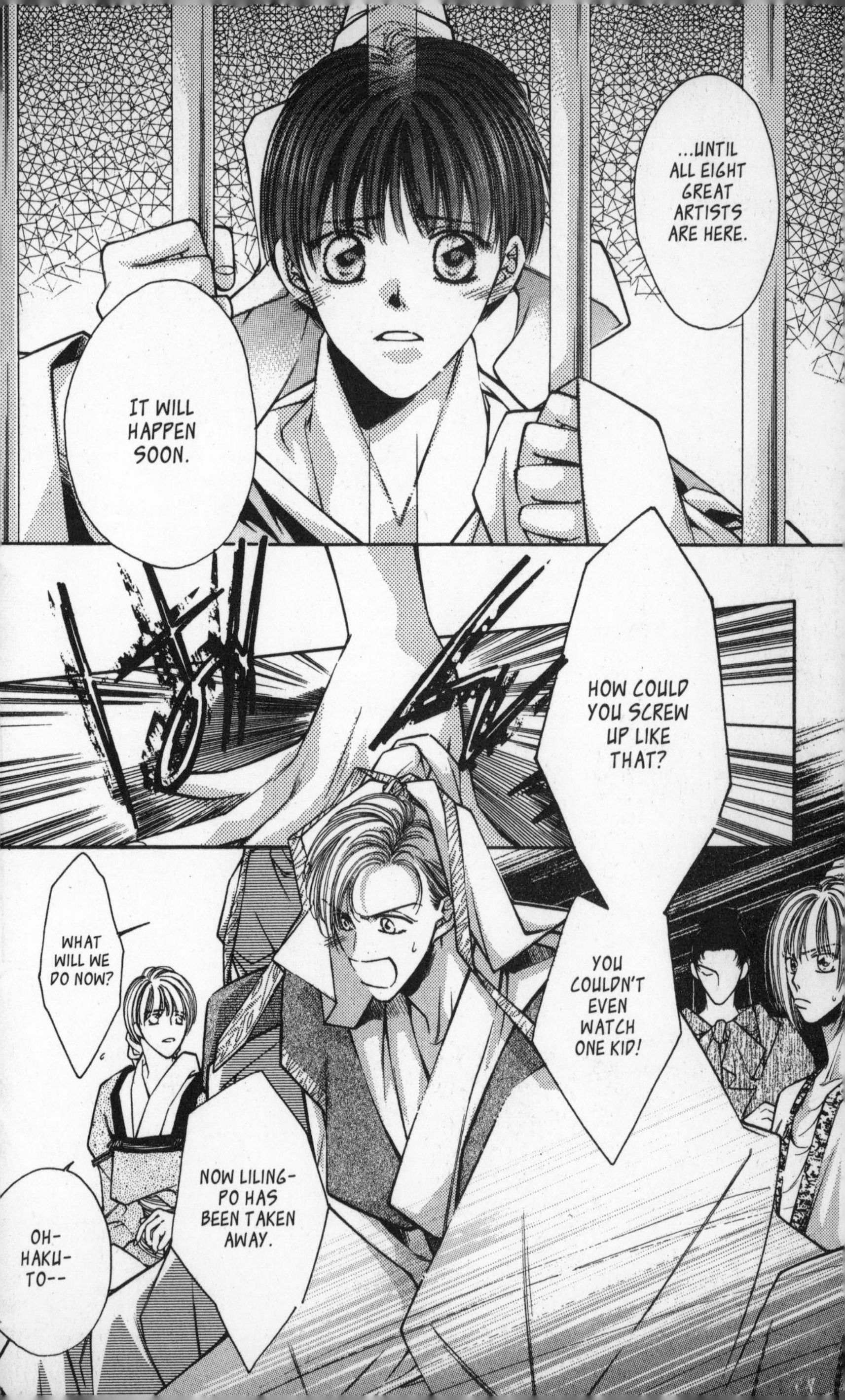
...UNTIL ALL EIGHT GREAT ARTISTS ARE HERE.
IT WILL HAPPEN SOON.
HOW COULD YOU SCREW UP LIKE THAT?
YOU COULDN'T EVEN WATCH ONE KID!
NOW LILING-PO HAS BEEN TAKEN AWAY.
WHAT WILL WE DO NOW?
OH- HAKU-TO--

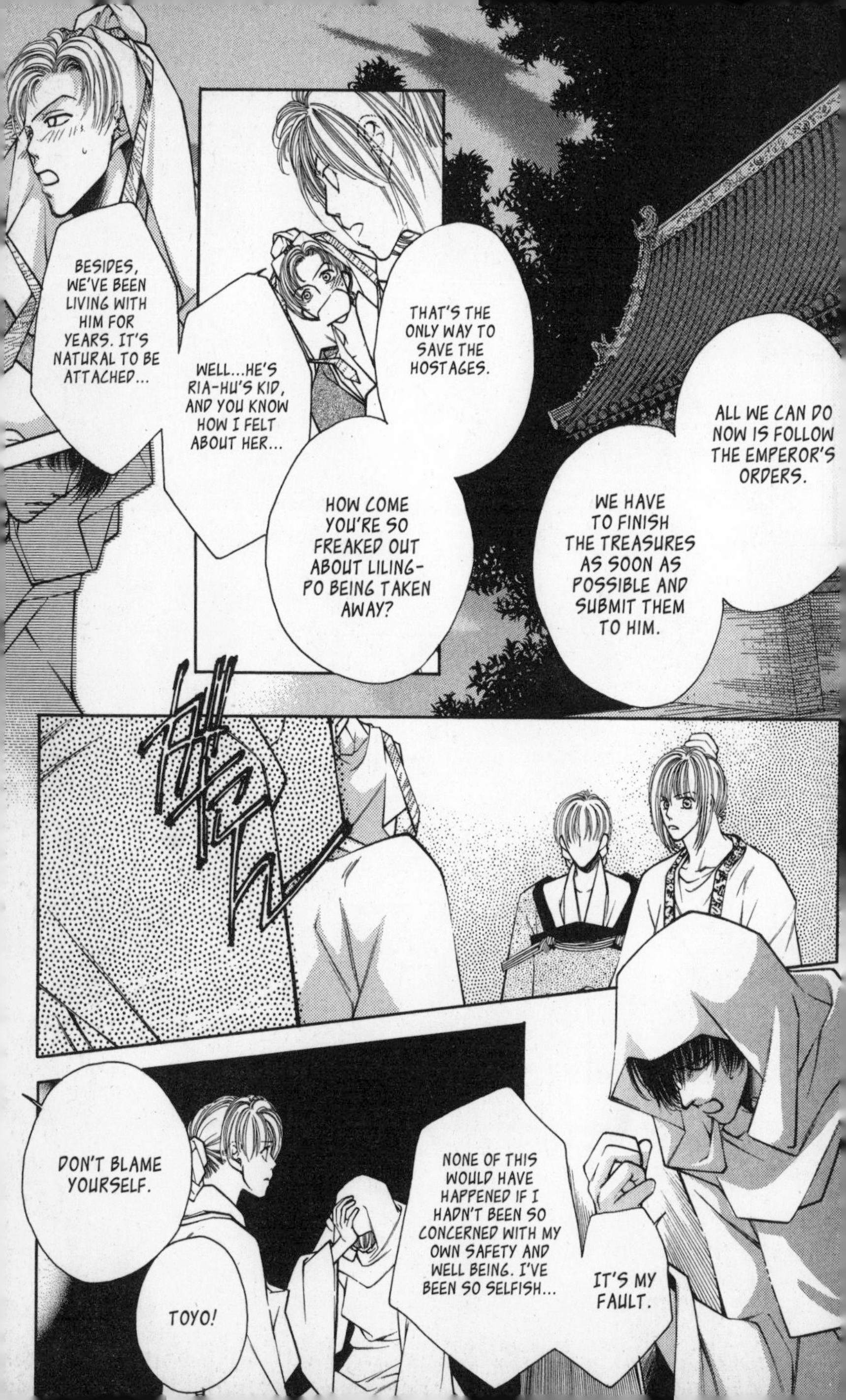
ALL WE CAN DO NOW IS FOLLOW THE EMPEROR'S ORDERS.
WE HAVE TO FINISH THE TREASURES AS SOON AS POSSIBLE AND SUBMIT THEM TO HIM.
THAT'S THE ONLY WAY TO SAVE THE HOSTAGES.
HOW COME YOU'RE SO FREAKED OUT ABOUT LILING-PO BEING TAKEN AWAY?
WELL...HE'S RIA-HU'S KID, AND YOU KNOW HOW I FELT ABOUT HER...
BESIDES, WE'VE BEEN LIVING WITH HIM FOR YEARS. IT'S NATURAL TO BE ATTACHED...
IT'S MY FAULT.
NONE OF THIS WOULD HAVE HAPPENED IF I HADN'T BEEN SO CONCERNED WITH MY OWN SAFETY AND WELL BEING. I'VE BEEN SO SELFISH...
DON'T BLAME YOURSELF.
TOYO!

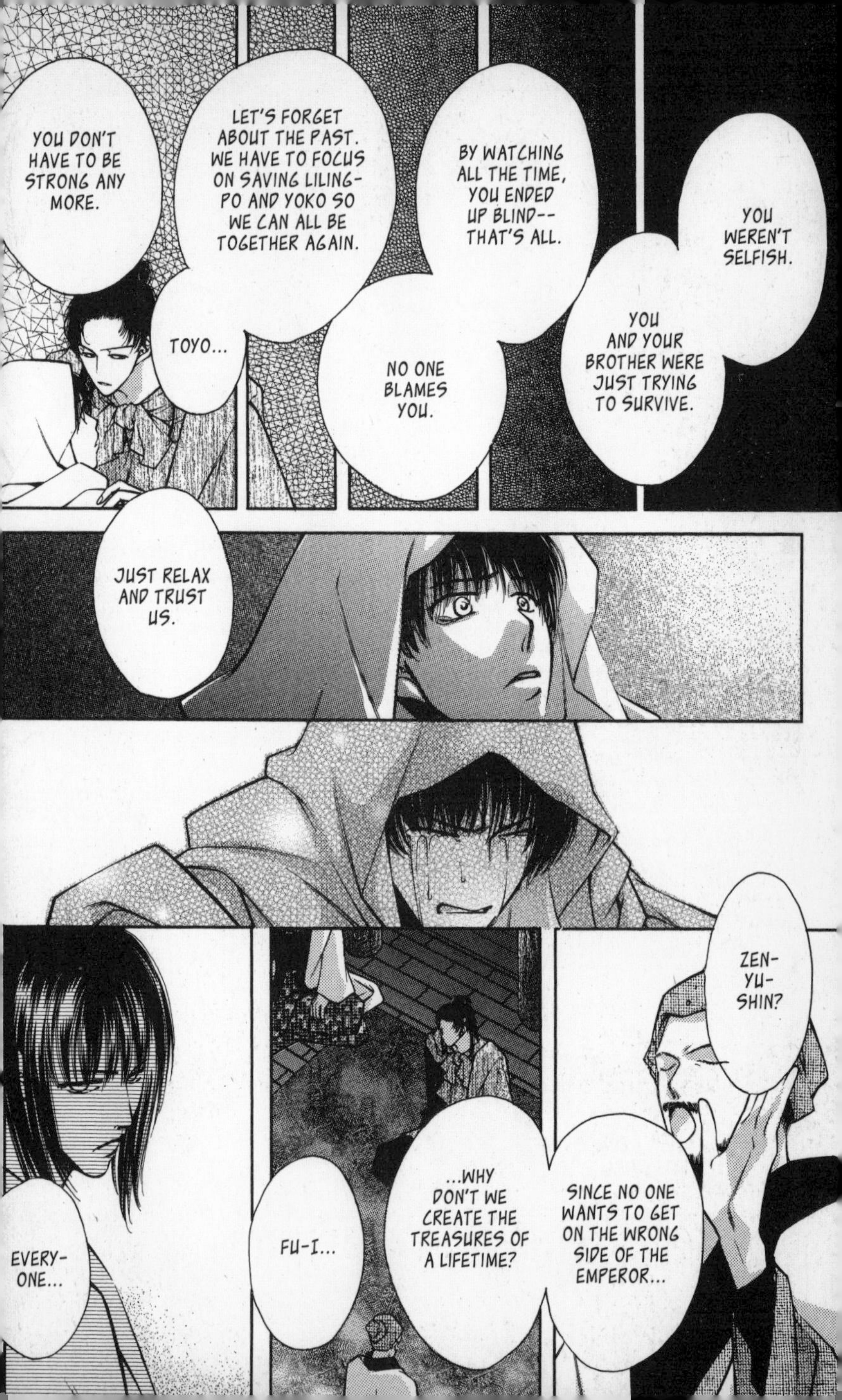
YOU WEREN'T SELFISH.
YOU AND YOUR BROTHER WERE JUST TRYING TO SURVIVE.
BY WATCHING ALL THE TIME, YOU ENDED UP BLIND-- THAT'S ALL.
NO ONE BLAMES YOU.
LET'S FORGET ABOUT THE PAST. WE HAVE TO FOCUS ON SAVING LILING-PO AND YOKO SO WE CAN ALL BE TOGETHER AGAIN.
TOYO...
YOU DON'T HAVE TO BE STRONG ANY MORE.
JUST RELAX AND TRUST US.
ZEN-YU-SHIN?
SINCE NO ONE WANTS TO GET ON THE WRONG SIDE OF THE EMPEROR...
...WHY DON'T WE CREATE THE TREASURES OF A LIFETIME?
FU-I...
EVERY-ONE...

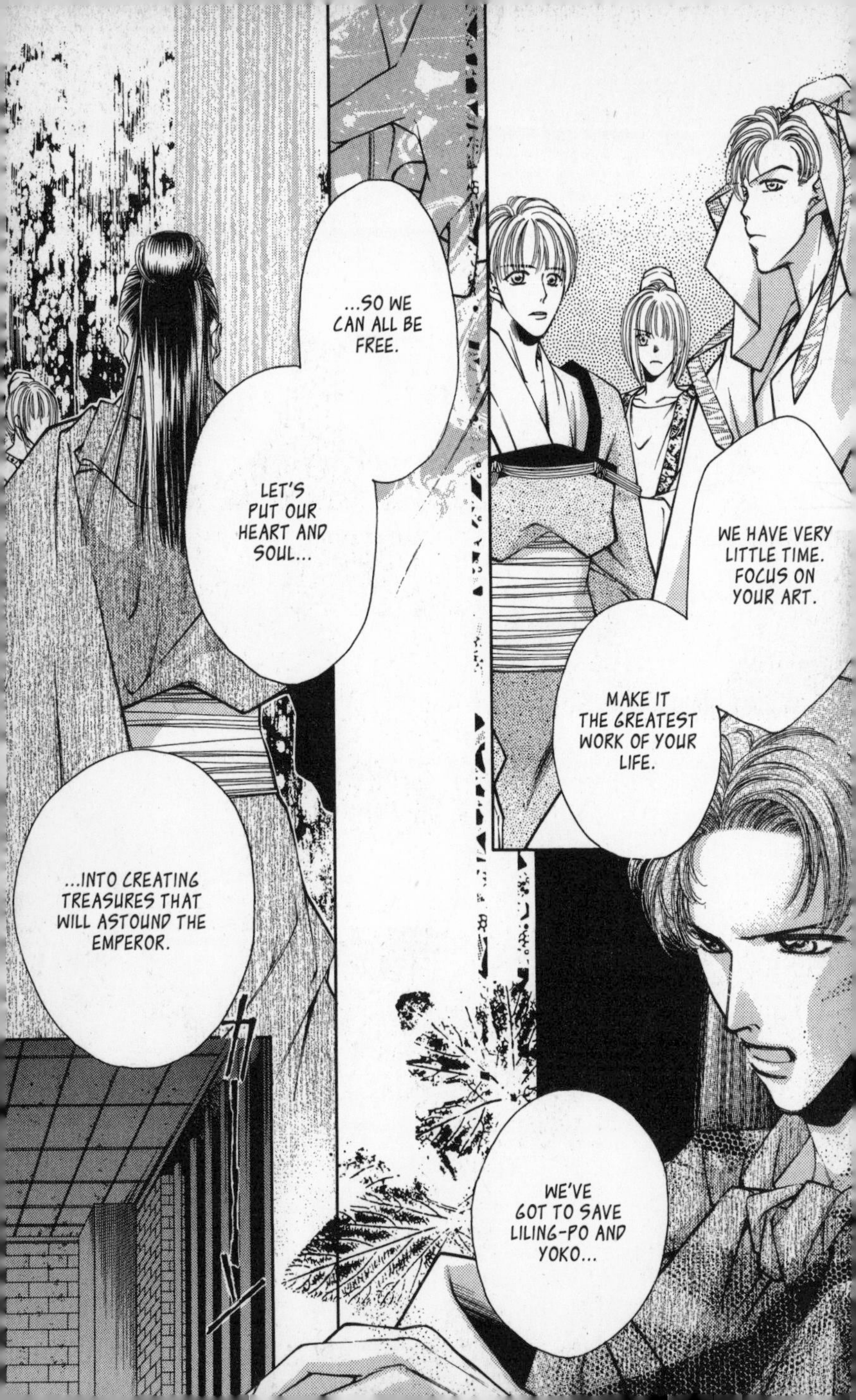

WE HAVE VERY LITTLE TIME. FOCUS ON YOUR ART.
MAKE IT THE GREATEST WORK OF YOUR LIFE.
WE'VE GOT TO SAVE LILING-PO AND YOKO...
...SO WE CAN ALL BE FREE.
LET'S PUT OUR HEART AND SOUL...
...INTO CREATING TREASURES THAT WILL ASTOUND THE EMPEROR.

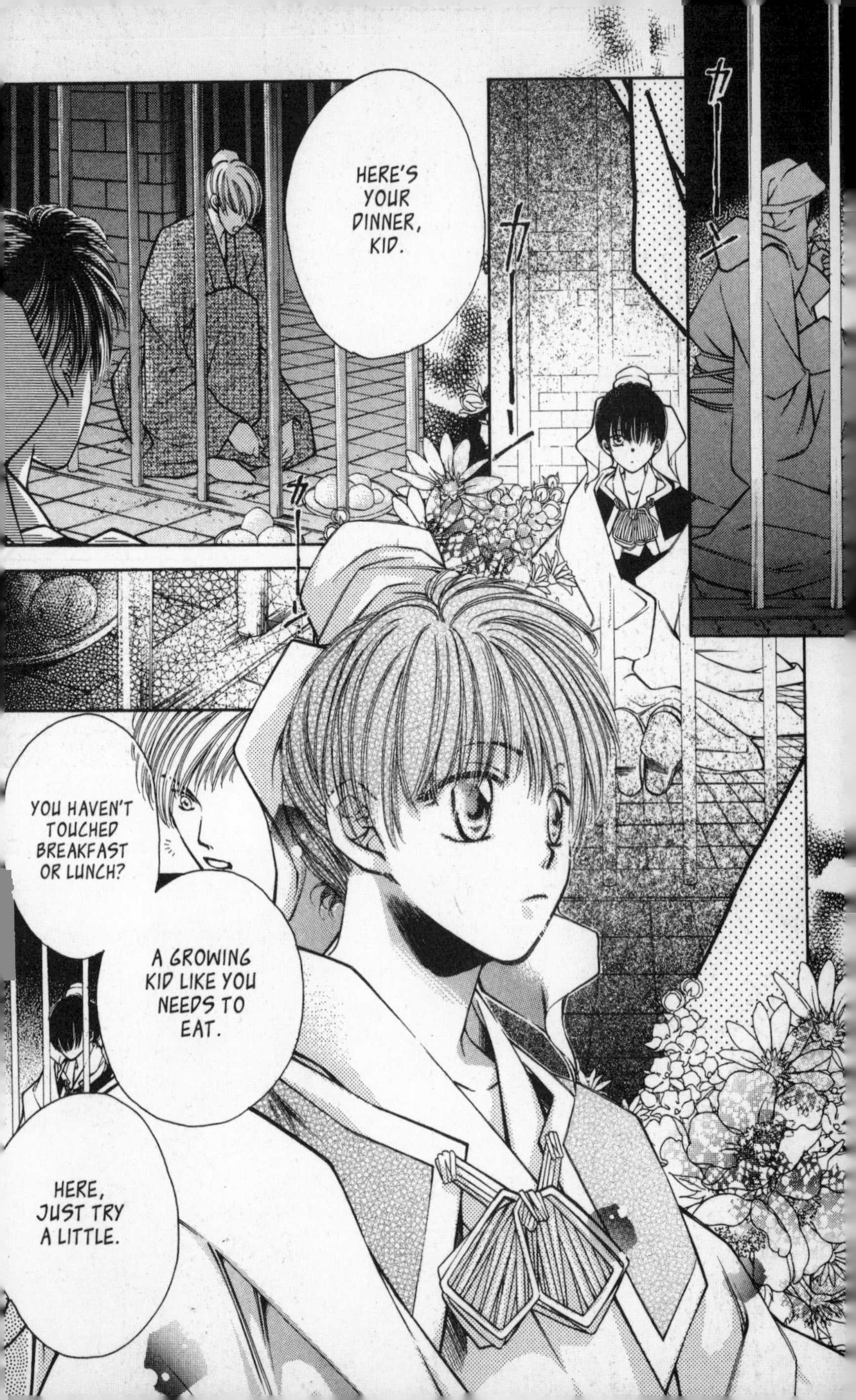
HERE'S YOUR DINNER, KID.
YOU HAVEN'T TOUCHED BREAKFAST OR LUNCH?
A GROWING KID LIKE YOU NEEDS TO EAT.
HERE, JUST TRY A LITTLE.

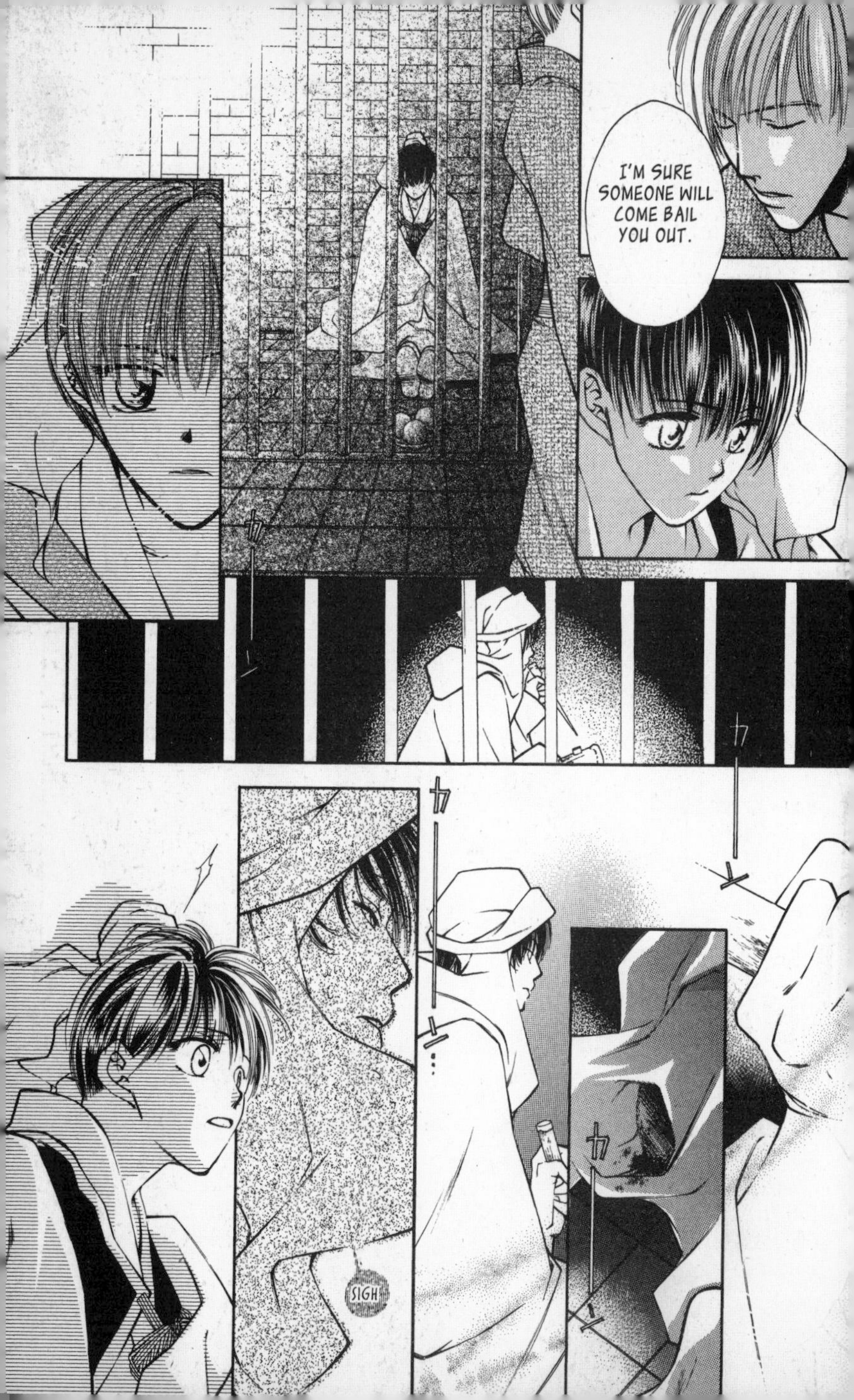
I'M SURE SOMEONE WILL COME BAIL YOU OUT.
SIGH

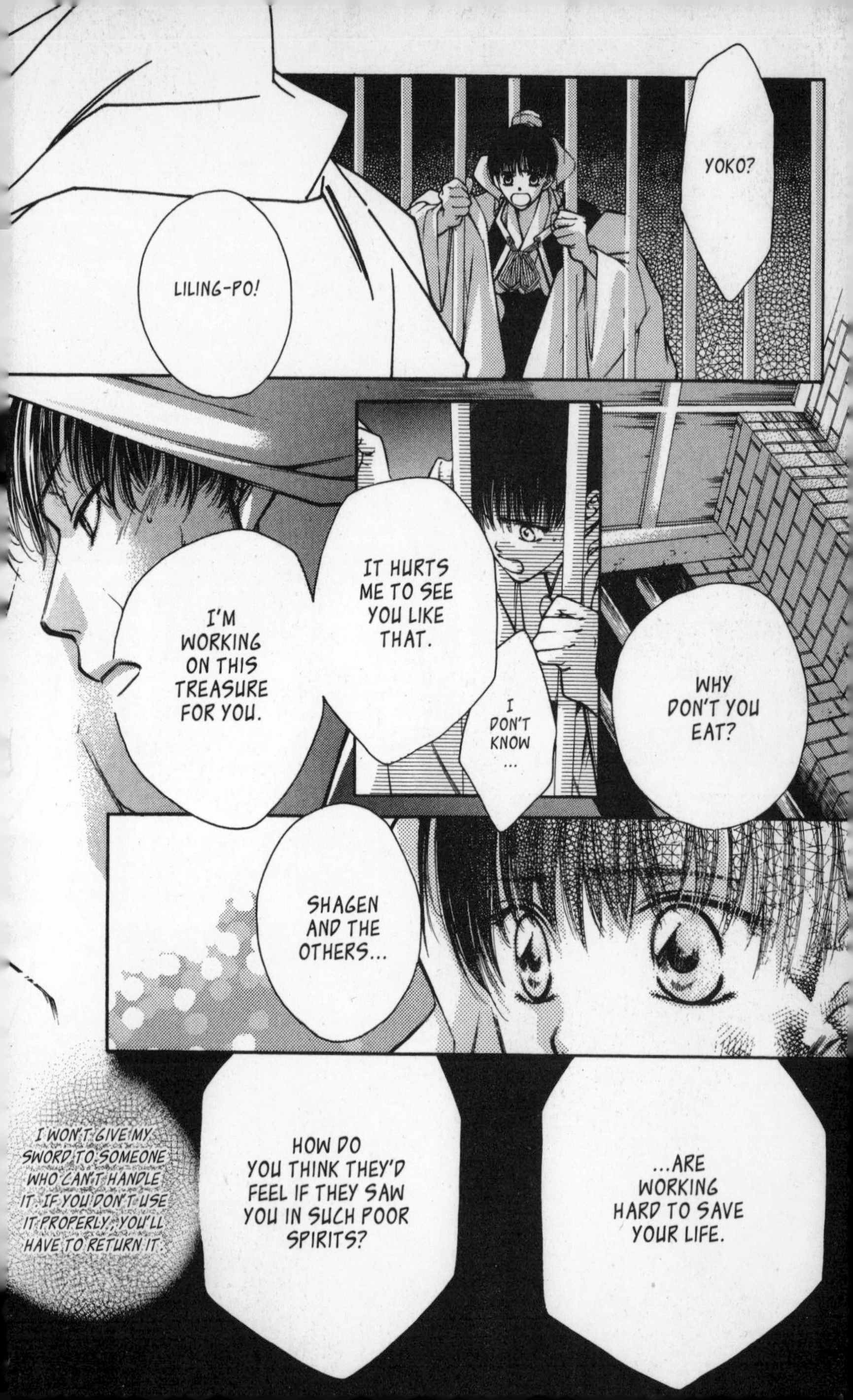
YOKO?
LILING-PO!
WHY DON'T YOU EAT?
I DON'T KNOW...
IT HURTS ME TO SEE YOU LIKE THAT.
I'M WORKING ON THIS TREASURE FOR YOU.
SHAGEN AND THE OTHERS...
...ARE WORKING HARD TO SAVE YOUR LIFE.
HOW DO YOU THINK THEY'D FEEL IF THEY SAW YOU IN SUCH POOR SPIRITS?
I WON'T GIVE MY SWORD TO SOMEONE WHO CAN'T HANDLE IT. IF YOU DON'T USE IT PROPERLY, YOU'LL HAVE TO RETURN IT.

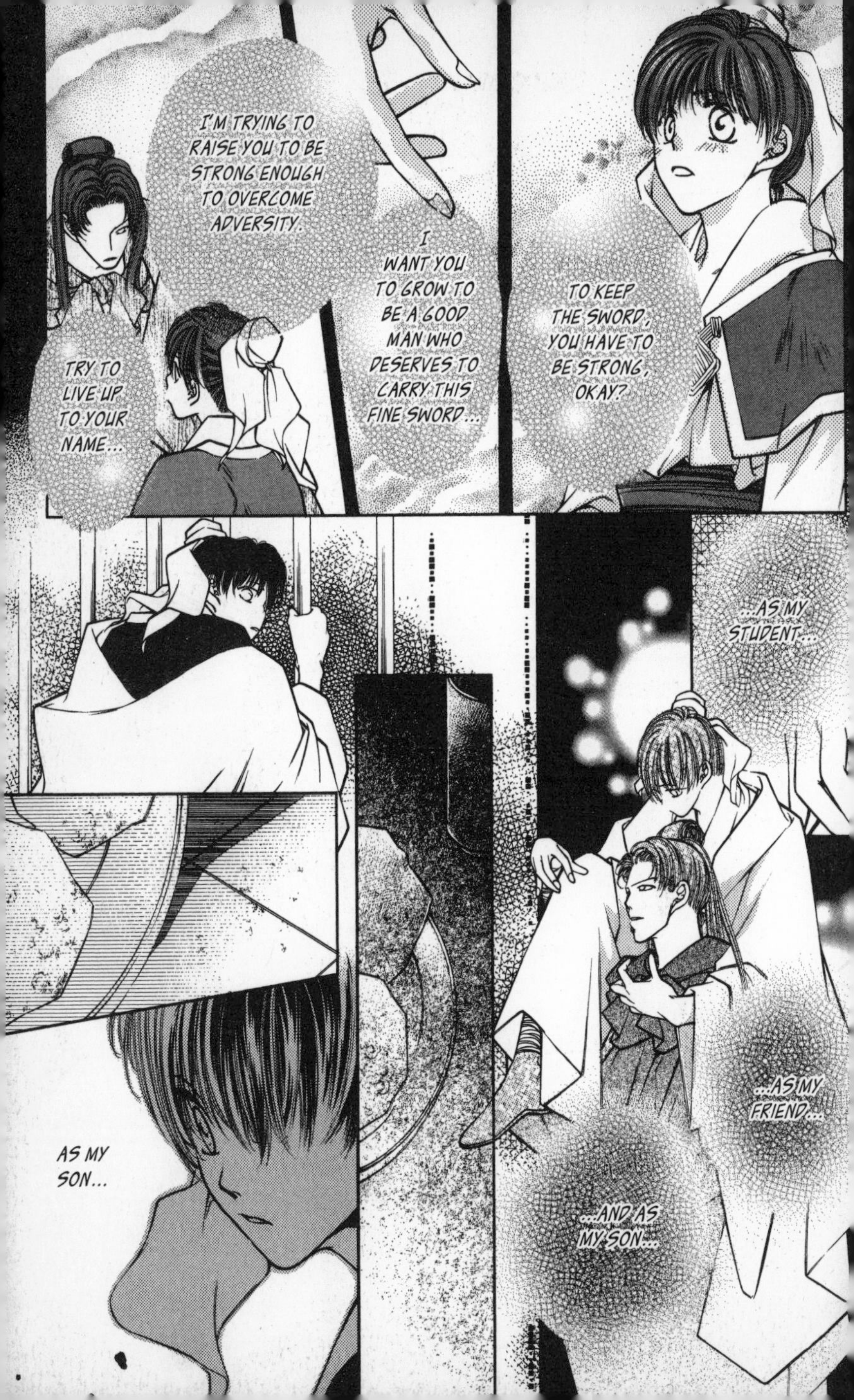
TO KEEP THE SWORD, YOU HAVE TO BE STRONG, OKAY?
I'M TRYING TO RAISE YOU TO BE STRONG ENOUGH TO OVERCOME ADVERSITY.
I WANT YOU TO GROW TO BE A GOOD MAN WHO DESERVES TO CARRY THIS FINE SWORD...
TRY TO LIVE UP TO YOUR NAME...
...AS MY STUDENT...
...AS MY FRIEND...
...AND AS MY SON...
AS MY SON...

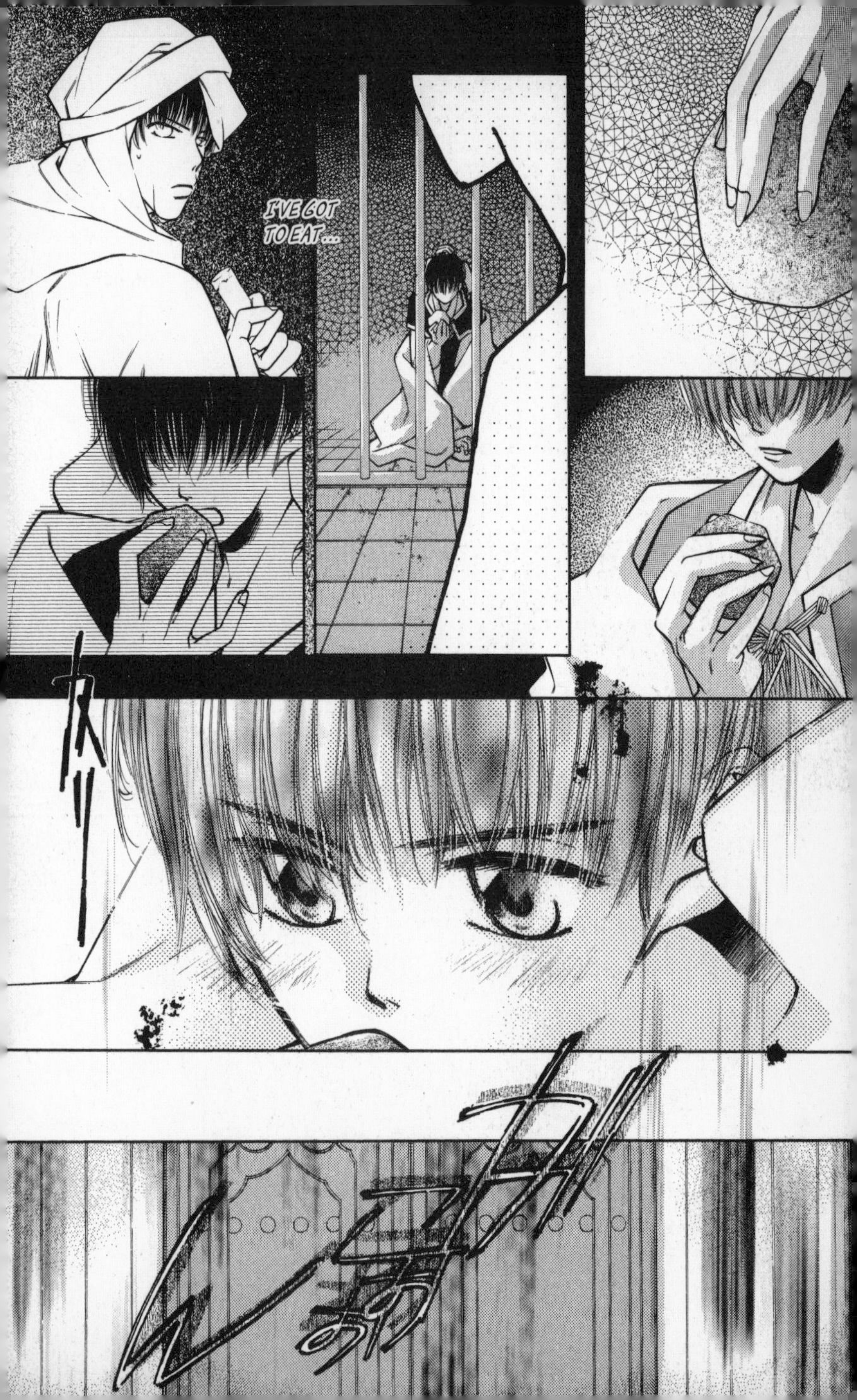
I'VE GOT TO EAT...

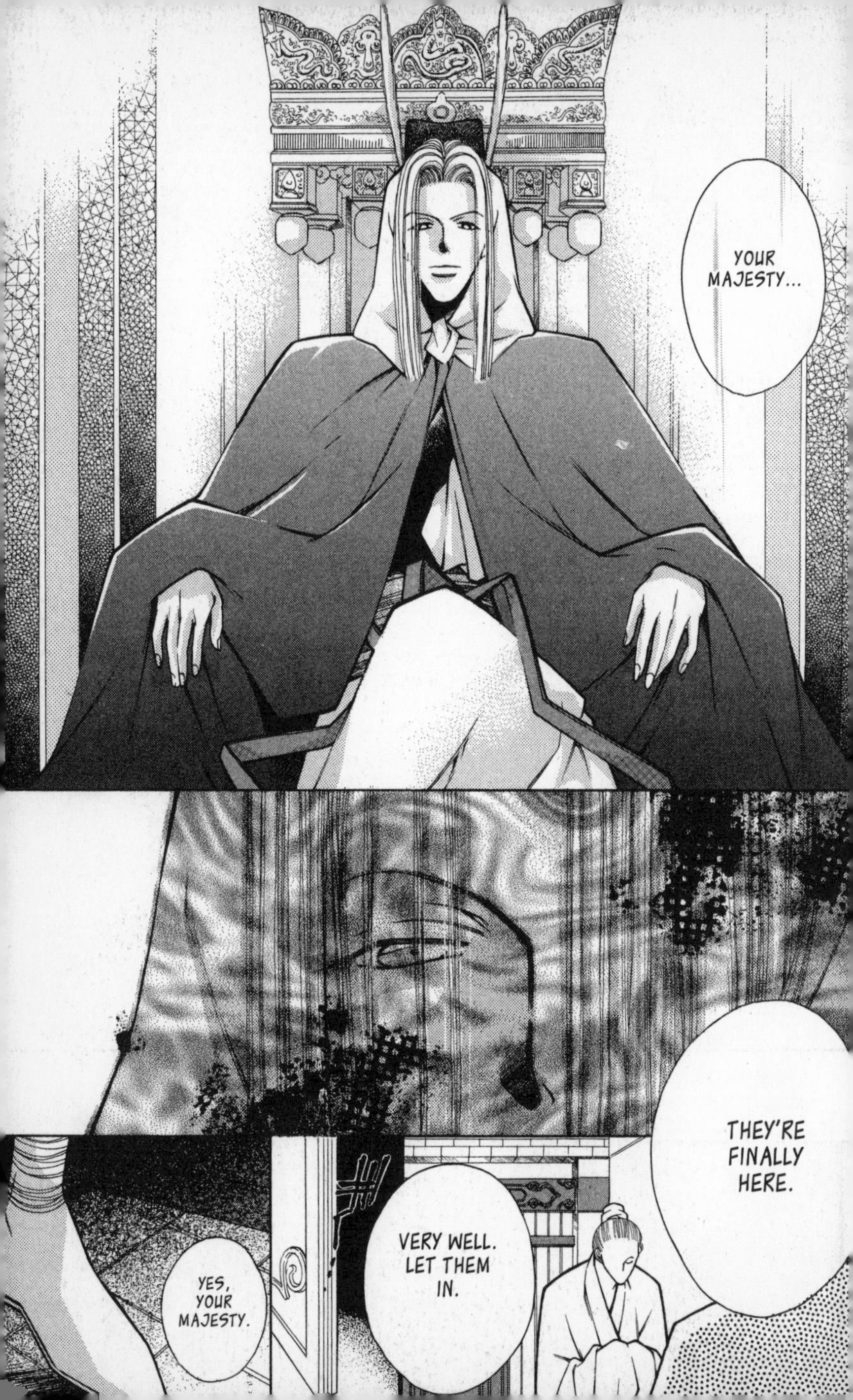
YOUR MAJESTY...
THEY'RE FINALLY HERE.
VERY WELL. LET THEM IN.
YES, YOUR MAJESTY.

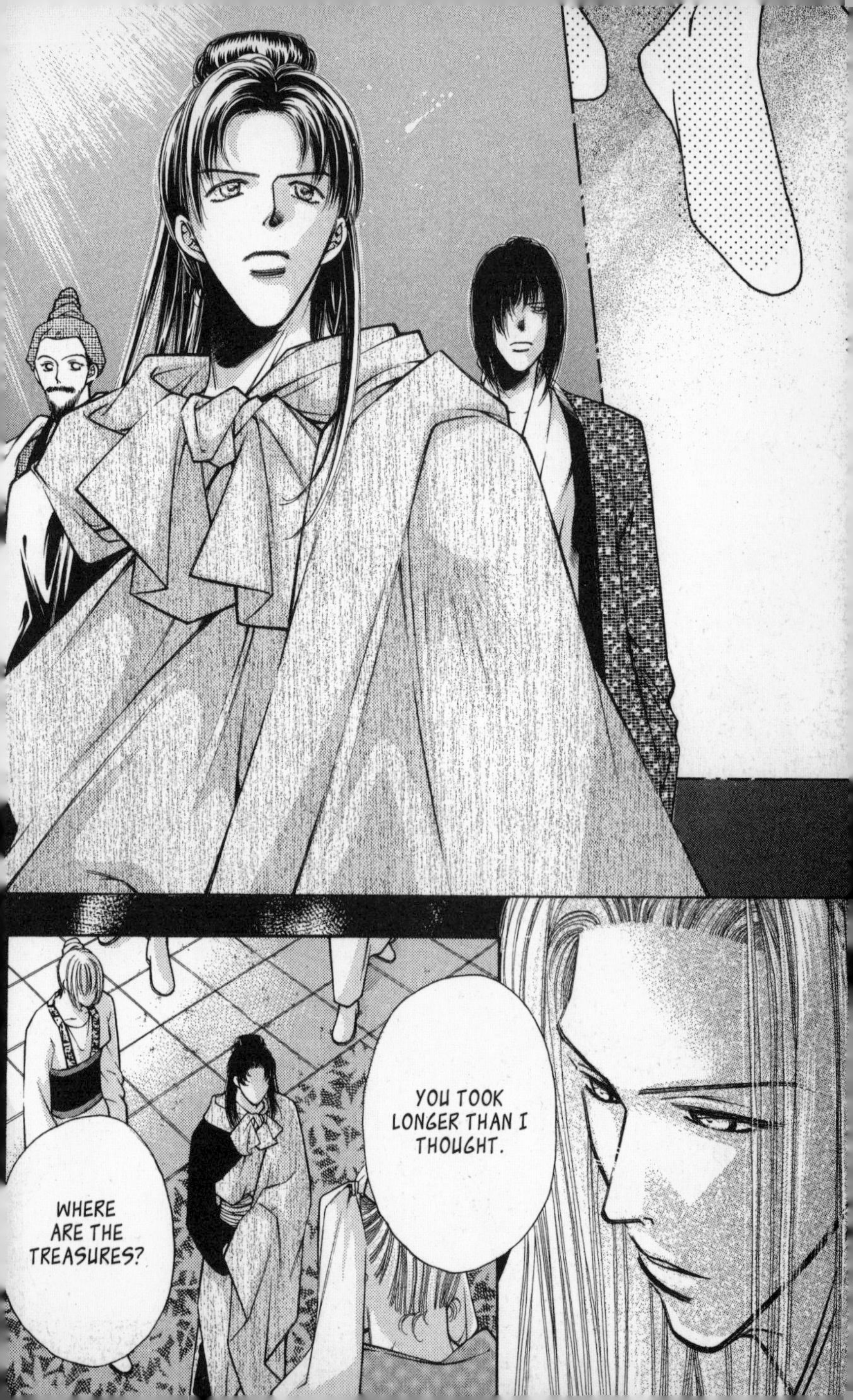
YOU TOOK LONGER THAN I THOUGHT.
WHERE ARE THE TREASURES?

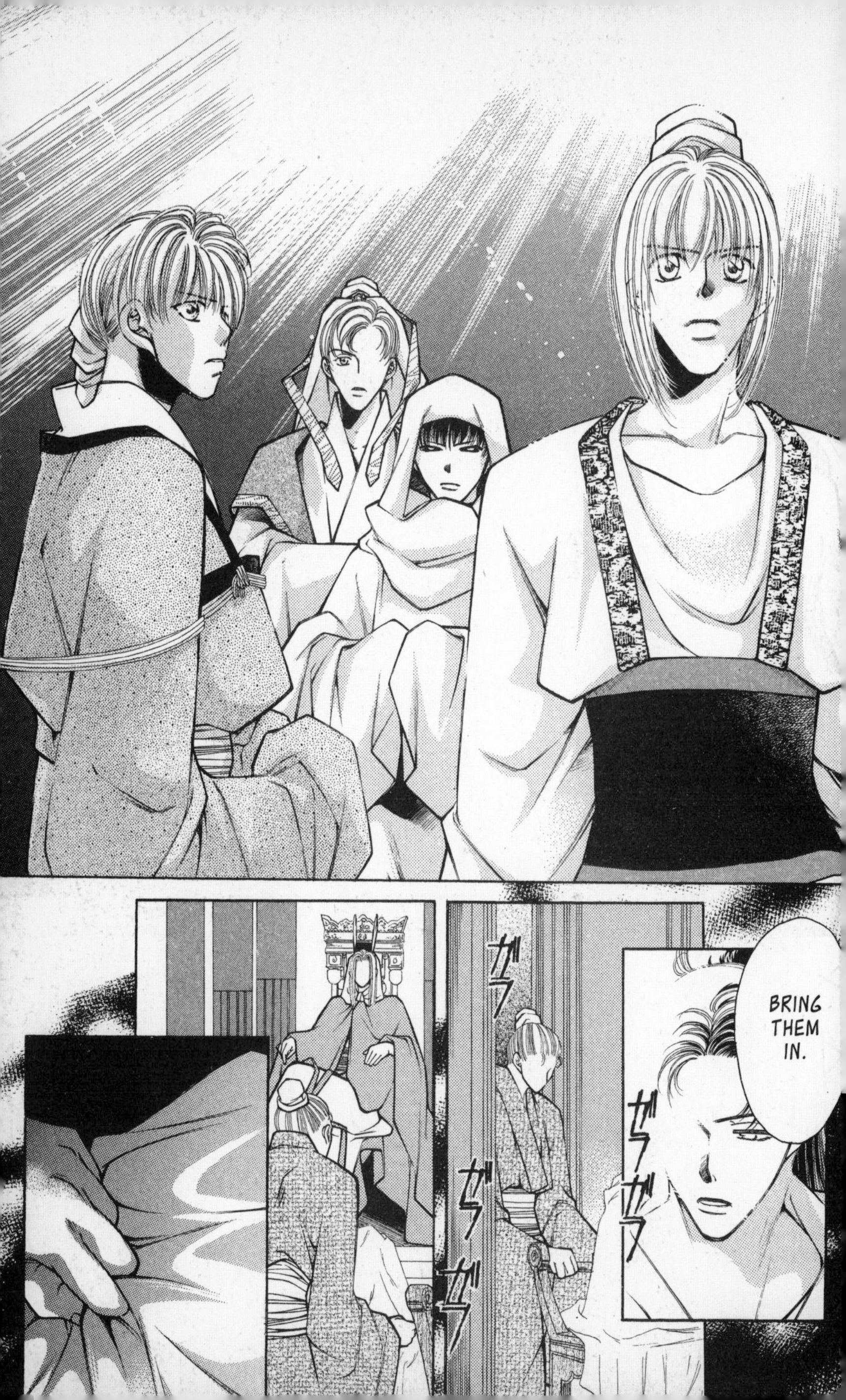
BRING THEM IN.

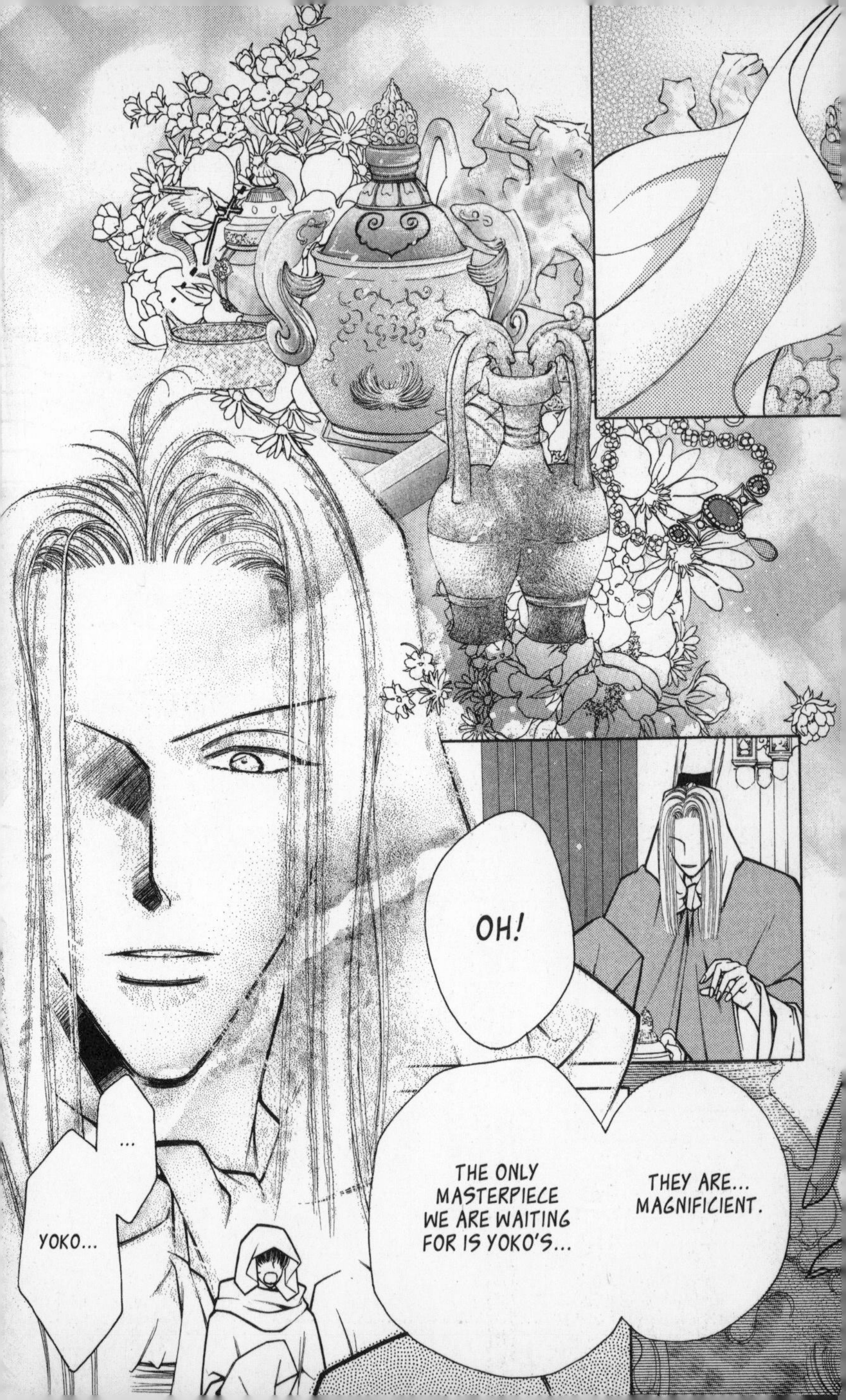
OH!
THEY ARE... MAGNIFICIENT.
THE ONLY MASTERPIECE WE ARE WAITING FOR IS YOKO'S...
...
YOKO...

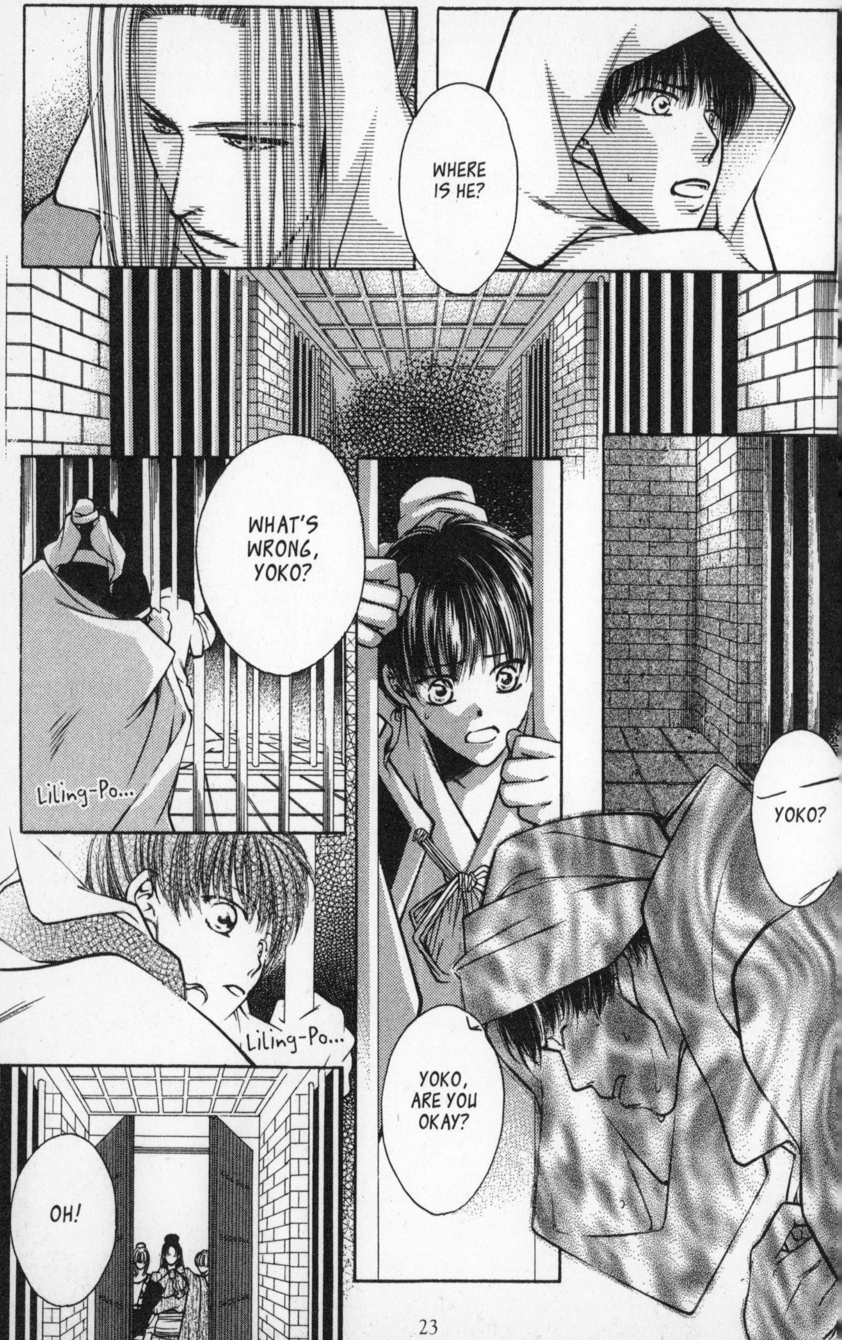
WHERE IS HE?
YOKO?
WHAT'S WRONG, YOKO?
Liling-Po...
YOKO, ARE YOU OKAY?
Liling-Po...
OH!

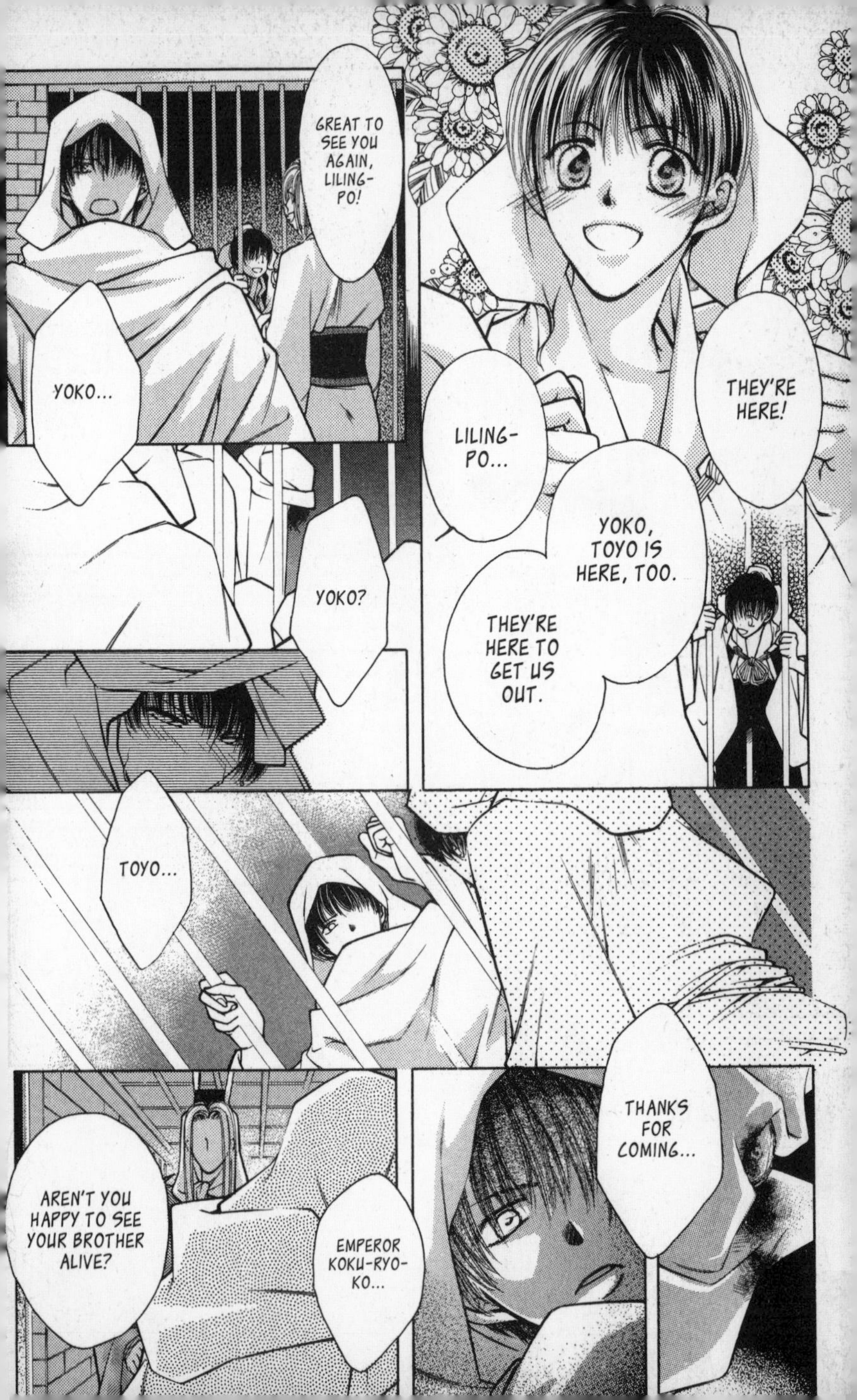
THEY'RE HERE!
LILING-PO...
YOKO, TOYO IS HERE, TOO.
THEY'RE HERE TO GET US OUT.
GREAT TO SEE YOU AGAIN, LILING-PO!
YOKO...
YOKO?
TOYO...
THANKS FOR COMING...
EMPEROR KOKU-RYO-KO...
AREN'T YOU HAPPY TO SEE YOUR BROTHER ALIVE?

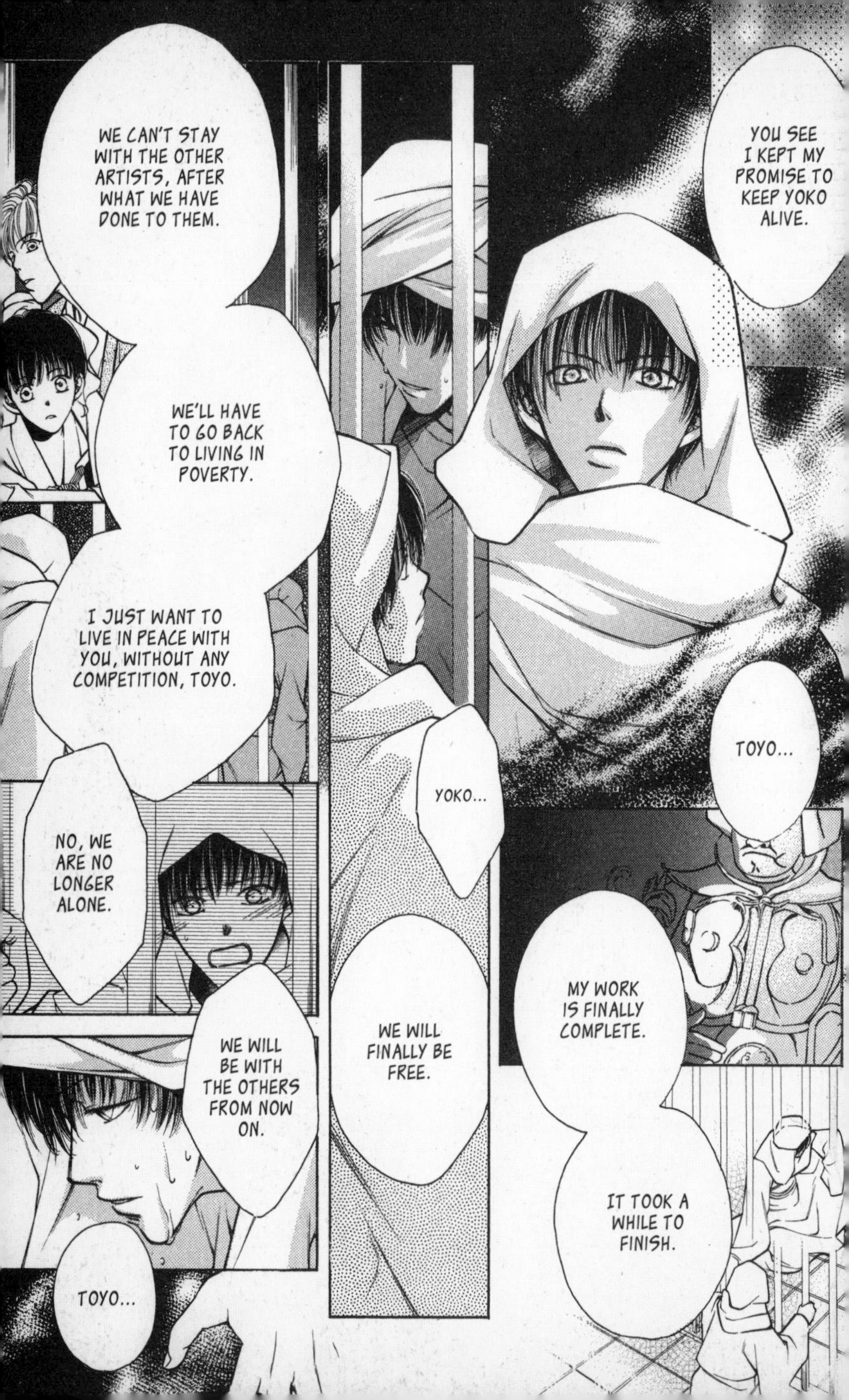
YOU SEE I KEPT MY PROMISE TO KEEP YOKO ALIVE.
TOYO...
MY WORK IS FINALLY COMPLETE.
IT TOOK A WHILE TO FINISH.
YOKO...
WE WILL FINALLY BE FREE.
WE CAN'T STAY WITH THE OTHER ARTISTS, AFTER WHAT WE HAVE DONE TO THEM.
WE'LL HAVE TO GO BACK TO LIVING IN POVERTY.
I JUST WANT TO LIVE IN PEACE WITH YOU, WITHOUT ANY COMPETITION, TOYO.
NO, WE ARE NO LONGER ALONE.
WE WILL BE WITH THE OTHERS FROM NOW ON.
TOYO...

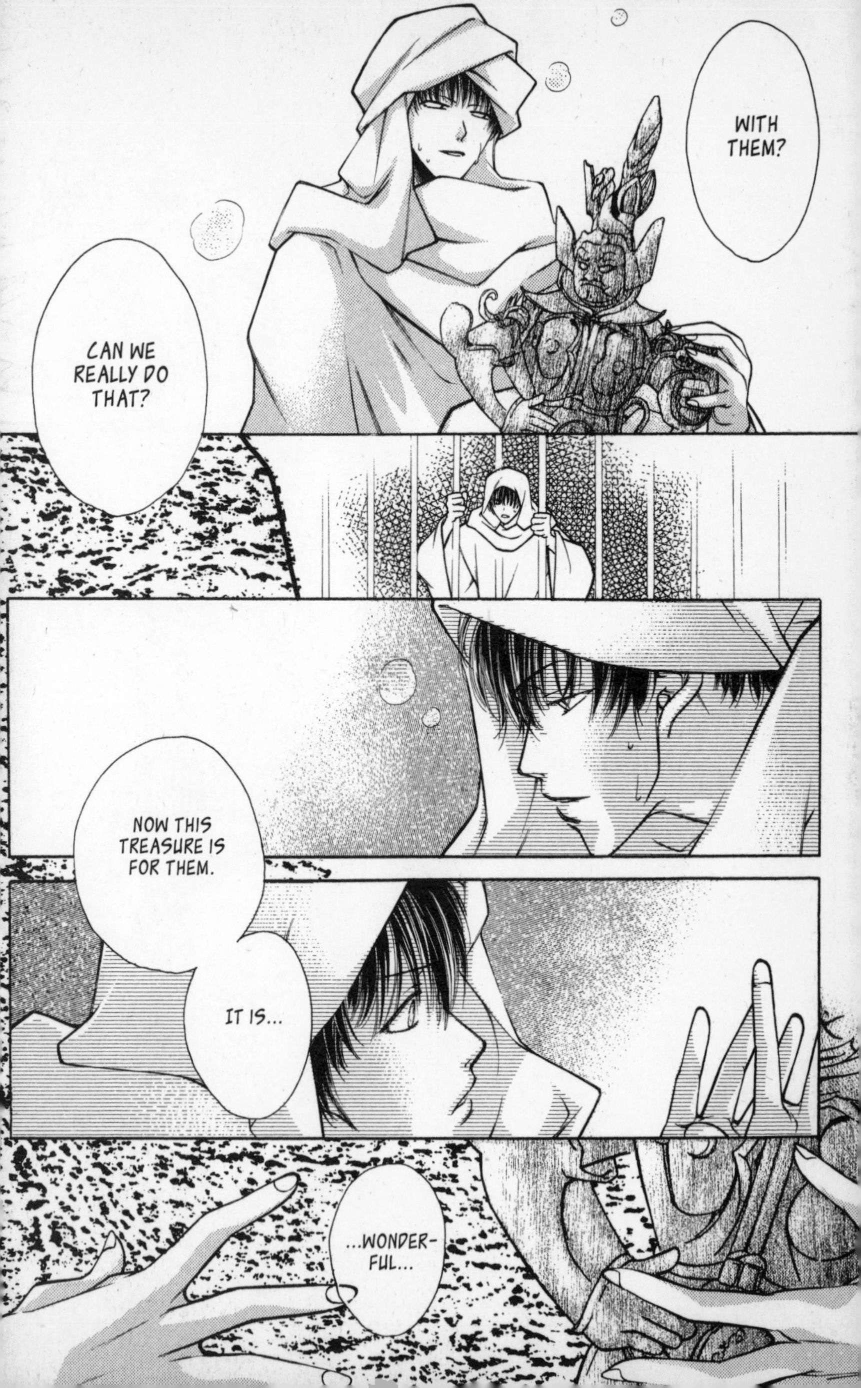
WITH THEM?
CAN WE REALLY DO THAT?
NOW THIS TREASURE IS FOR THEM.
IT IS...
...WONDER-FUL...

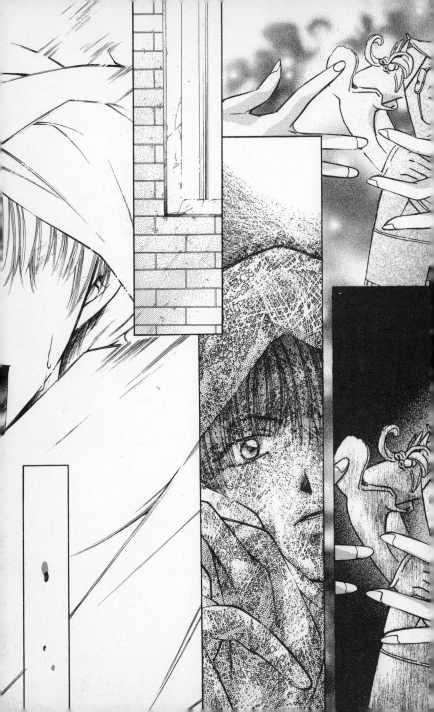

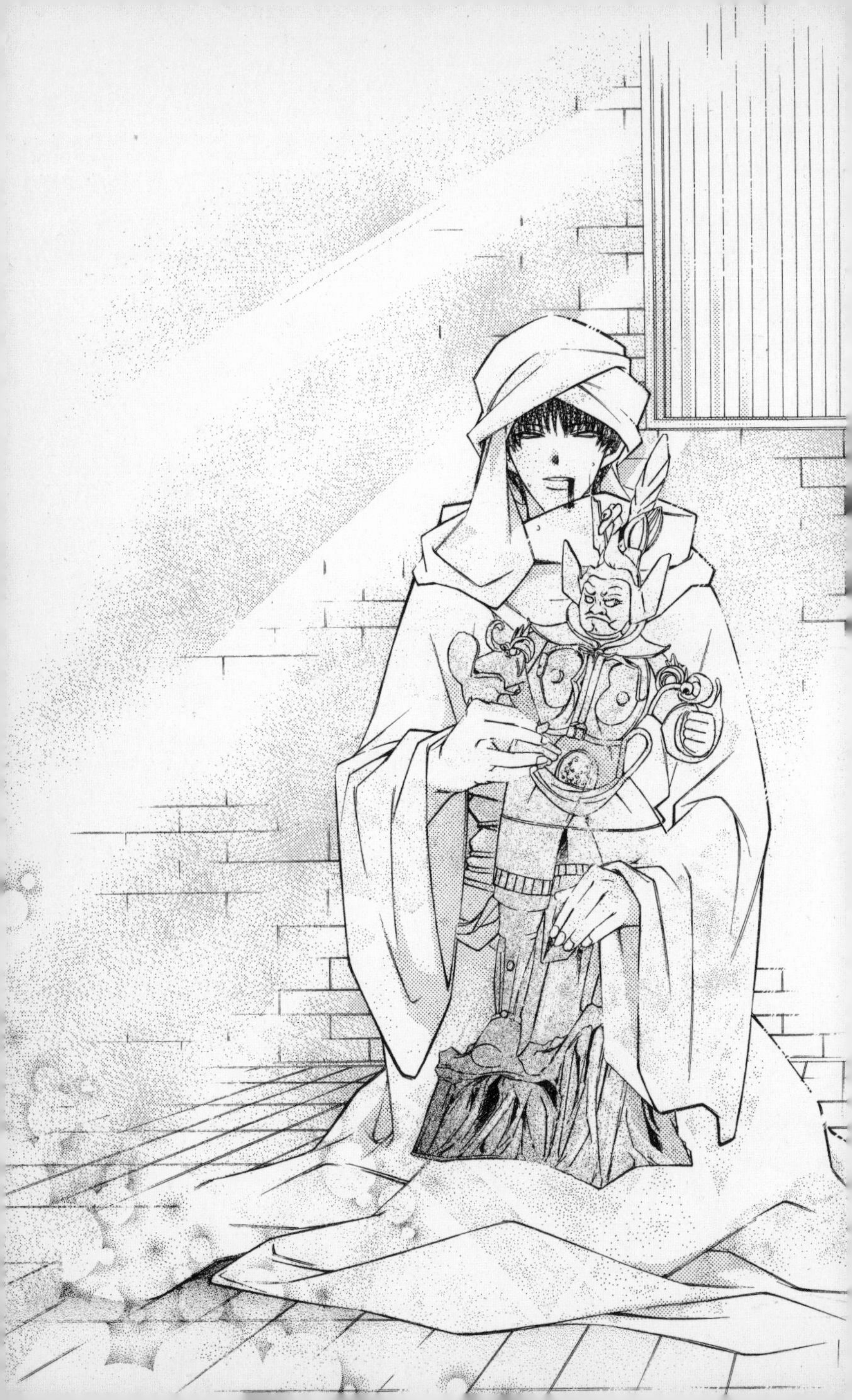

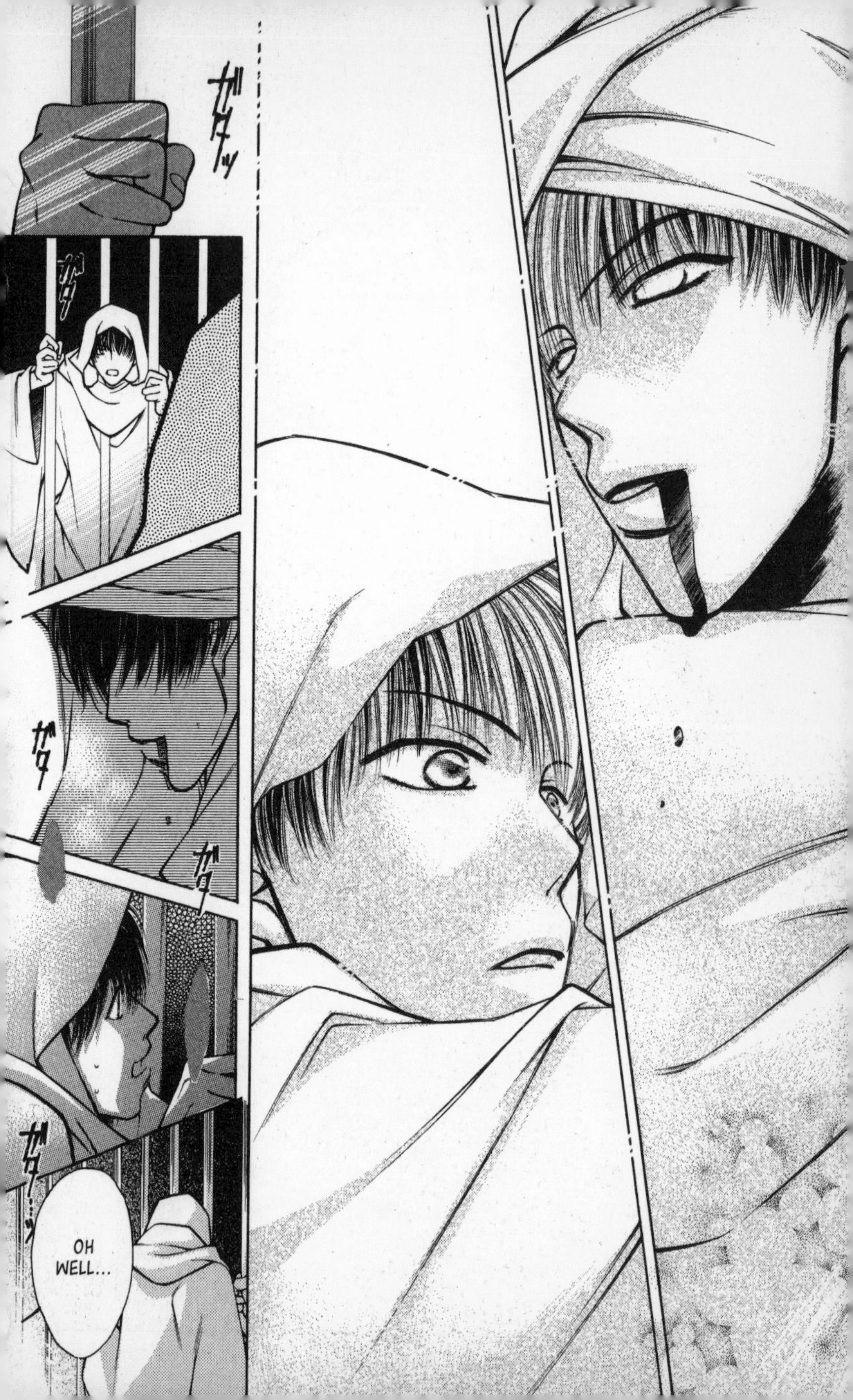

ガタッ
ガタ
ガタ
ガタ
ガタ…ッ
OH WELL...

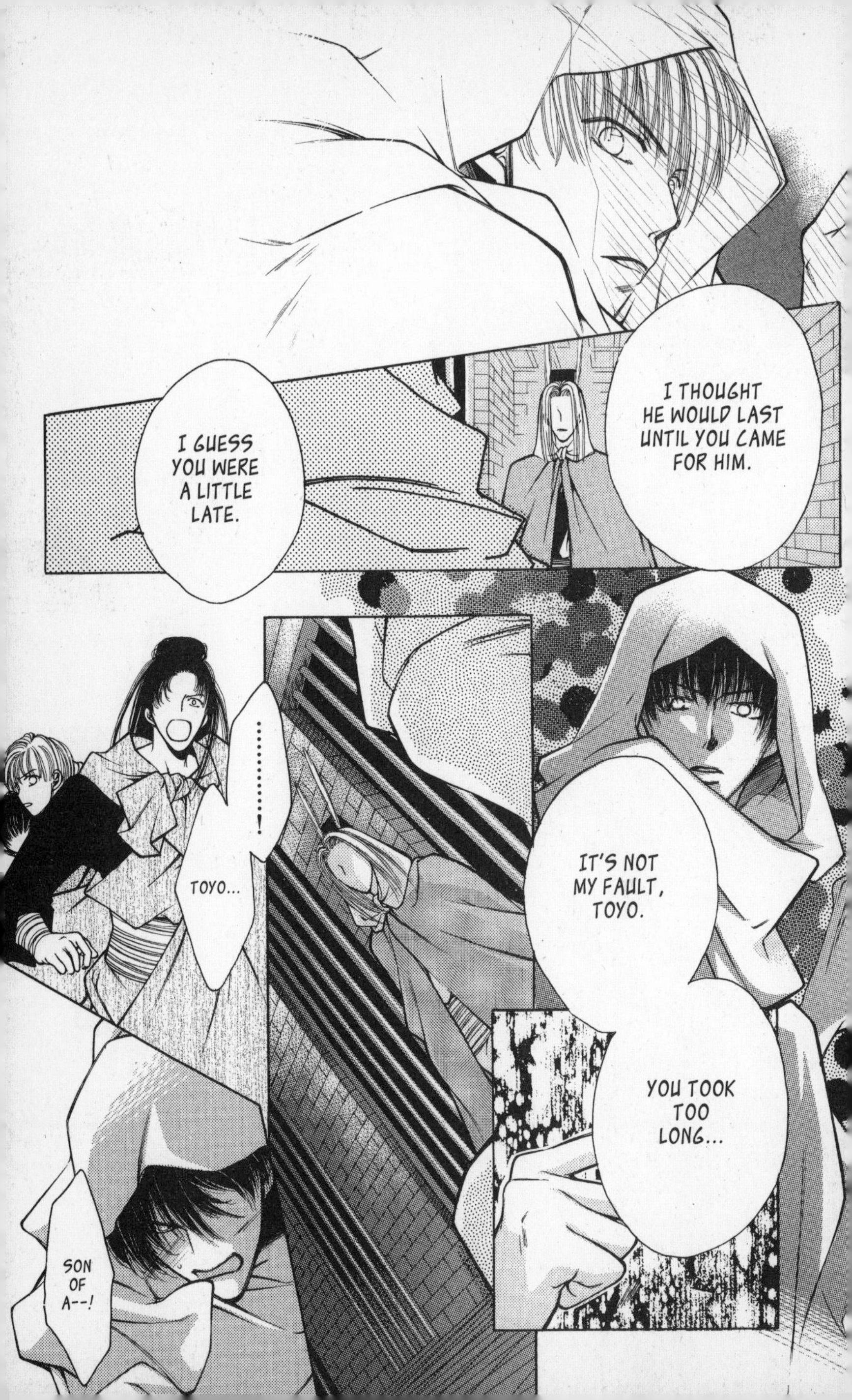
I THOUGHT HE WOULD LAST UNTIL YOU CAME FOR HIM.
I GUESS YOU WERE A LITTLE LATE.
IT'S NOT MY FAULT, TOYO.
YOU TOOK TOO LONG...
......!
TOYO...
SON OF A--!

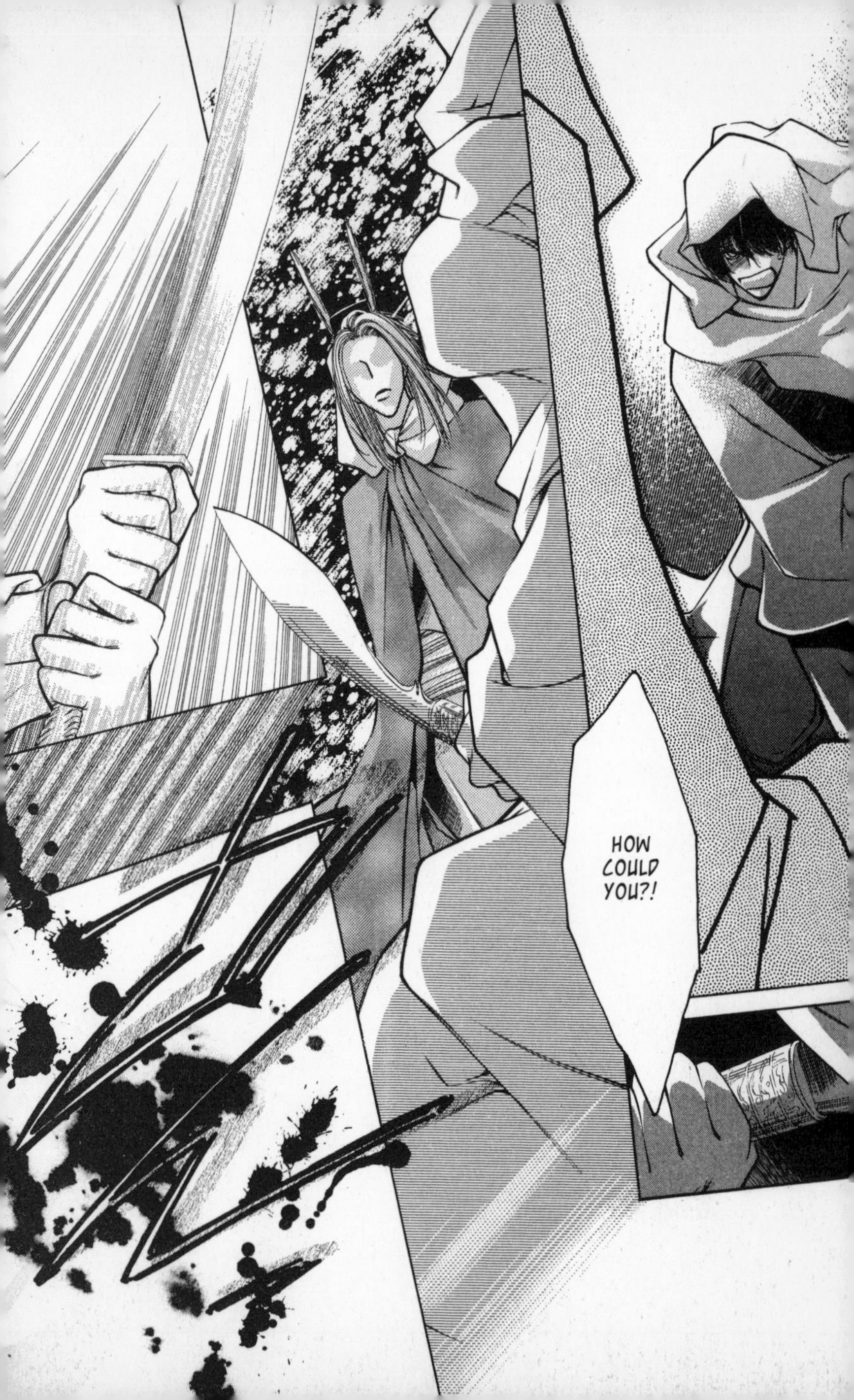
HOW COULD YOU?!

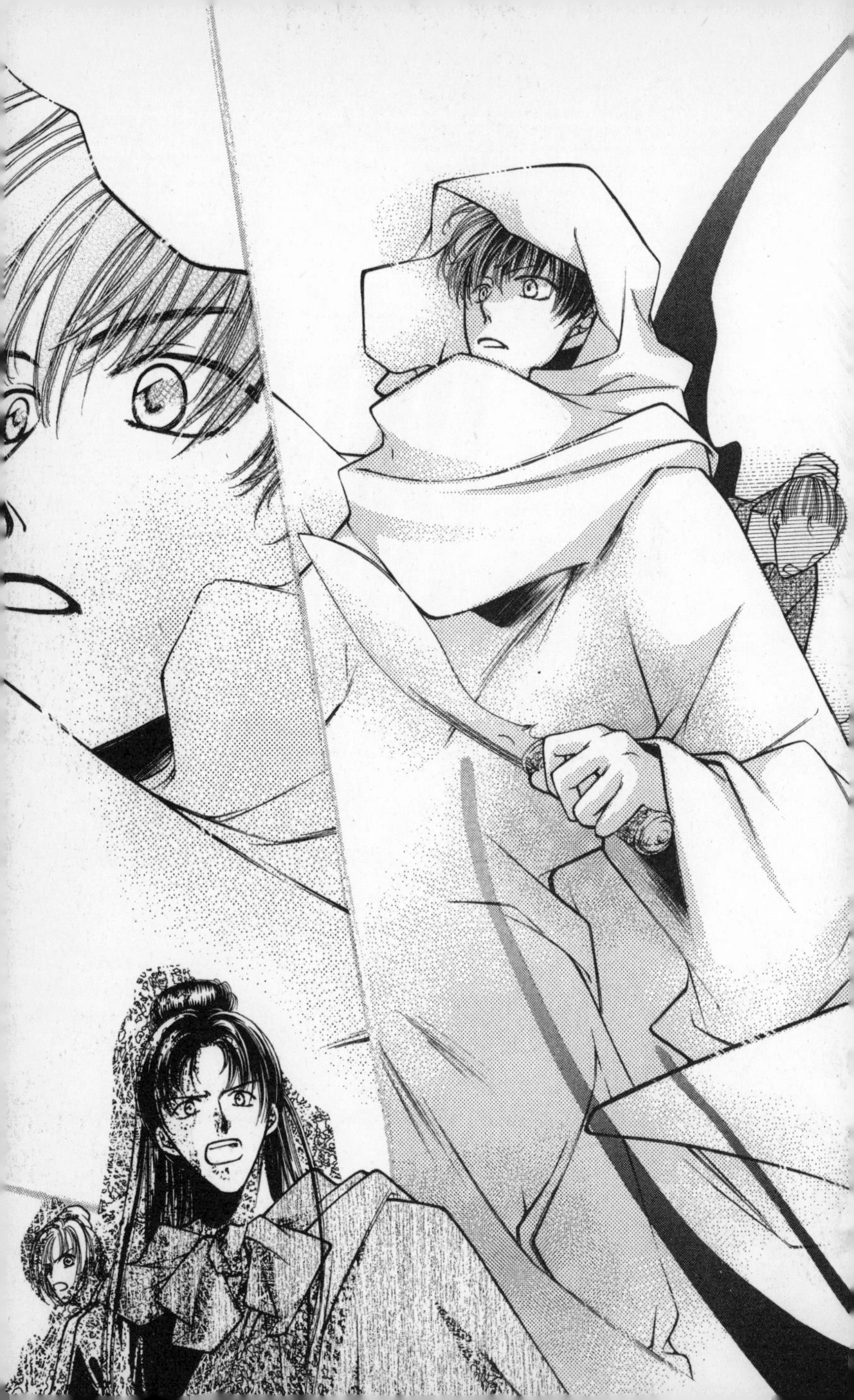

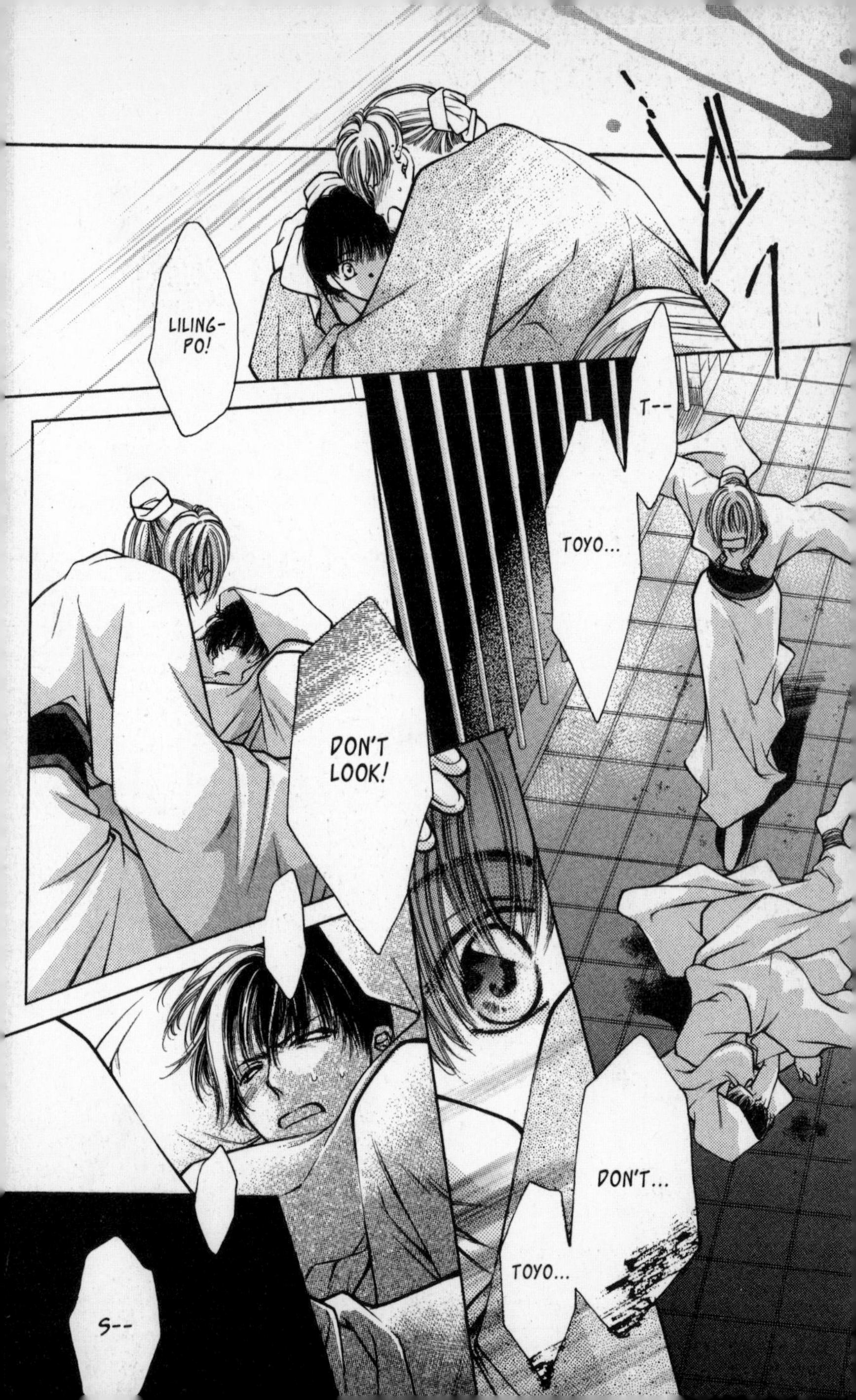
LILING-PO!
T--
TOYO...
DON'T LOOK!
DON'T...
TOYO...
S--

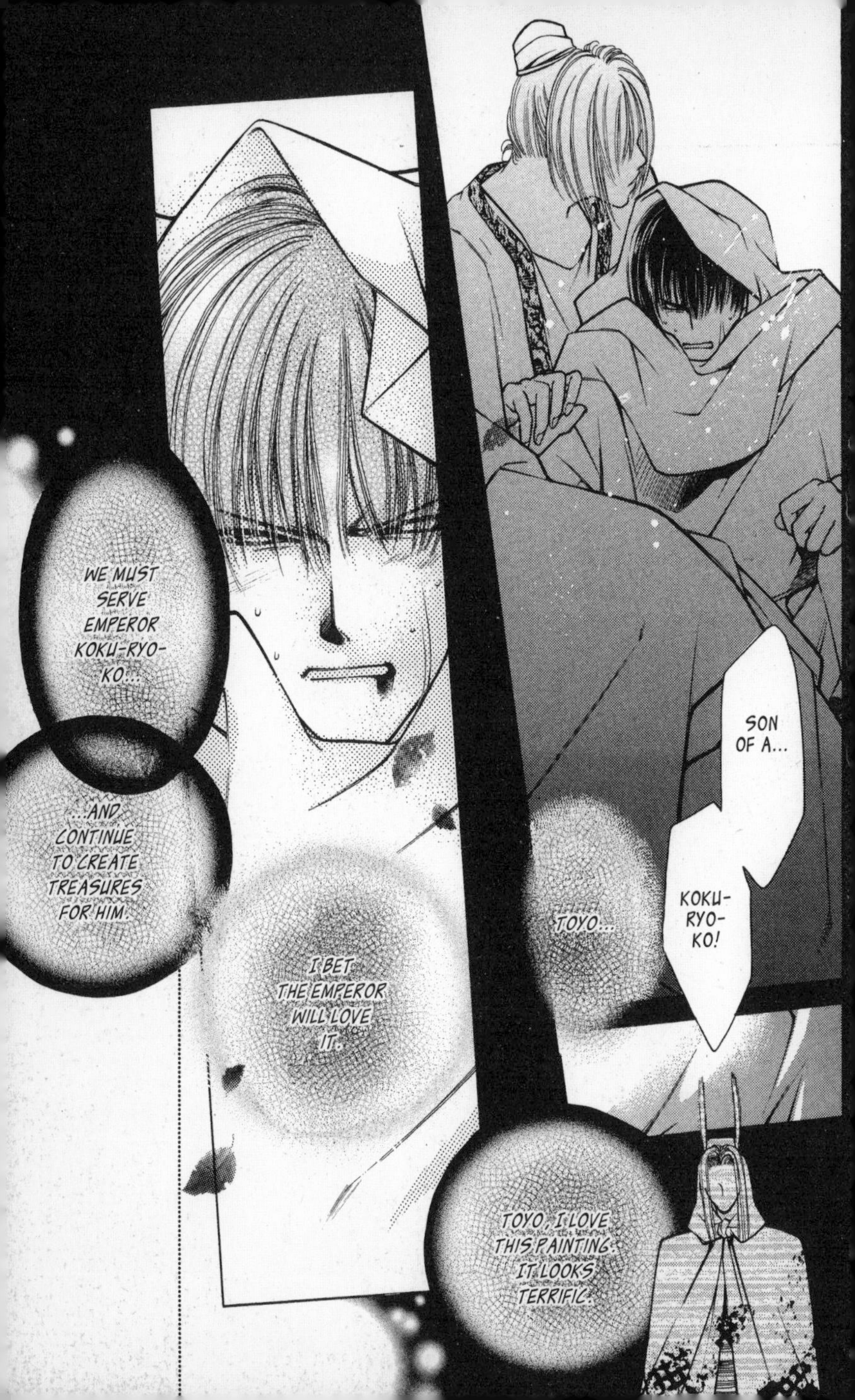
SON OF A...
KOKU-RYO-KO!
TOYO...
TOYO, I LOVE THIS PAINTING. IT LOOKS TERRIFIC.
WE MUST SERVE EMPEROR KOKU-RYO-KO...
...AND CONTINUE TO CREATE TREASURES FOR HIM.
I BET THE EMPEROR WILL LOVE IT.

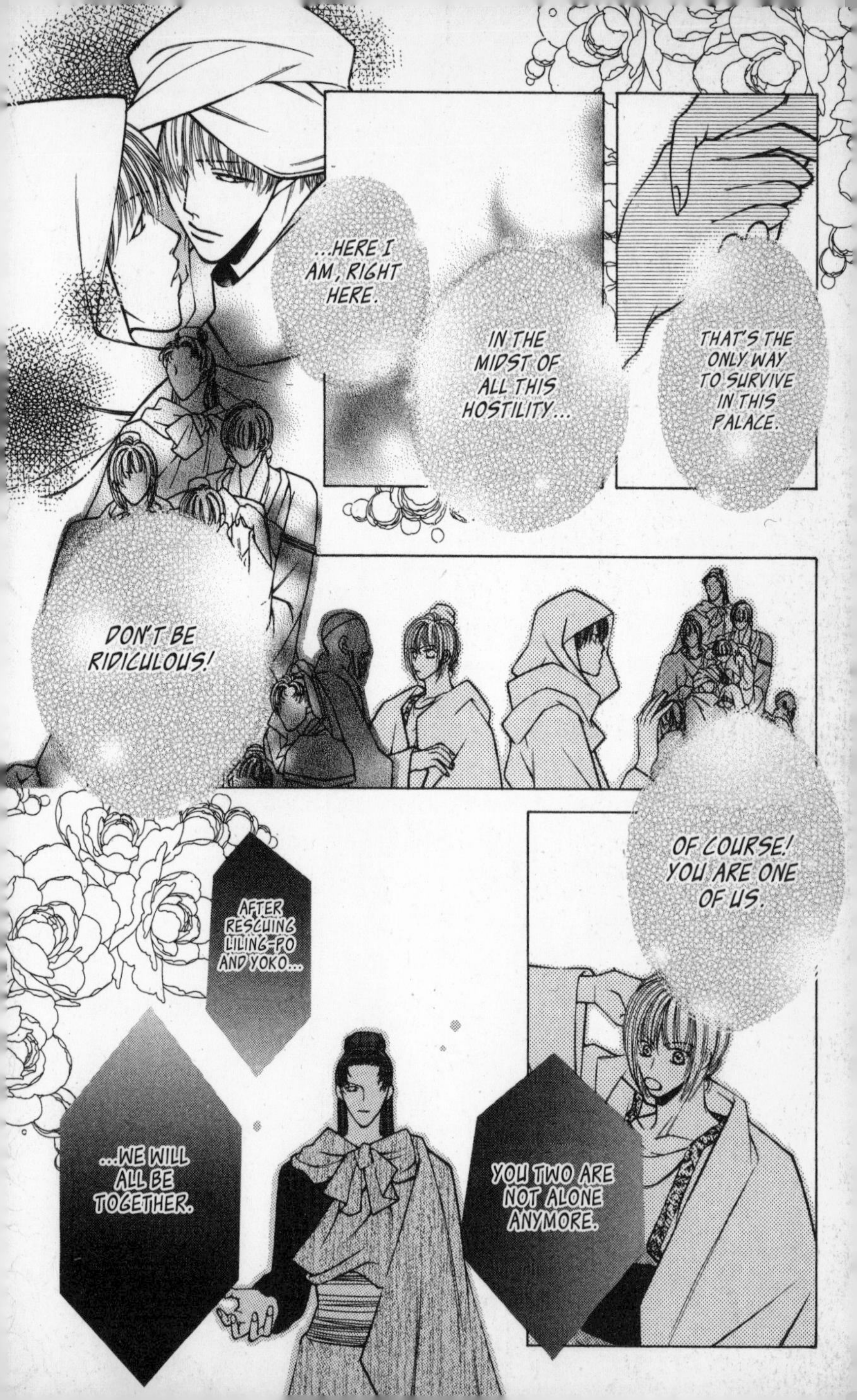
THAT'S THE ONLY WAY TO SURVIVE IN THIS PALACE.
IN THE MIDST OF ALL THIS HOSTILITY...
...HERE I AM, RIGHT HERE.
DON'T BE RIDICULOUS!
OF COURSE! YOU ARE ONE OF US.
YOU TWO ARE NOT ALONE ANYMORE.
AFTER RESCUING LILING-PO AND YOKO...
...WE WILL ALL BE TOGETHER.

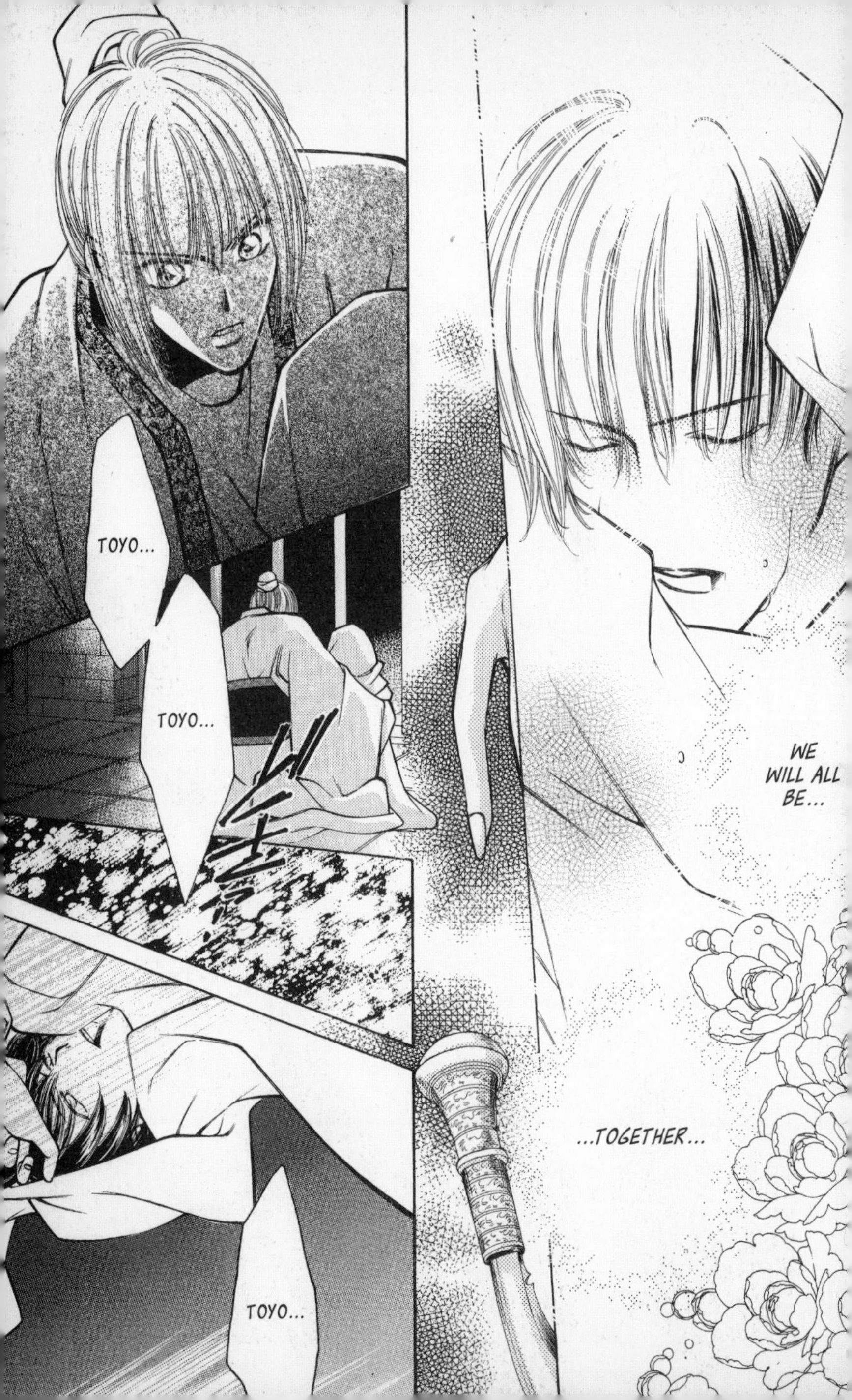
WE WILL ALL BE...
...TOGETHER...
TOYO...
TOYO...
TOYO...

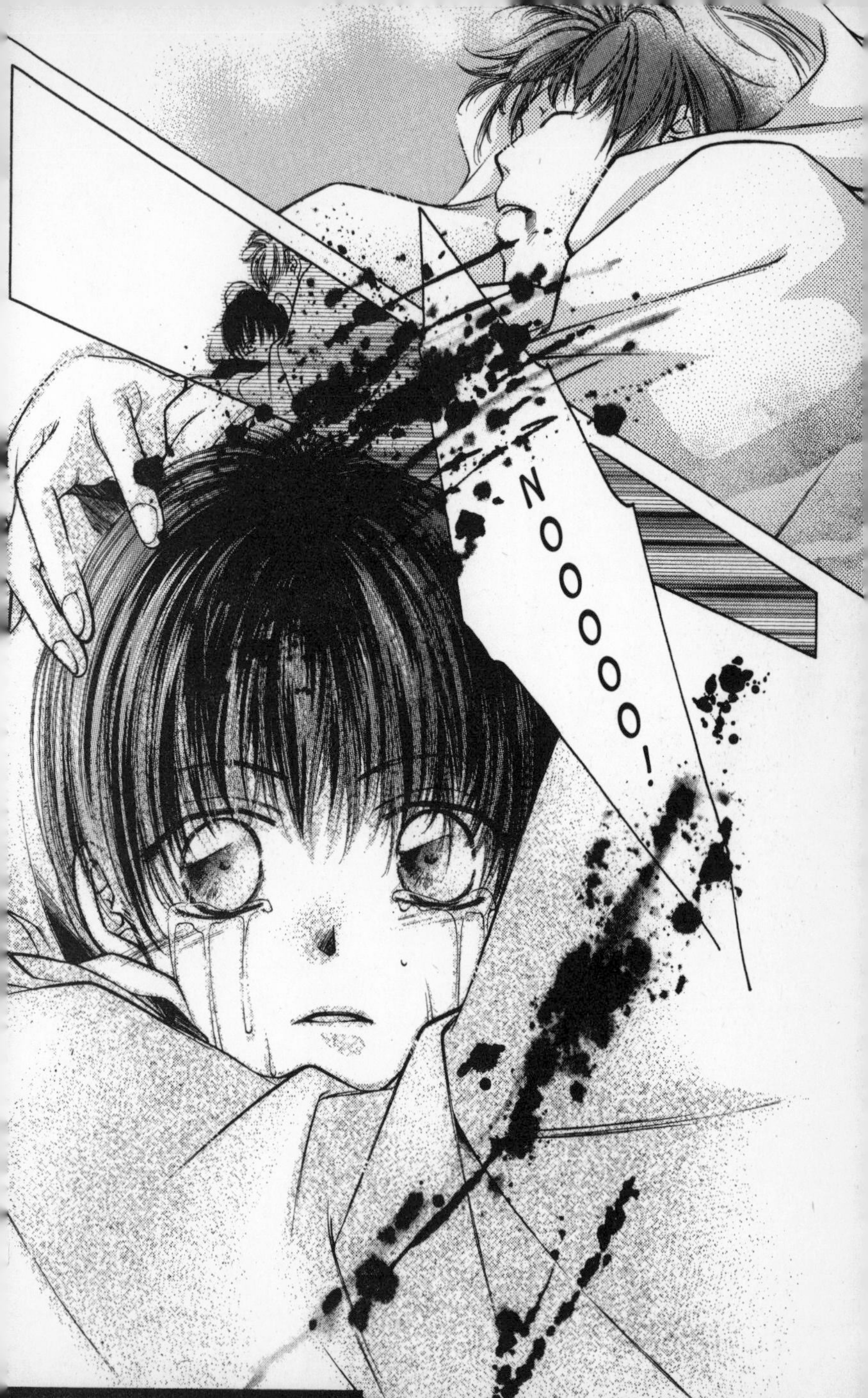
NOOOOO!

THE EIGHT GREAT ARTISTS, PART 8 – THE END

I am Liling-Po.

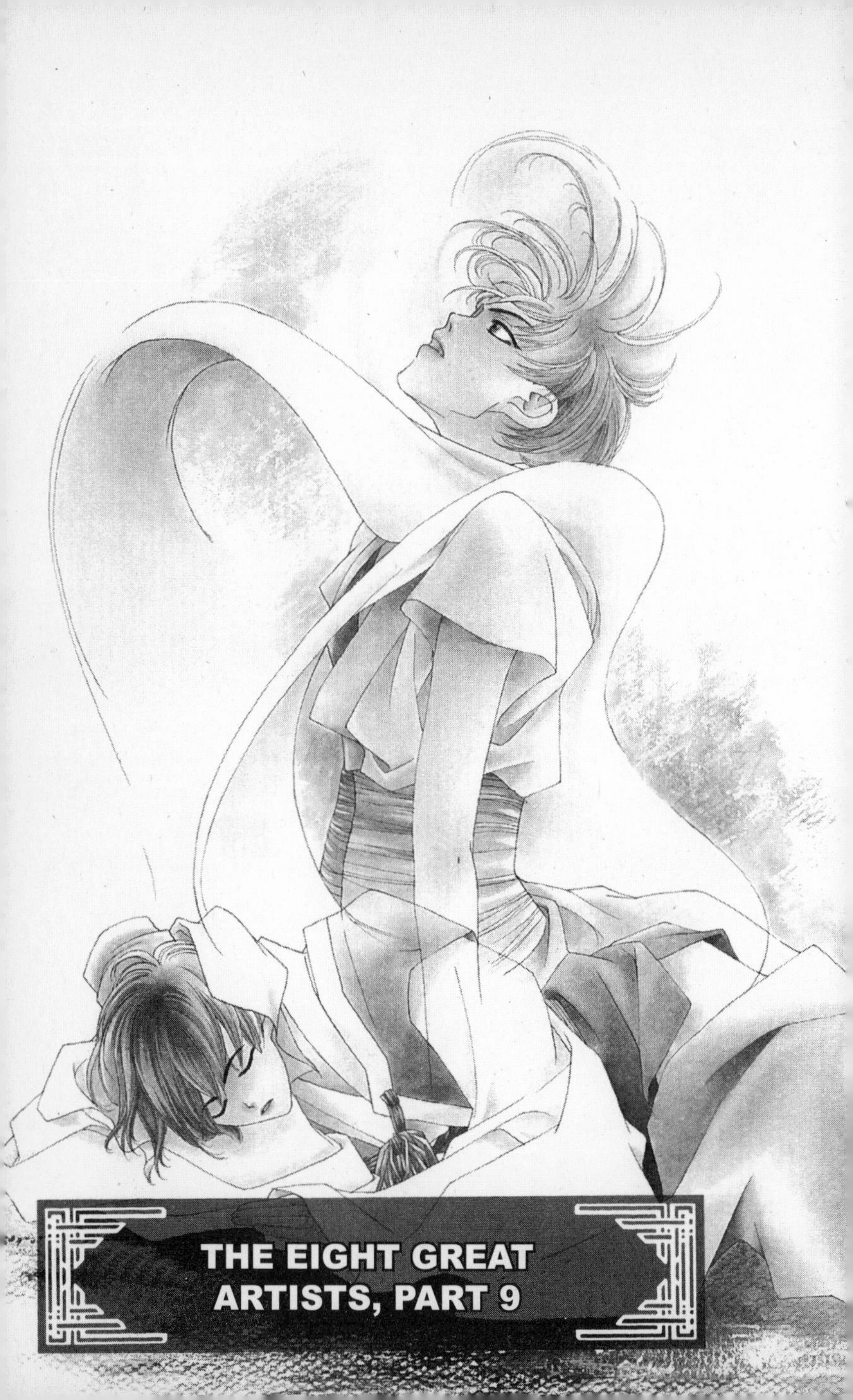
THE EIGHT GREAT ARTISTS, PART 9

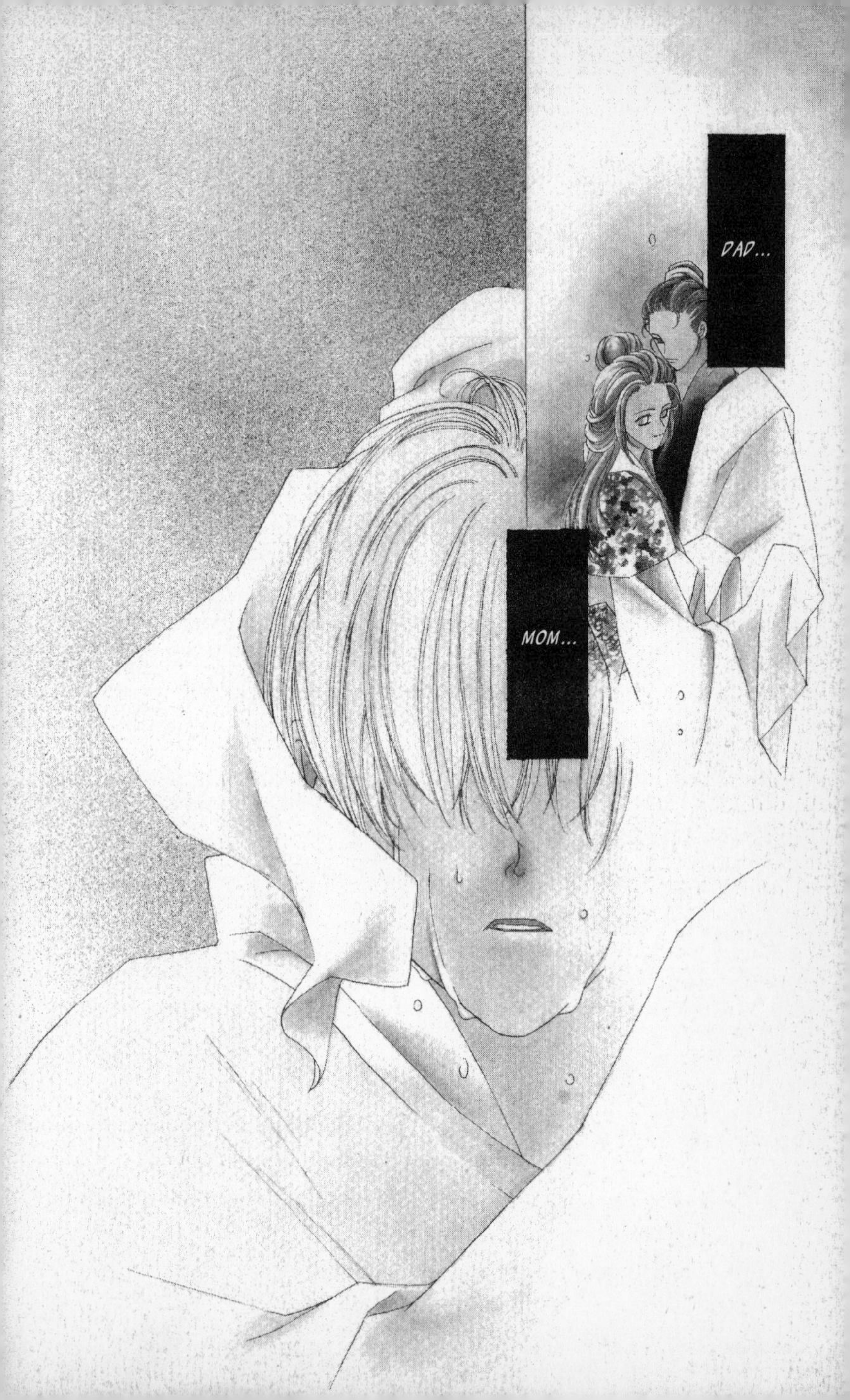
DAD...
MOM...

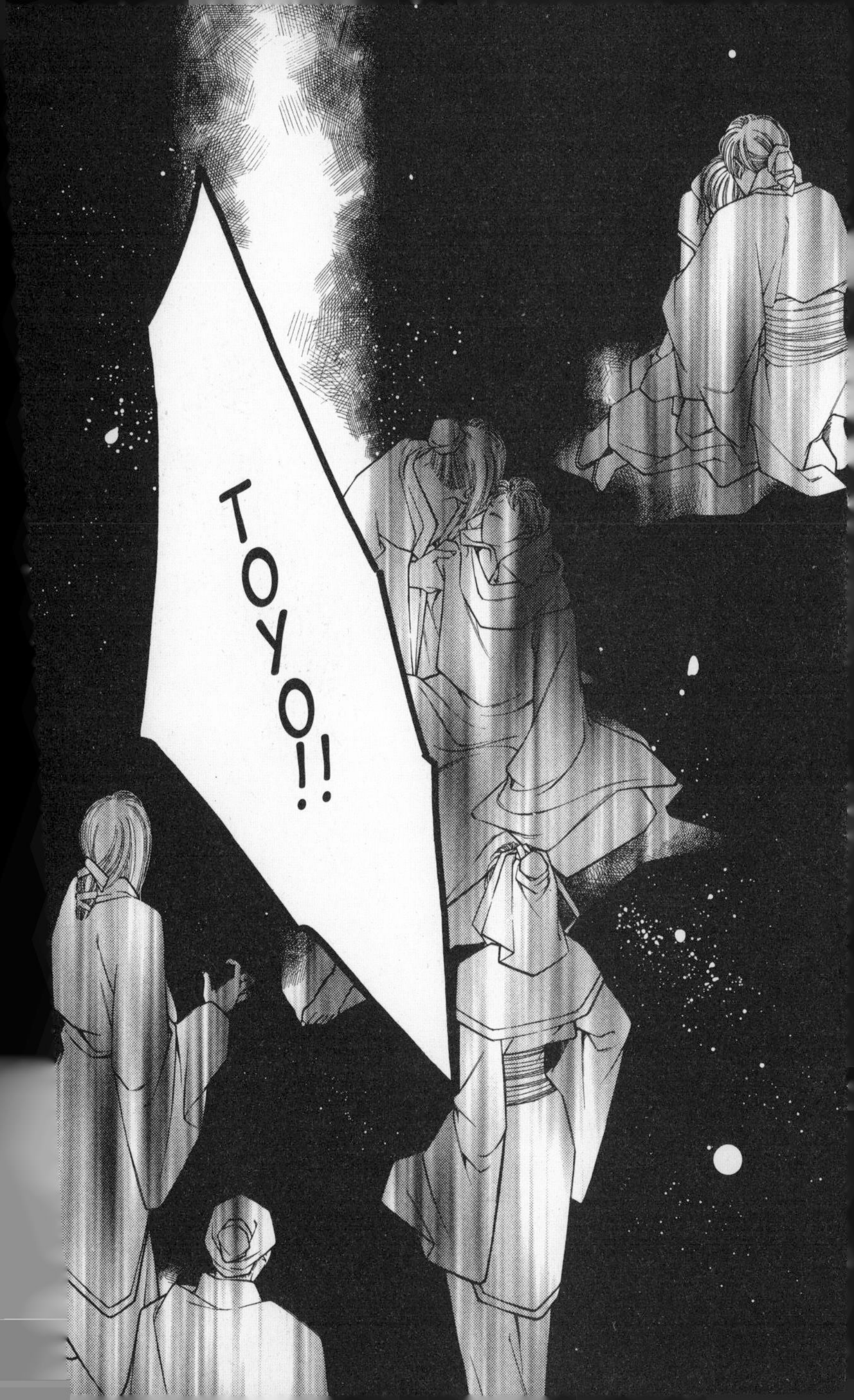
TOYO!!

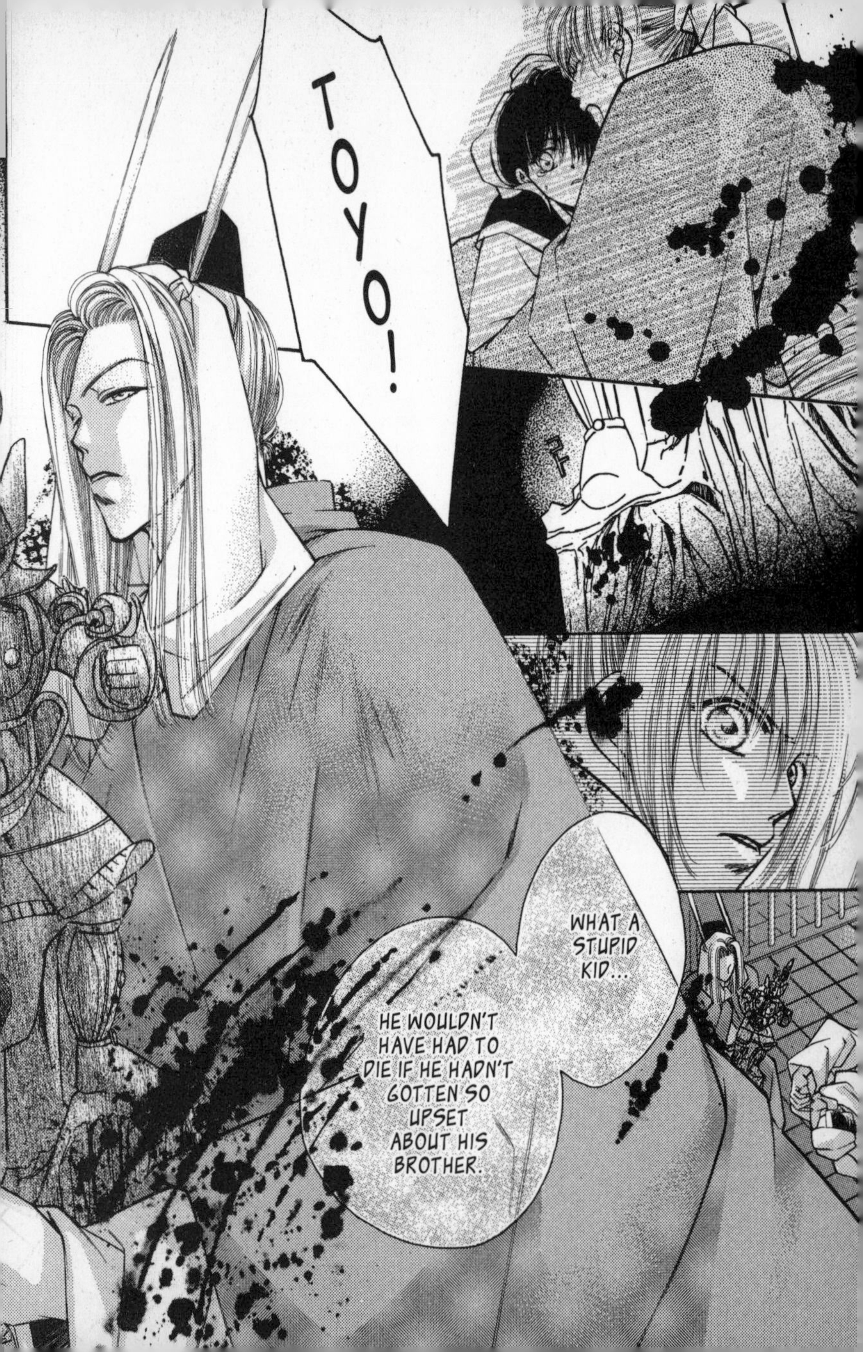
TOYO!
WHAT A STUPID KID...
HE WOULDN'T HAVE HAD TO DIE IF HE HADN'T GOTTEN SO UPSET ABOUT HIS BROTHER.

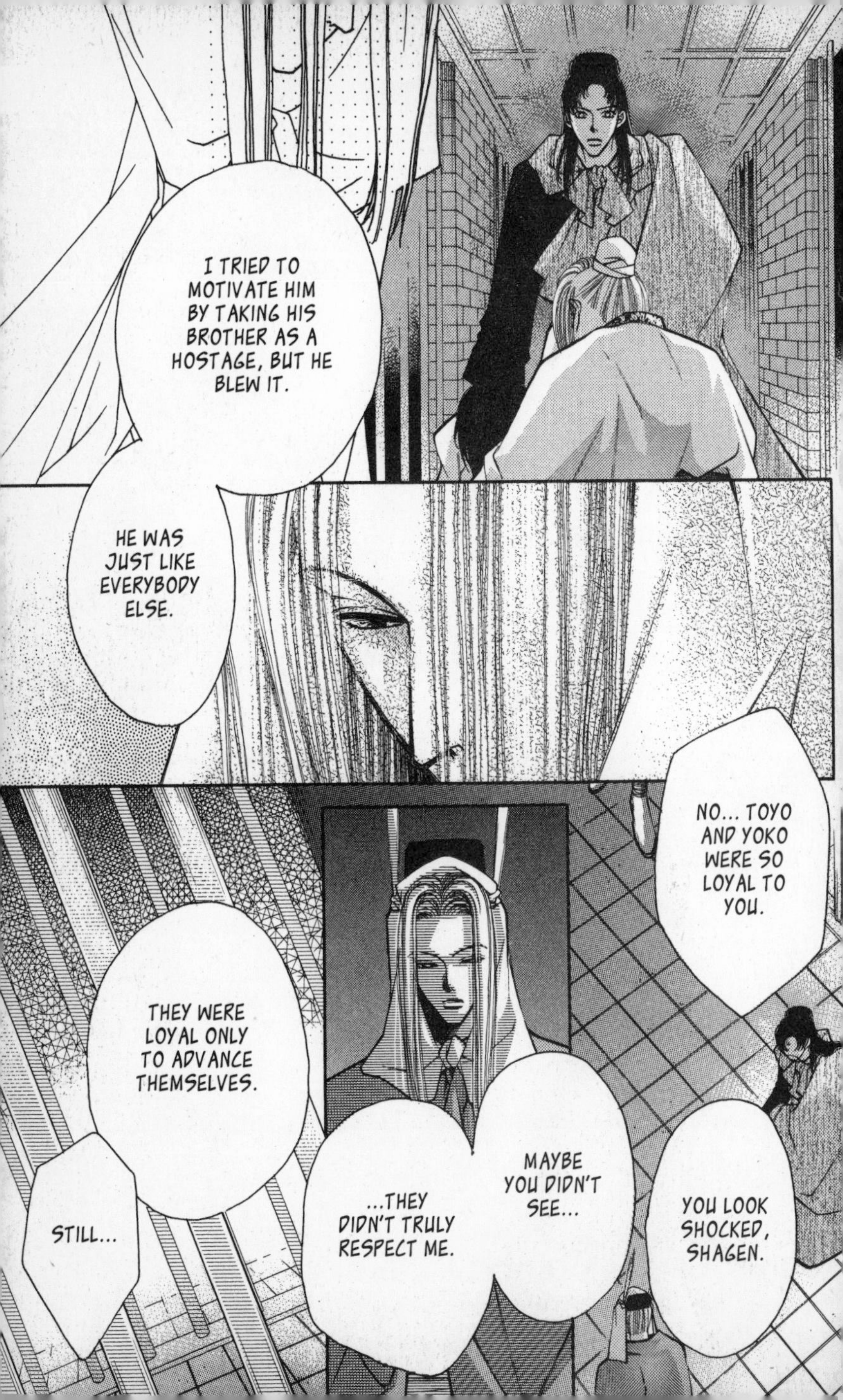
I TRIED TO MOTIVATE HIM BY TAKING HIS BROTHER AS A HOSTAGE, BUT HE BLEW IT.
HE WAS JUST LIKE EVERYBODY ELSE.
NO... TOYO AND YOKO WERE SO LOYAL TO YOU.
THEY WERE LOYAL ONLY TO ADVANCE THEMSELVES.
YOU LOOK SHOCKED, SHAGEN.
MAYBE YOU DIDN'T SEE...
...THEY DIDN'T TRULY RESPECT ME.
STILL...

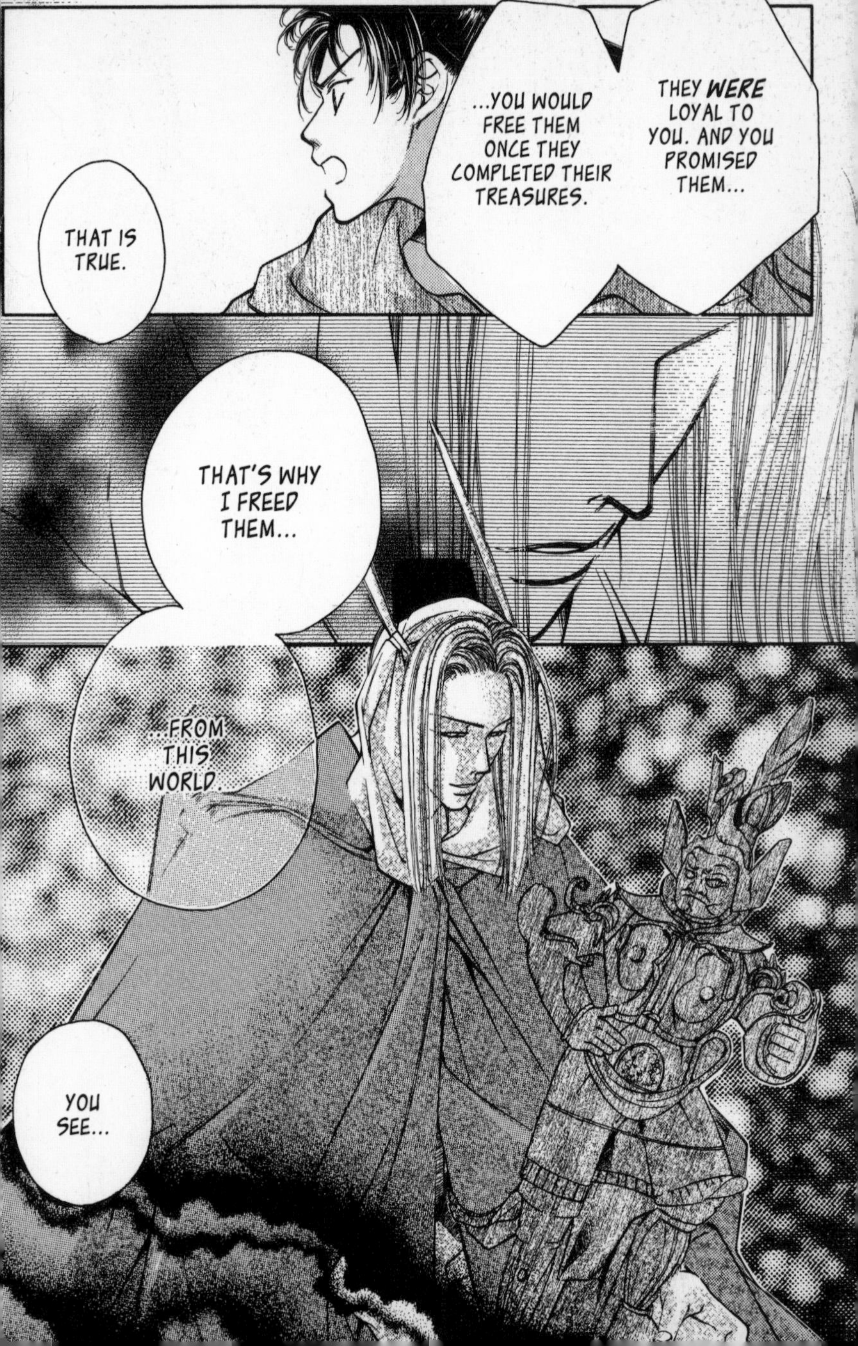
THEY **WERE** LOYAL TO YOU. AND YOU PROMISED THEM...
...YOU WOULD FREE THEM ONCE THEY COMPLETED THEIR TREASURES.
THAT IS TRUE.
THAT'S WHY I FREED THEM...
...FROM THIS WORLD.
YOU SEE...

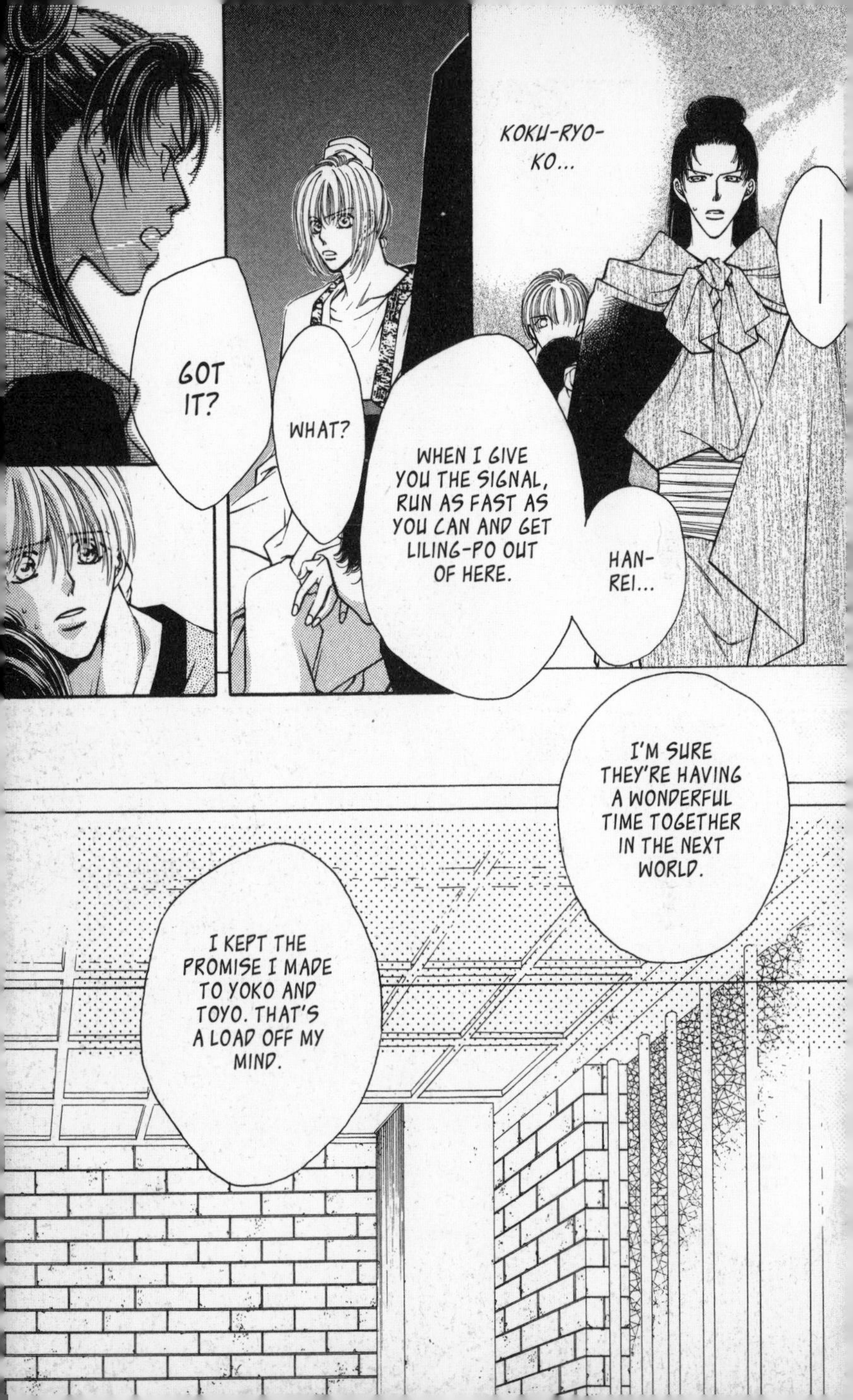
KOKU-RYO-KO...
HAN-REI...
WHEN I GIVE YOU THE SIGNAL, RUN AS FAST AS YOU CAN AND GET LILING-PO OUT OF HERE.
GOT IT?
WHAT?
I'M SURE THEY'RE HAVING A WONDERFUL TIME TOGETHER IN THE NEXT WORLD.
I KEPT THE PROMISE I MADE TO YOKO AND TOYO. THAT'S A LOAD OFF MY MIND.

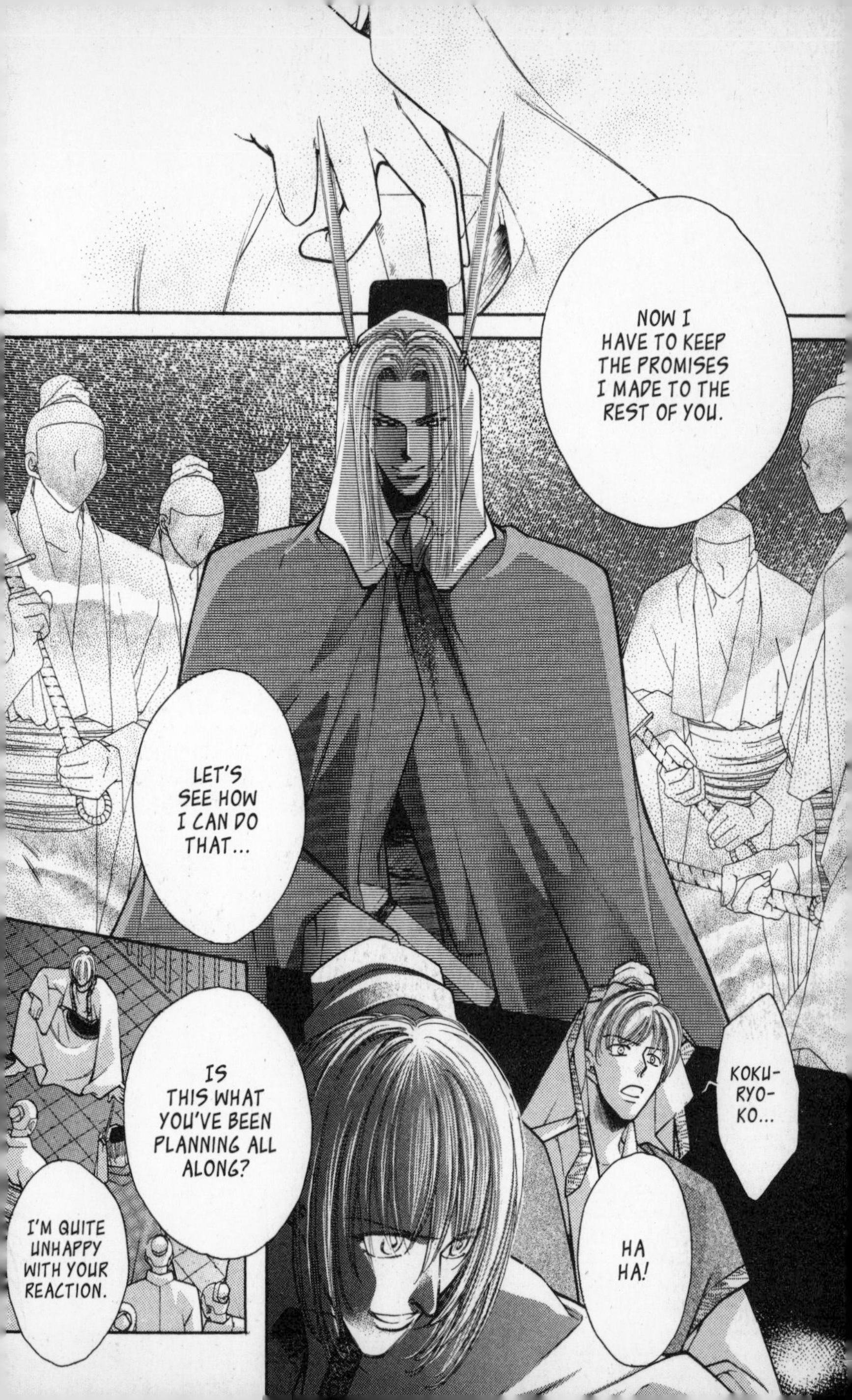
NOW I HAVE TO KEEP THE PROMISES I MADE TO THE REST OF YOU.
LET'S SEE HOW I CAN DO THAT...
KOKU-RYO-KO...
IS THIS WHAT YOU'VE BEEN PLANNING ALL ALONG?
HA HA!
I'M QUITE UNHAPPY WITH YOUR REACTION.

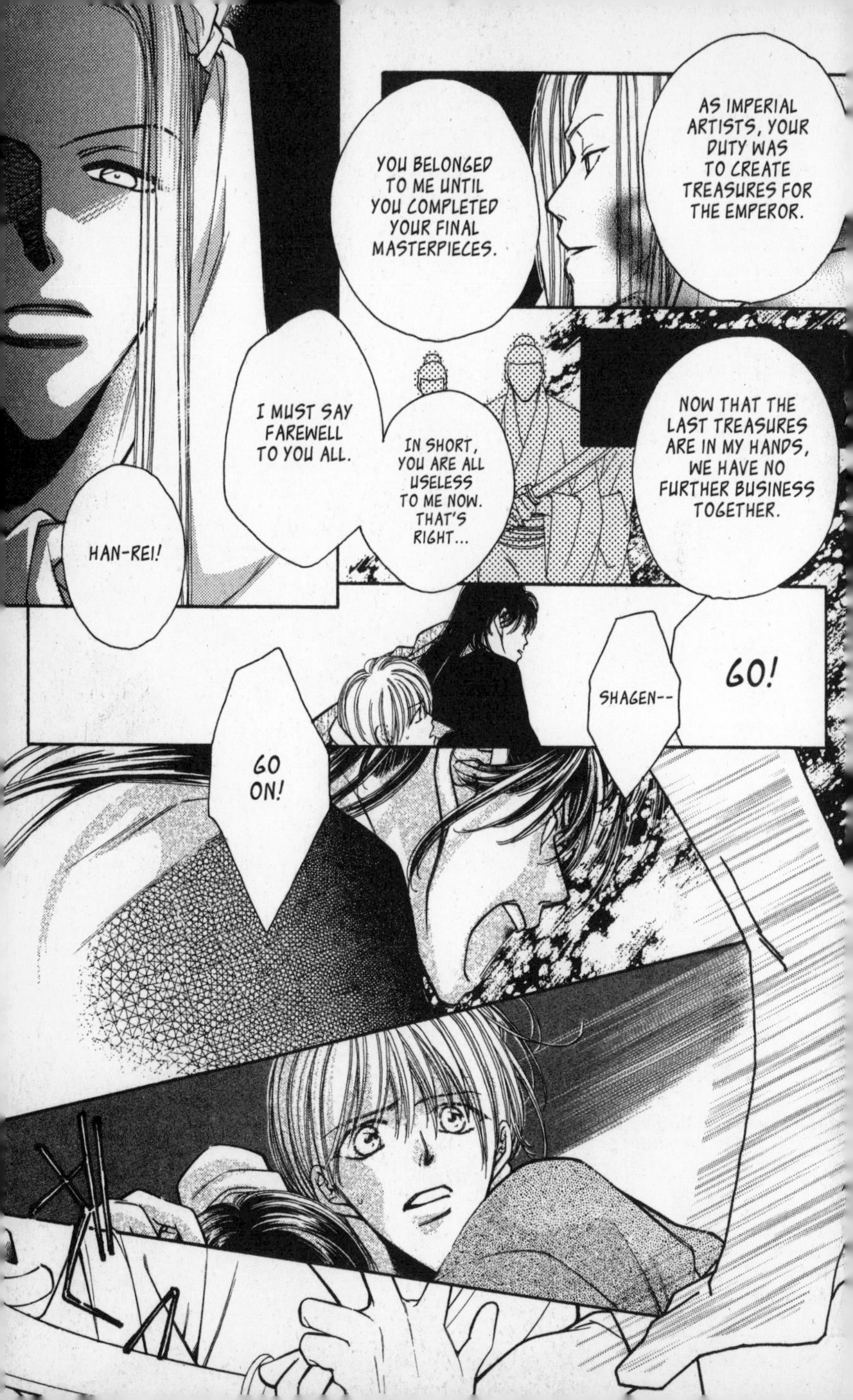
AS IMPERIAL ARTISTS, YOUR DUTY WAS TO CREATE TREASURES FOR THE EMPEROR.
YOU BELONGED TO ME UNTIL YOU COMPLETED YOUR FINAL MASTERPIECES.
NOW THAT THE LAST TREASURES ARE IN MY HANDS, WE HAVE NO FURTHER BUSINESS TOGETHER.
IN SHORT, YOU ARE ALL USELESS TO ME NOW. THAT'S RIGHT...
I MUST SAY FAREWELL TO YOU ALL.
HAN-REI!
GO!
SHAGEN--
GO ON!

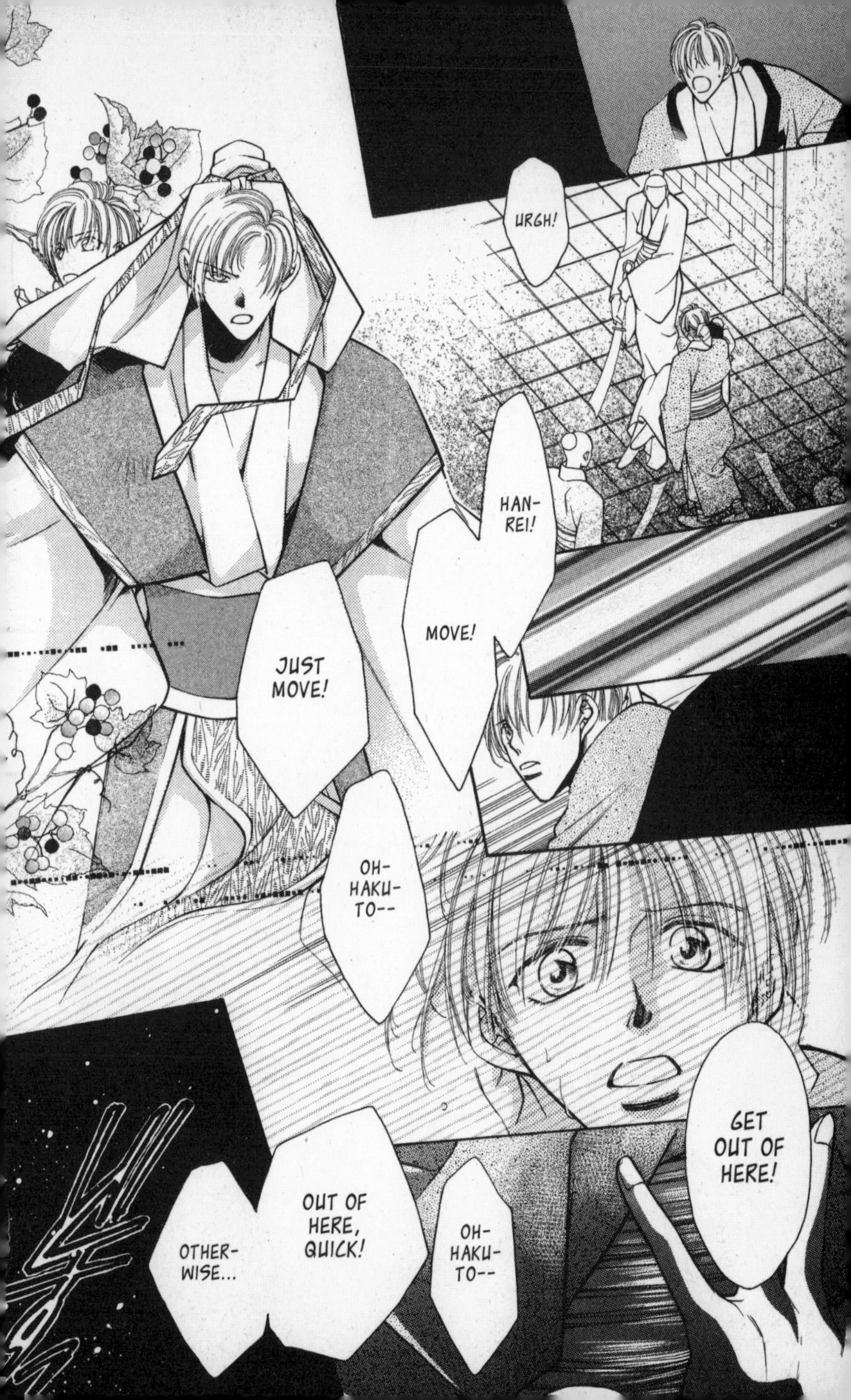
URGH!
HAN-REI!
MOVE!
JUST MOVE!
OH-HAKU-TO--
GET OUT OF HERE!
OH-HAKU-TO--
OUT OF HERE, QUICK!
OTHER-WISE...

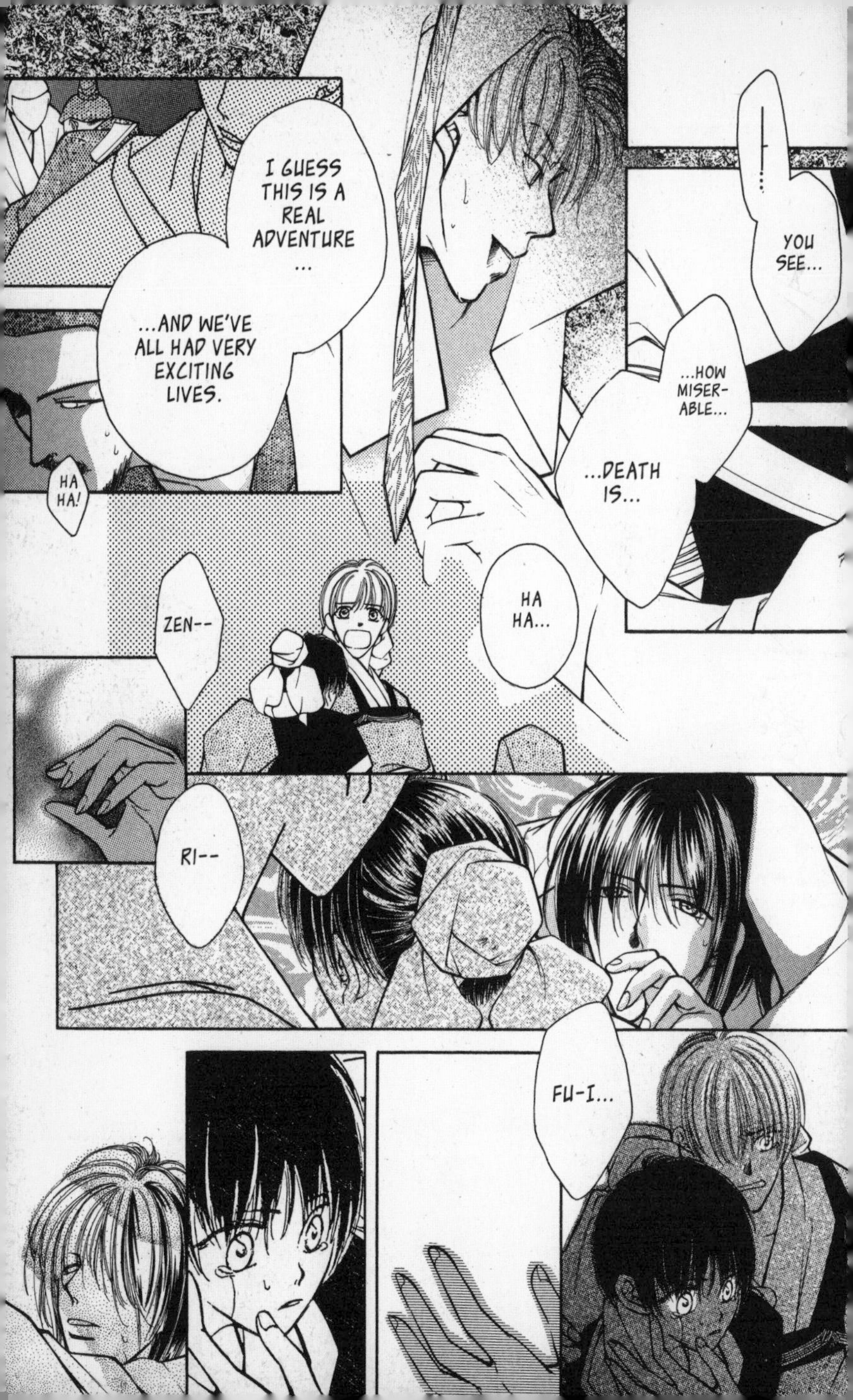
...
YOU SEE...
...HOW MISERABLE...
...DEATH IS...
HA HA...
I GUESS THIS IS A REAL ADVENTURE ...
...AND WE'VE ALL HAD VERY EXCITING LIVES.
HA HA!
ZEN--
RI--
FU-I...

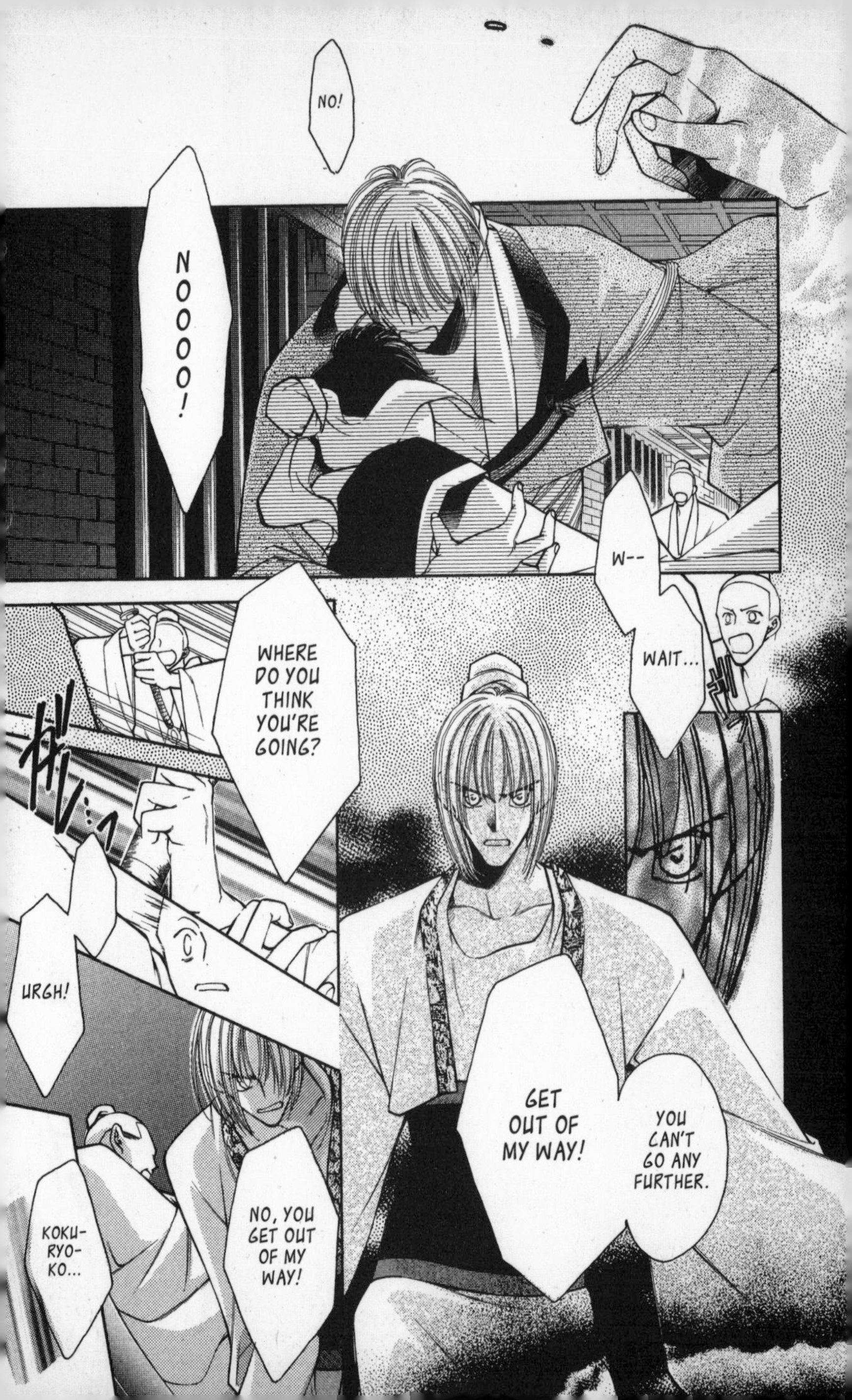
NO!
NOOOOO!
W--
WAIT...
WHERE DO YOU THINK YOU'RE GOING?
URGH!
YOU CAN'T GO ANY FURTHER.
GET OUT OF MY WAY!
NO, YOU GET OUT OF MY WAY!
KOKU-RYO-KO...

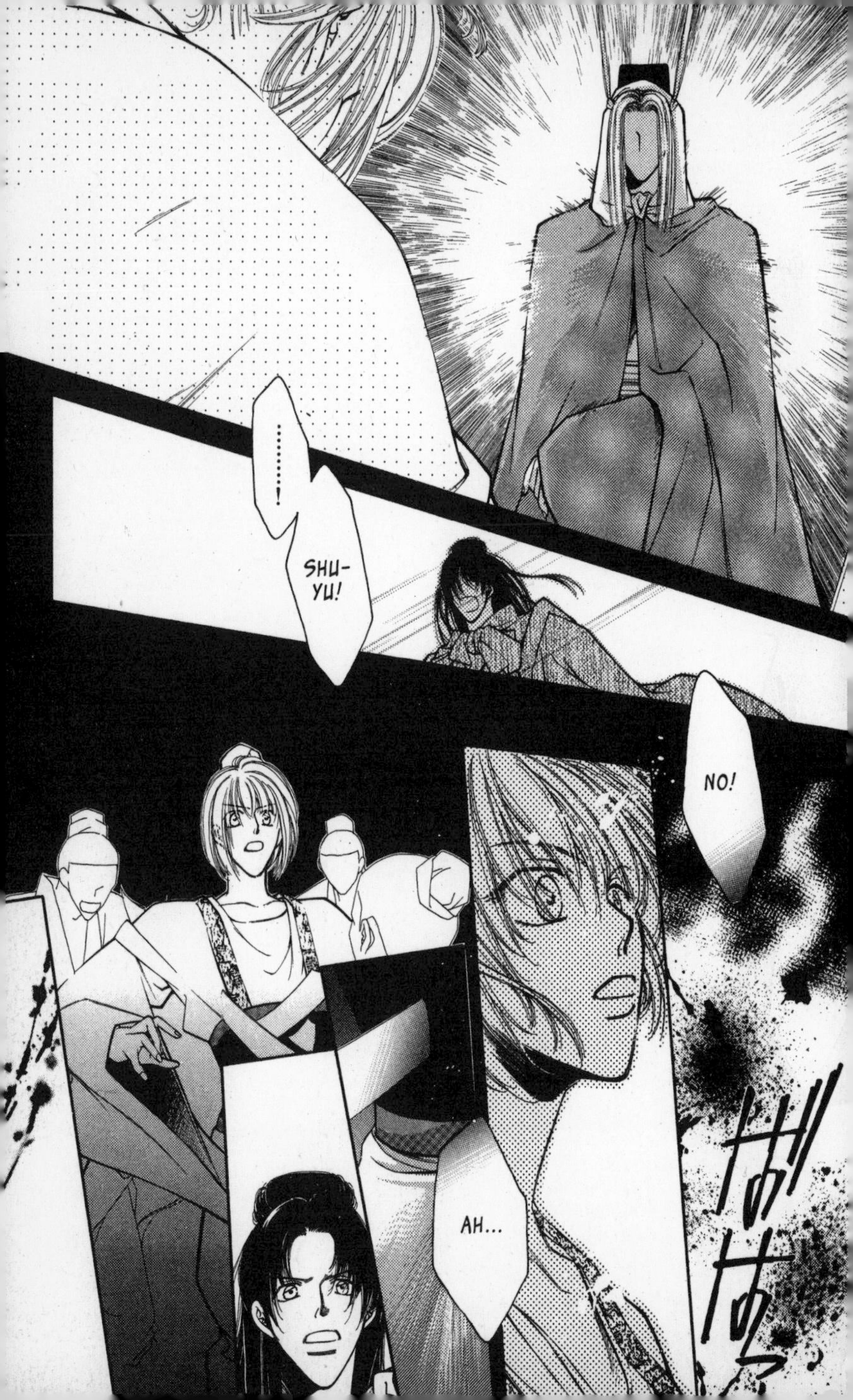
......!
SHU-YU!
NO!
AH...

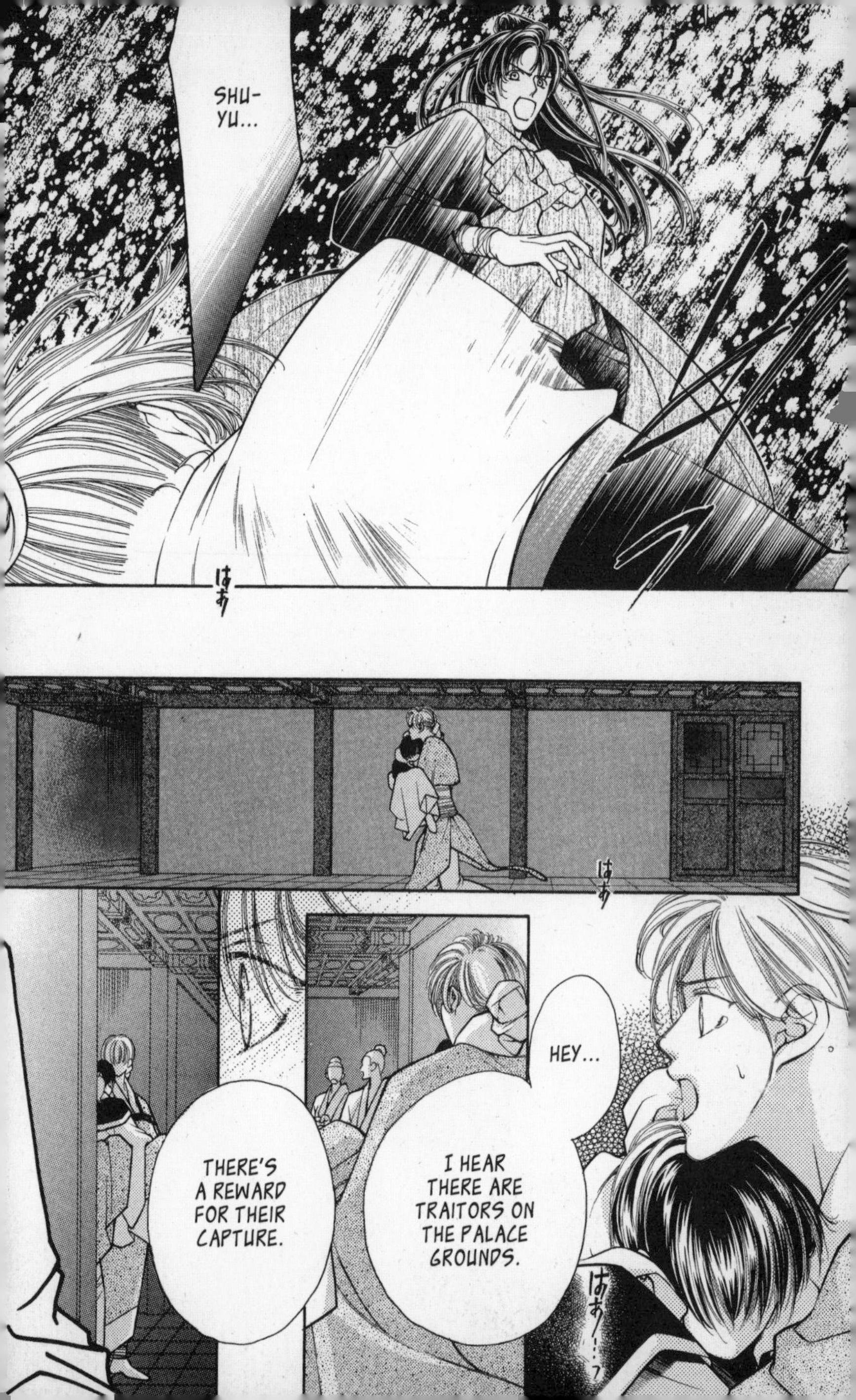
SHU-YU...
はあ
はあ
HEY...
はあ!?
I HEAR THERE ARE TRAITORS ON THE PALACE GROUNDS.
THERE'S A REWARD FOR THEIR CAPTURE.

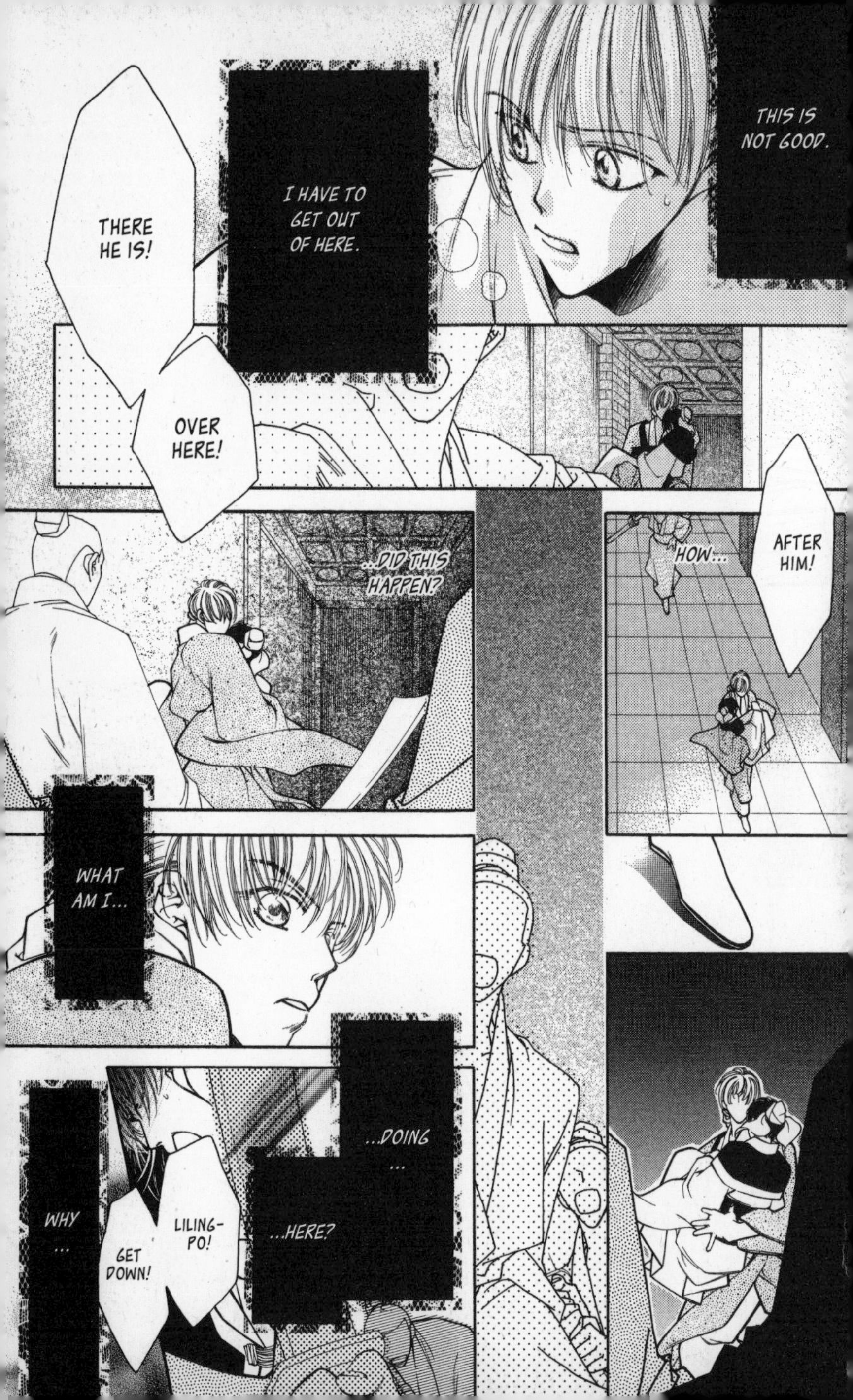
THIS IS NOT GOOD.
I HAVE TO GET OUT OF HERE.
THERE HE IS!
OVER HERE!
AFTER HIM!
HOW...
...DID THIS HAPPEN?
WHAT AM I...
...DOING ...
...HERE?
LILING-PO!
WHY ...
GET DOWN!

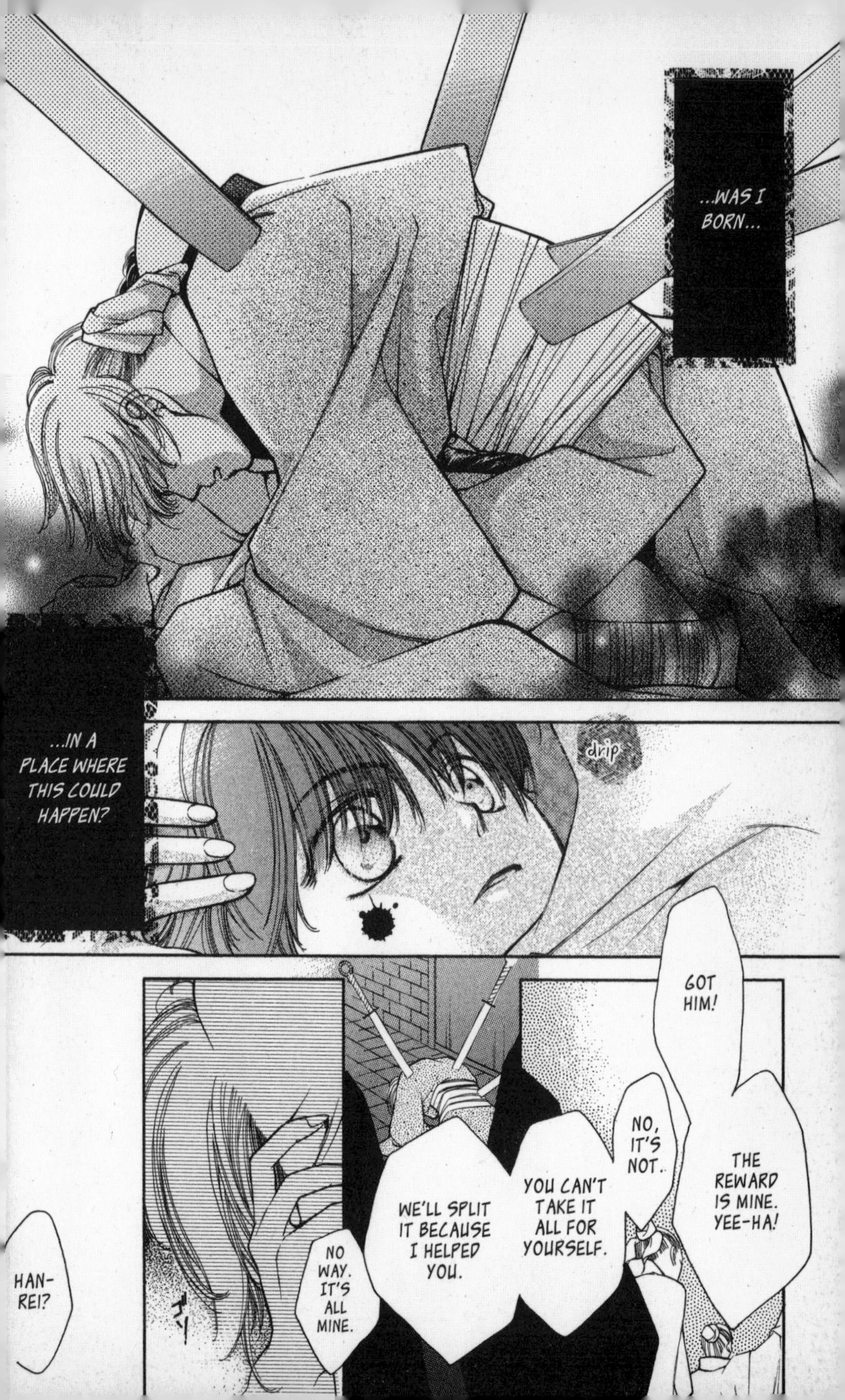
...WAS I BORN...
...IN A PLACE WHERE THIS COULD HAPPEN?
drip
GOT HIM!
THE REWARD IS MINE. YEE-HA!
NO, IT'S NOT.
YOU CAN'T TAKE IT ALL FOR YOURSELF.
WE'LL SPLIT IT BECAUSE I HELPED YOU.
NO WAY. IT'S ALL MINE.
HAN-REI?

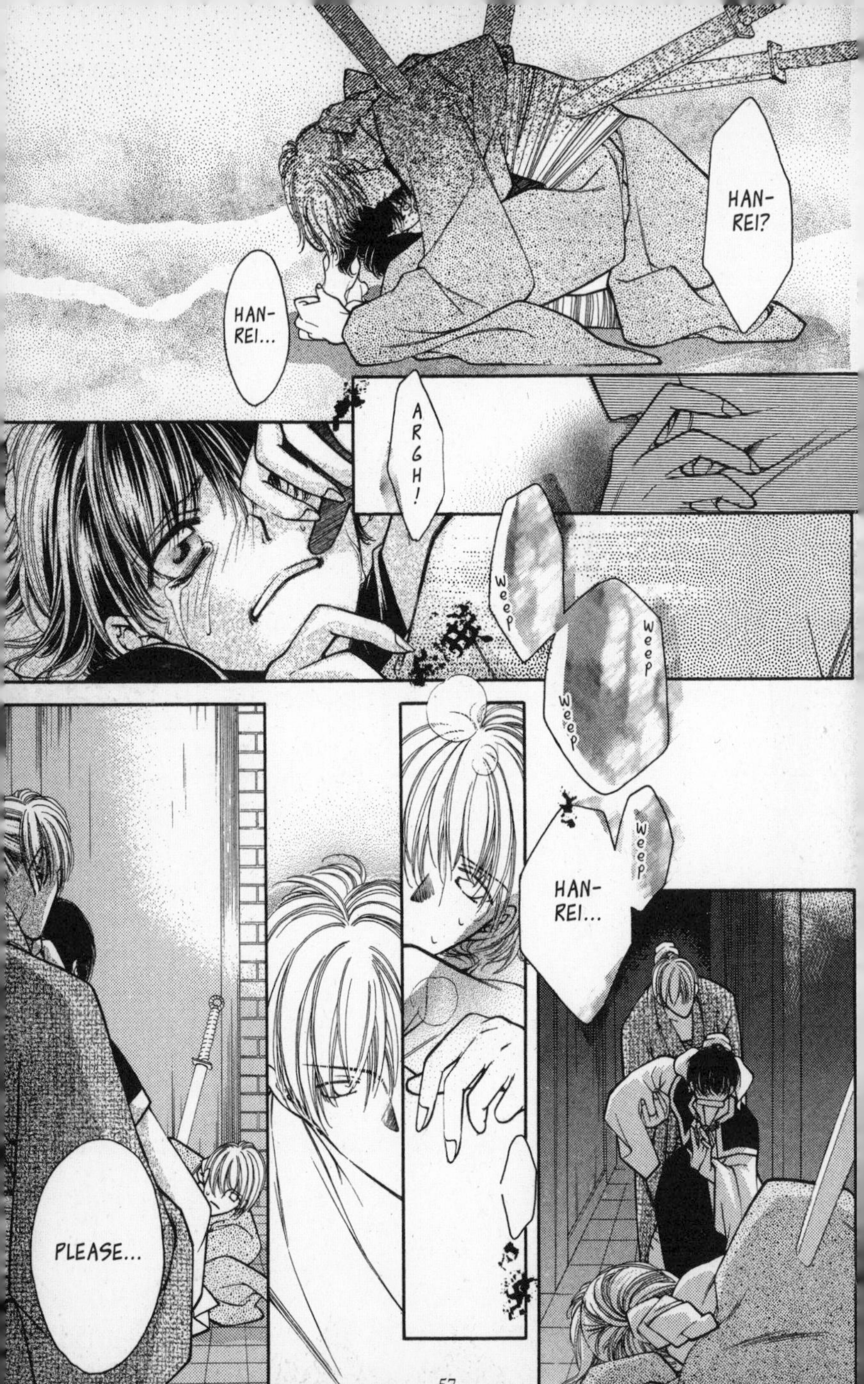
HAN-REI?
HAN-REI...
ARGH!
WEEP
WEEP
WEEP
WEEP
HAN-REI...
PLEASE...

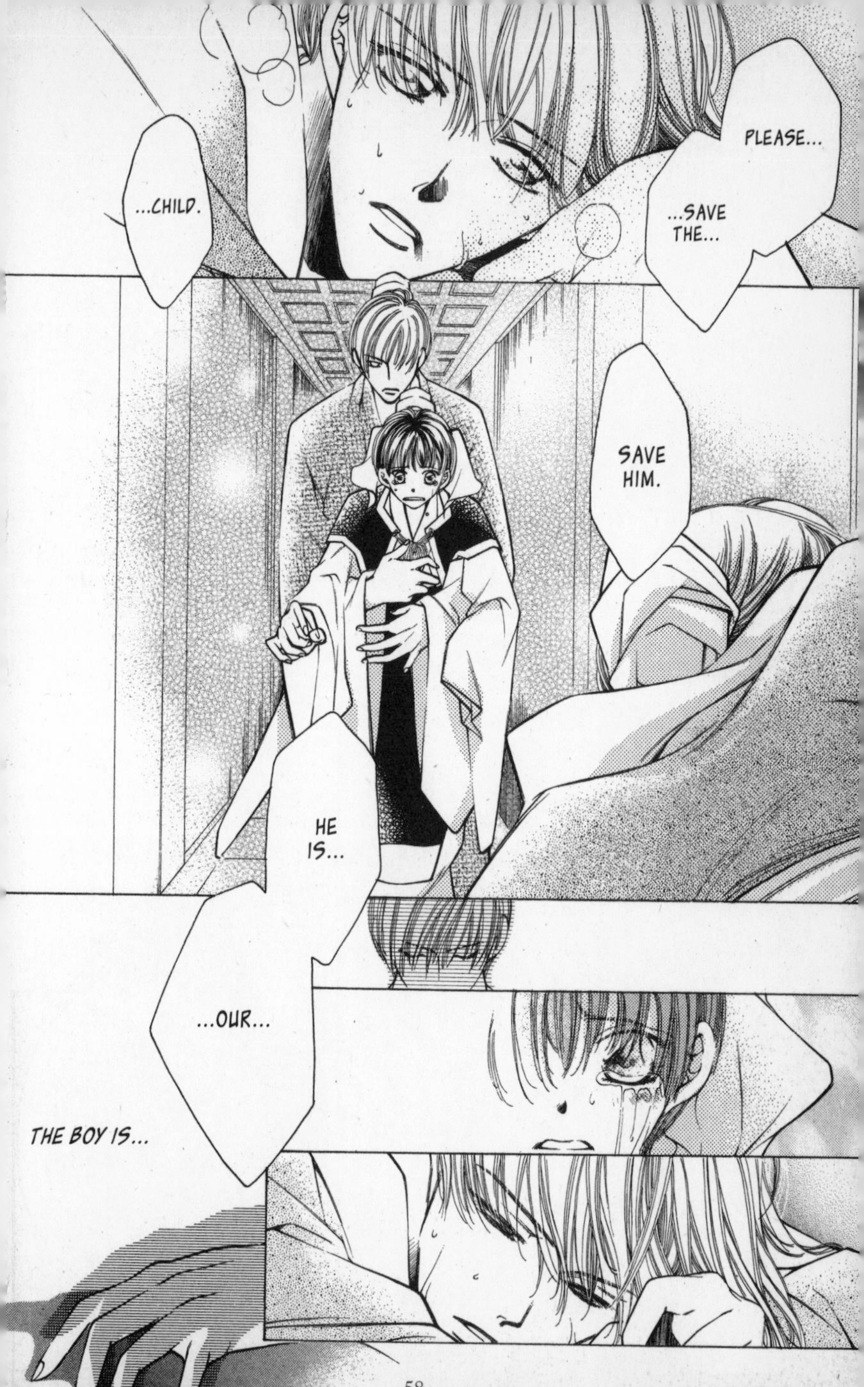
PLEASE...
...SAVE THE...
...CHILD.
SAVE HIM.
HE IS...
...OUR...
THE BOY IS...

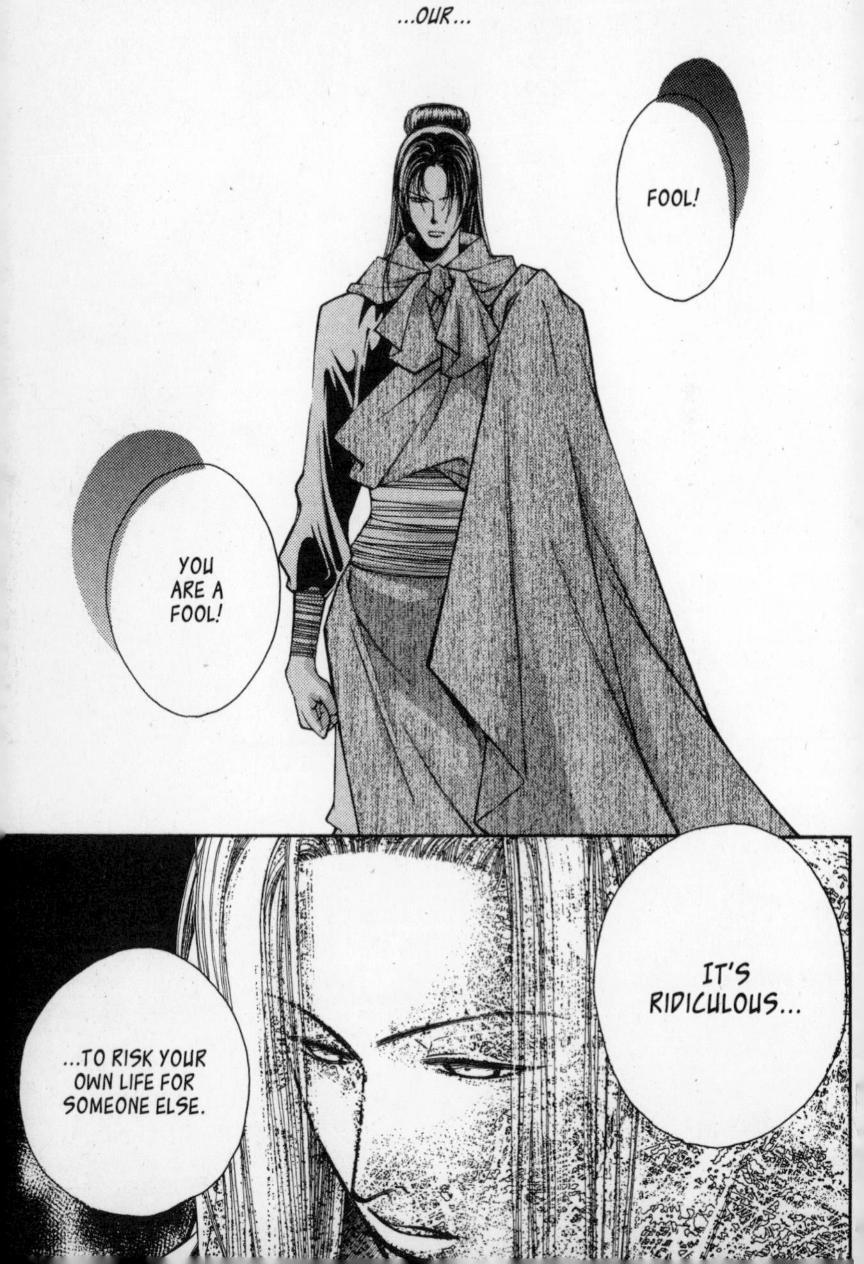
...OUR...
FOOL!
YOU ARE A FOOL!
IT'S RIDICULOUS...
...TO RISK YOUR OWN LIFE FOR SOMEONE ELSE.

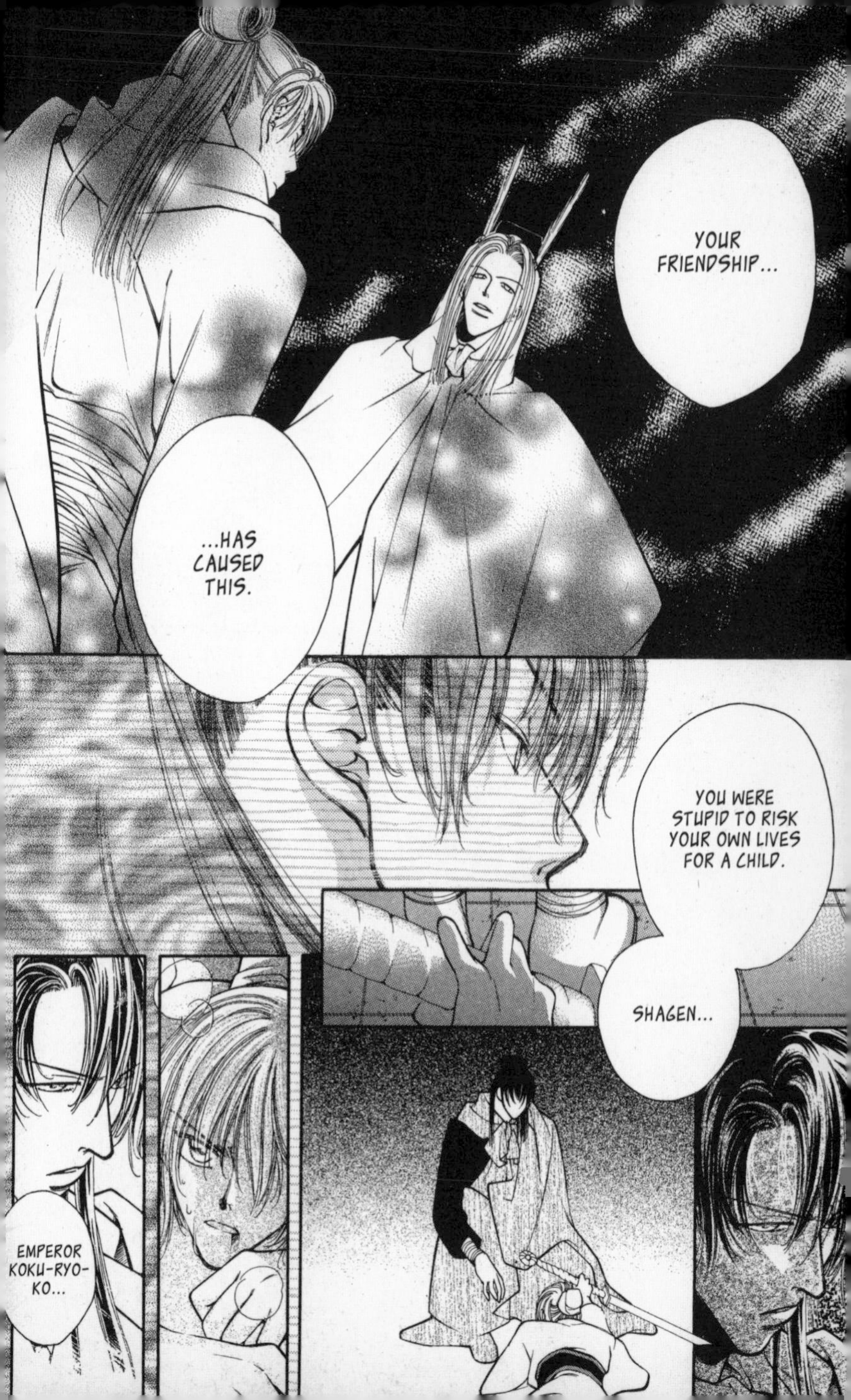
YOUR FRIENDSHIP...
...HAS CAUSED THIS.
YOU WERE STUPID TO RISK YOUR OWN LIVES FOR A CHILD.
SHAGEN...
EMPEROR KOKU-RYOKO...

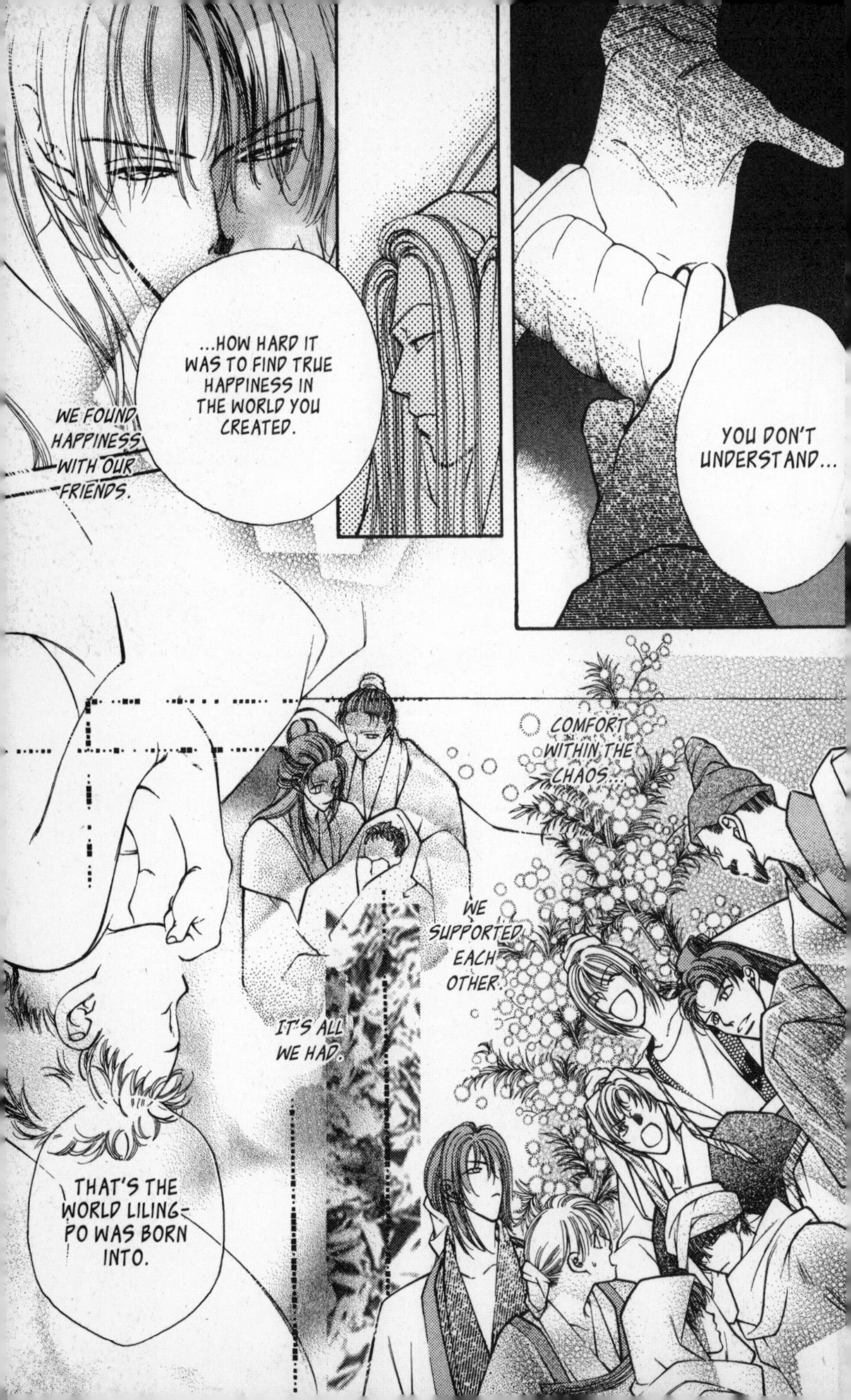
YOU DON'T UNDERSTAND...
...HOW HARD IT WAS TO FIND TRUE HAPPINESS IN THE WORLD YOU CREATED.
WE FOUND HAPPINESS WITH OUR FRIENDS.
COMFORT WITHIN THE CHAOS...
WE SUPPORTED EACH OTHER.
IT'S ALL WE HAD.
THAT'S THE WORLD LILING-PO WAS BORN INTO.

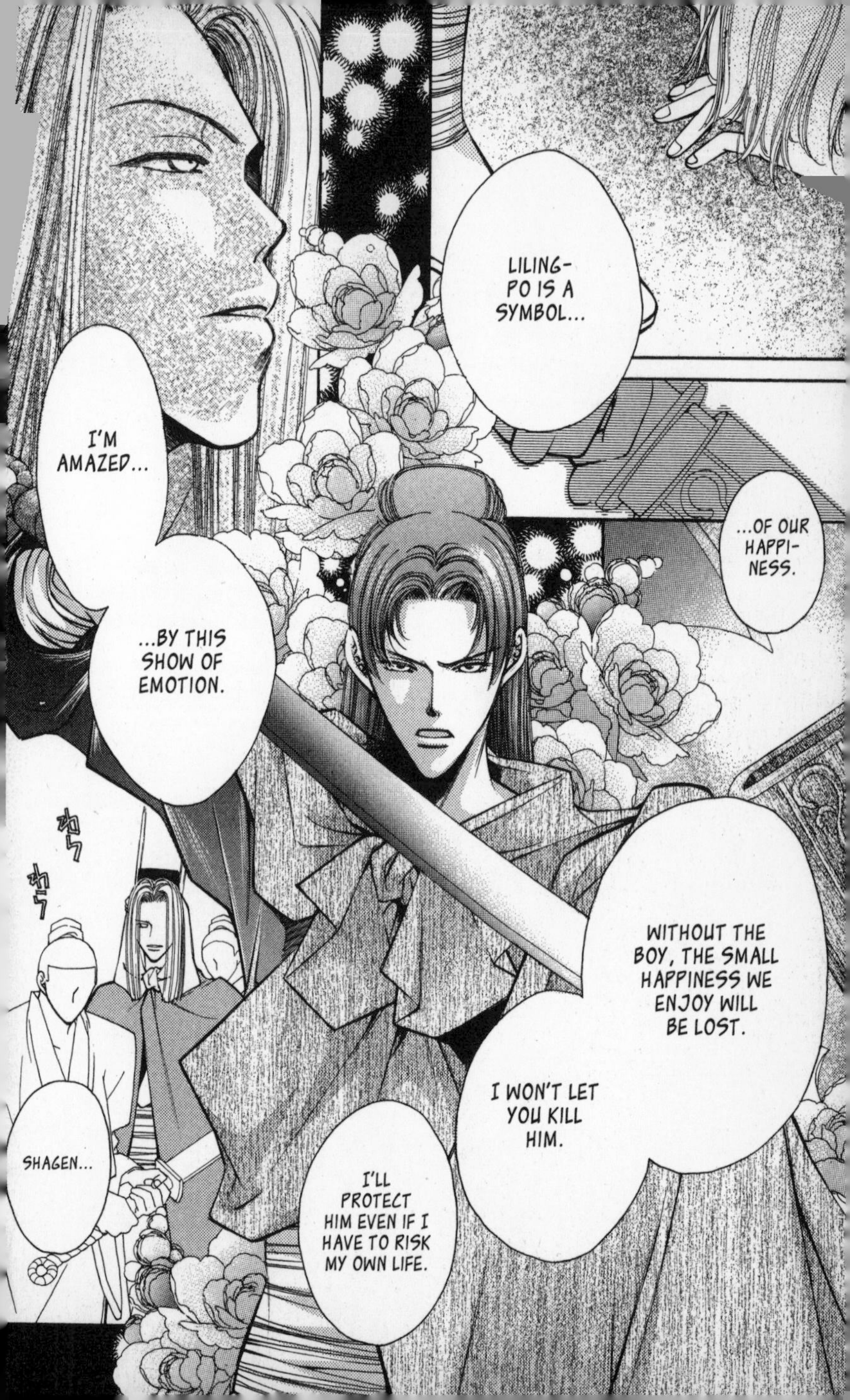
LILING-PO IS A SYMBOL...
...OF OUR HAPPINESS.
I'M AMAZED...
...BY THIS SHOW OF EMOTION.
WITHOUT THE BOY, THE SMALL HAPPINESS WE ENJOY WILL BE LOST.
I WON'T LET YOU KILL HIM.
I'LL PROTECT HIM EVEN IF I HAVE TO RISK MY OWN LIFE.
SHAGEN...

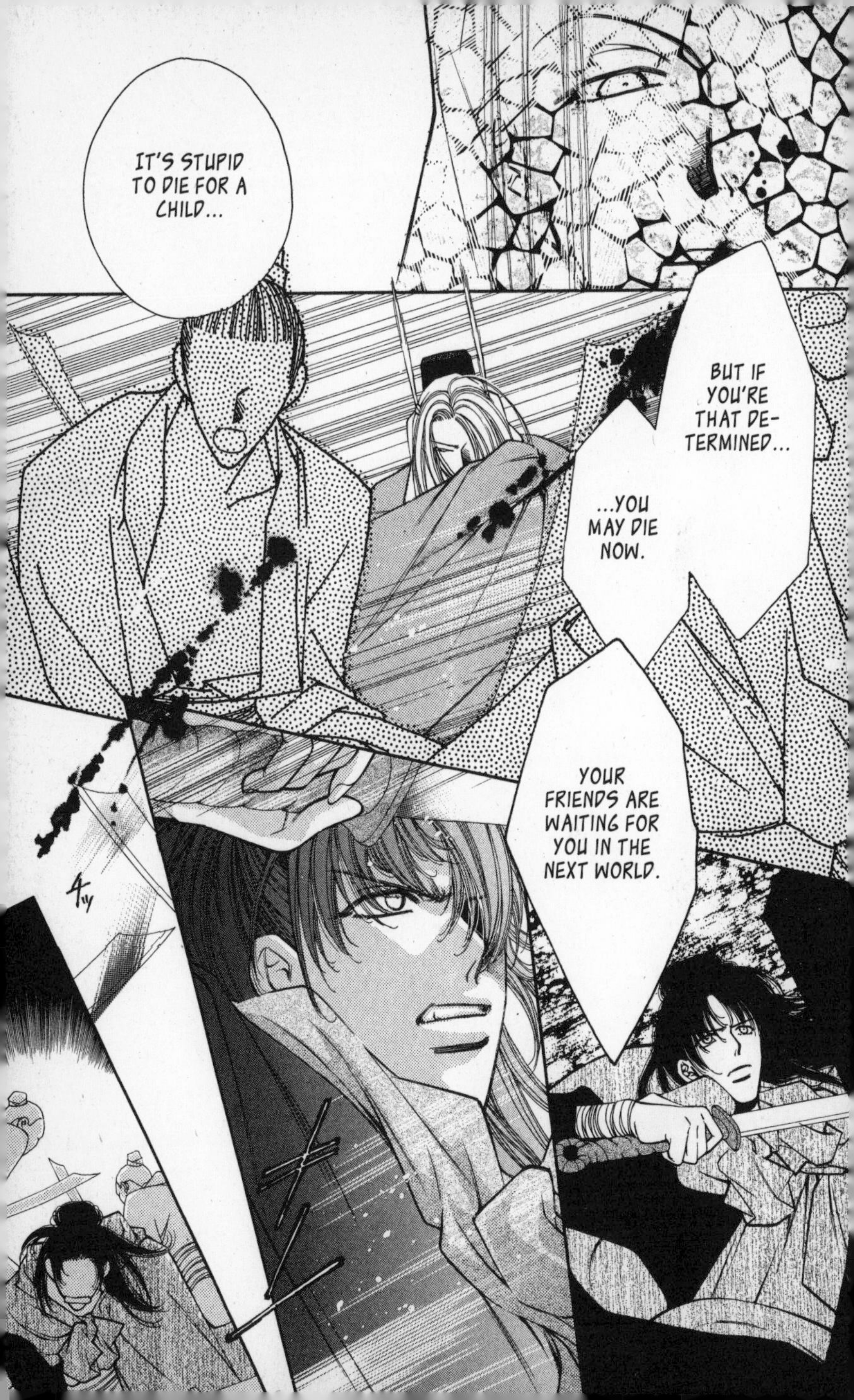
IT'S STUPID TO DIE FOR A CHILD...
BUT IF YOU'RE THAT DE-TERMINED...
...YOU MAY DIE NOW.
YOUR FRIENDS ARE WAITING FOR YOU IN THE NEXT WORLD.

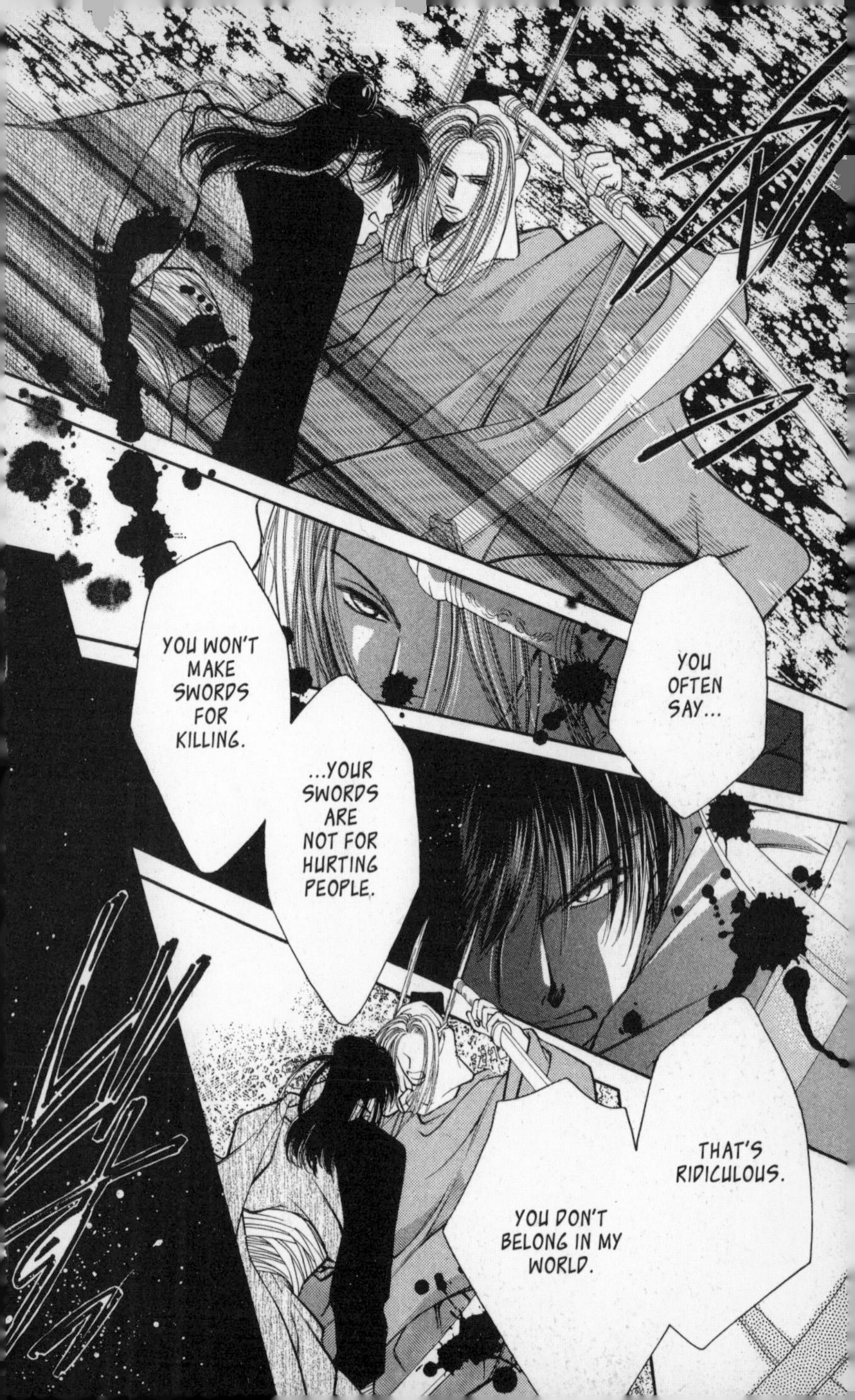
YOU OFTEN SAY...
YOU WON'T MAKE SWORDS FOR KILLING.
...YOUR SWORDS ARE NOT FOR HURTING PEOPLE.
THAT'S RIDICULOUS.
YOU DON'T BELONG IN MY WORLD.

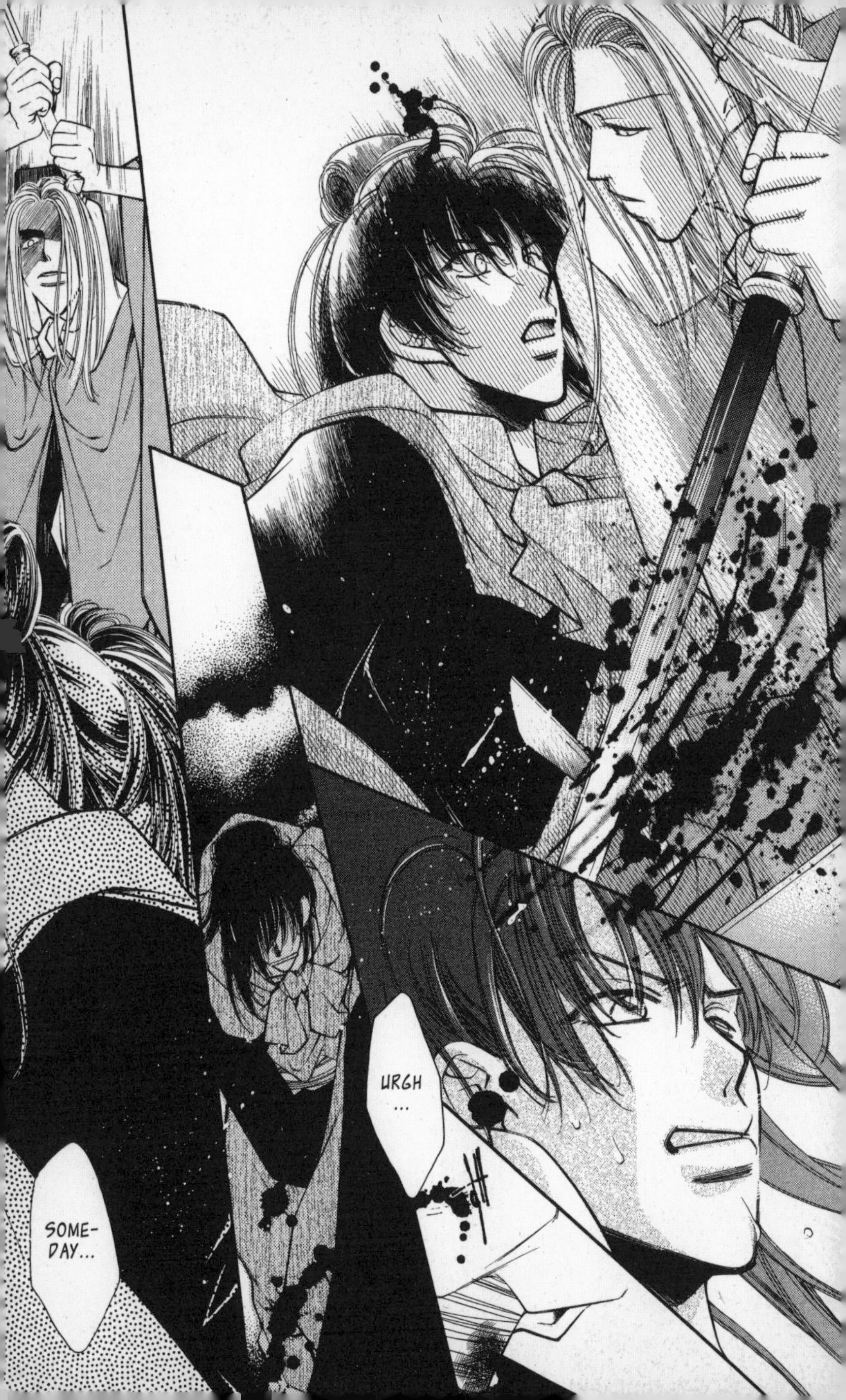
URGH ...
SOME-DAY...

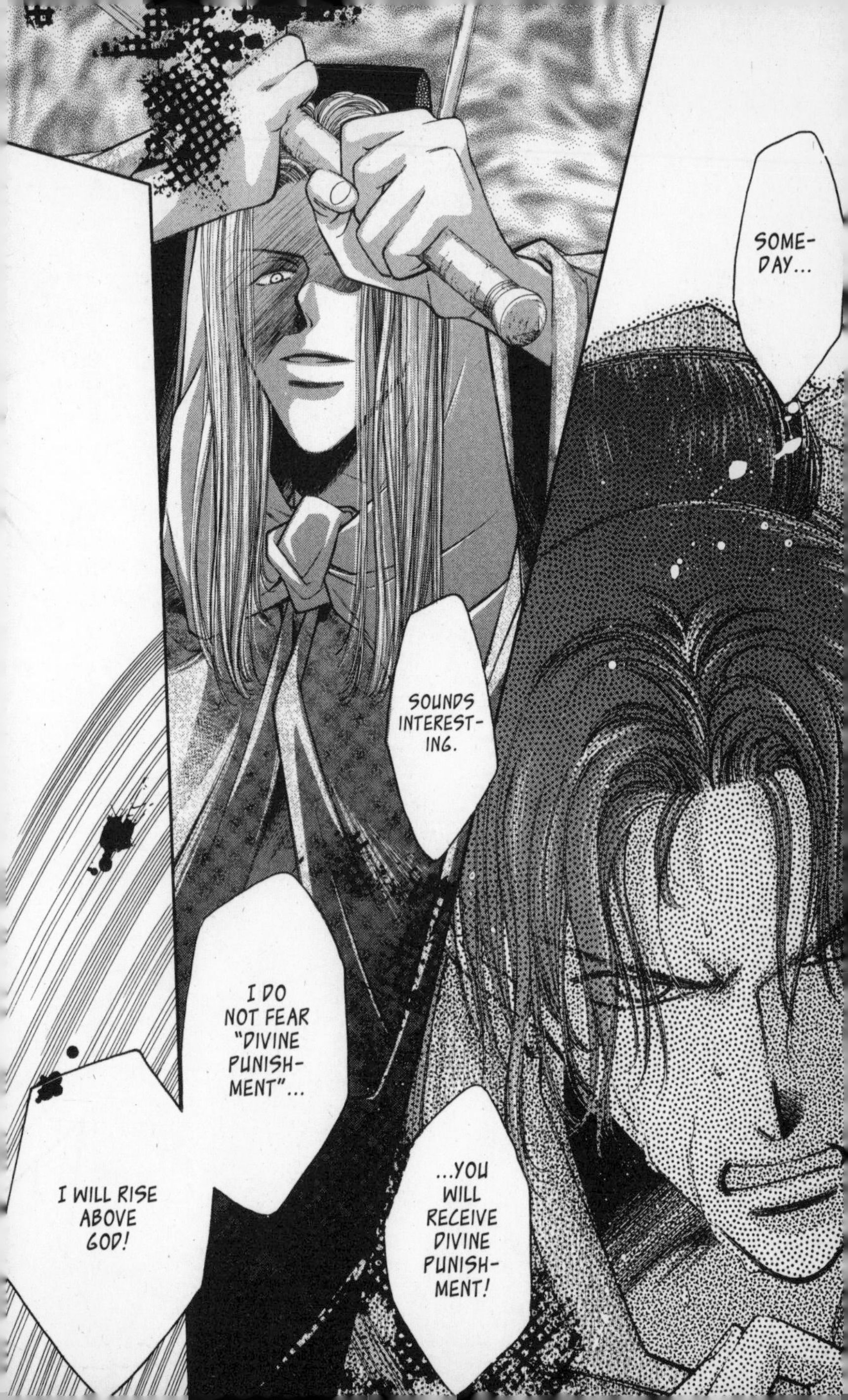

SOME-DAY...
...YOU WILL RECEIVE DIVINE PUNISH-MENT!
SOUNDS INTEREST-ING.
I DO NOT FEAR "DIVINE PUNISH-MENT"...
I WILL RISE ABOVE GOD!

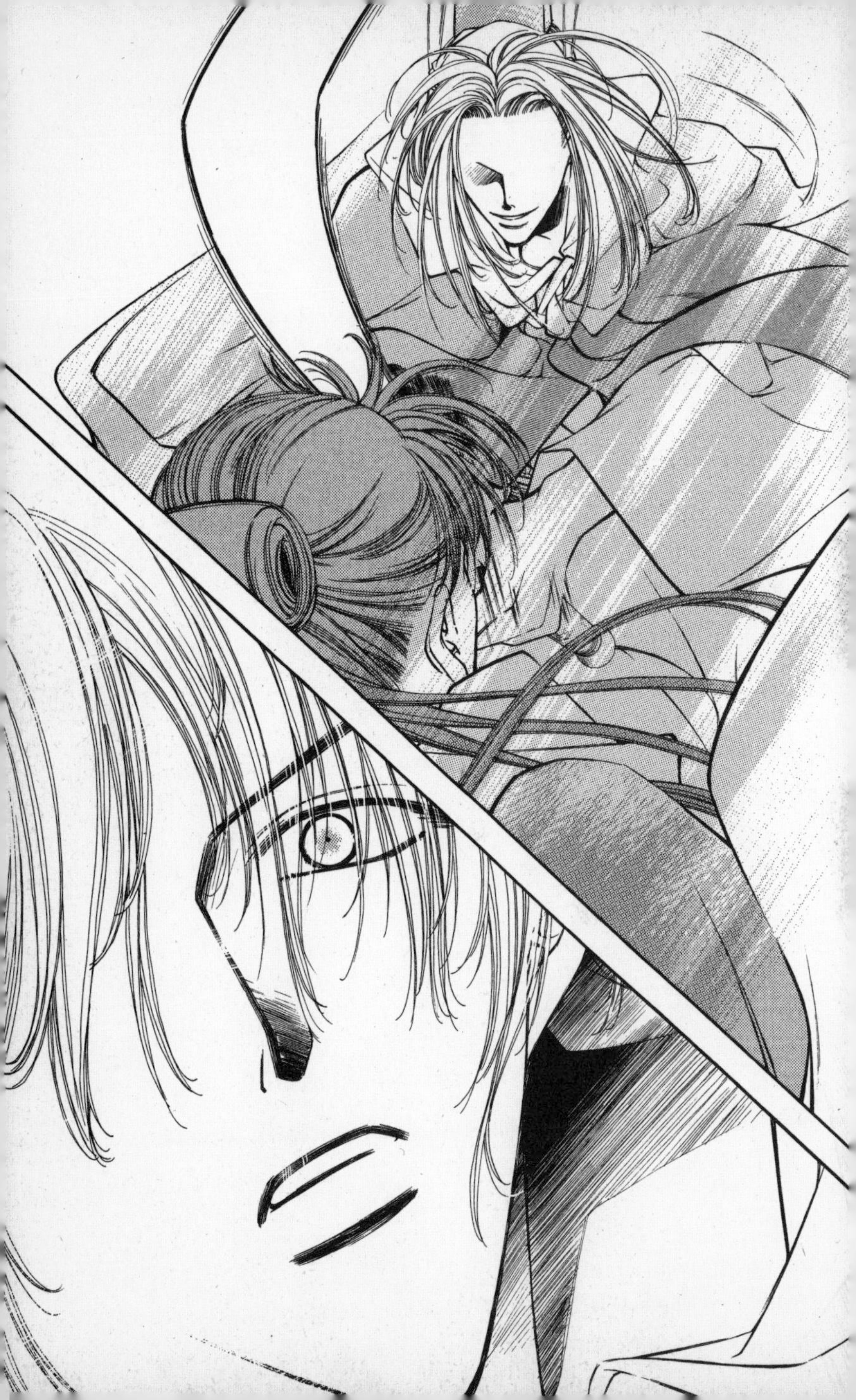

LILING-PO...

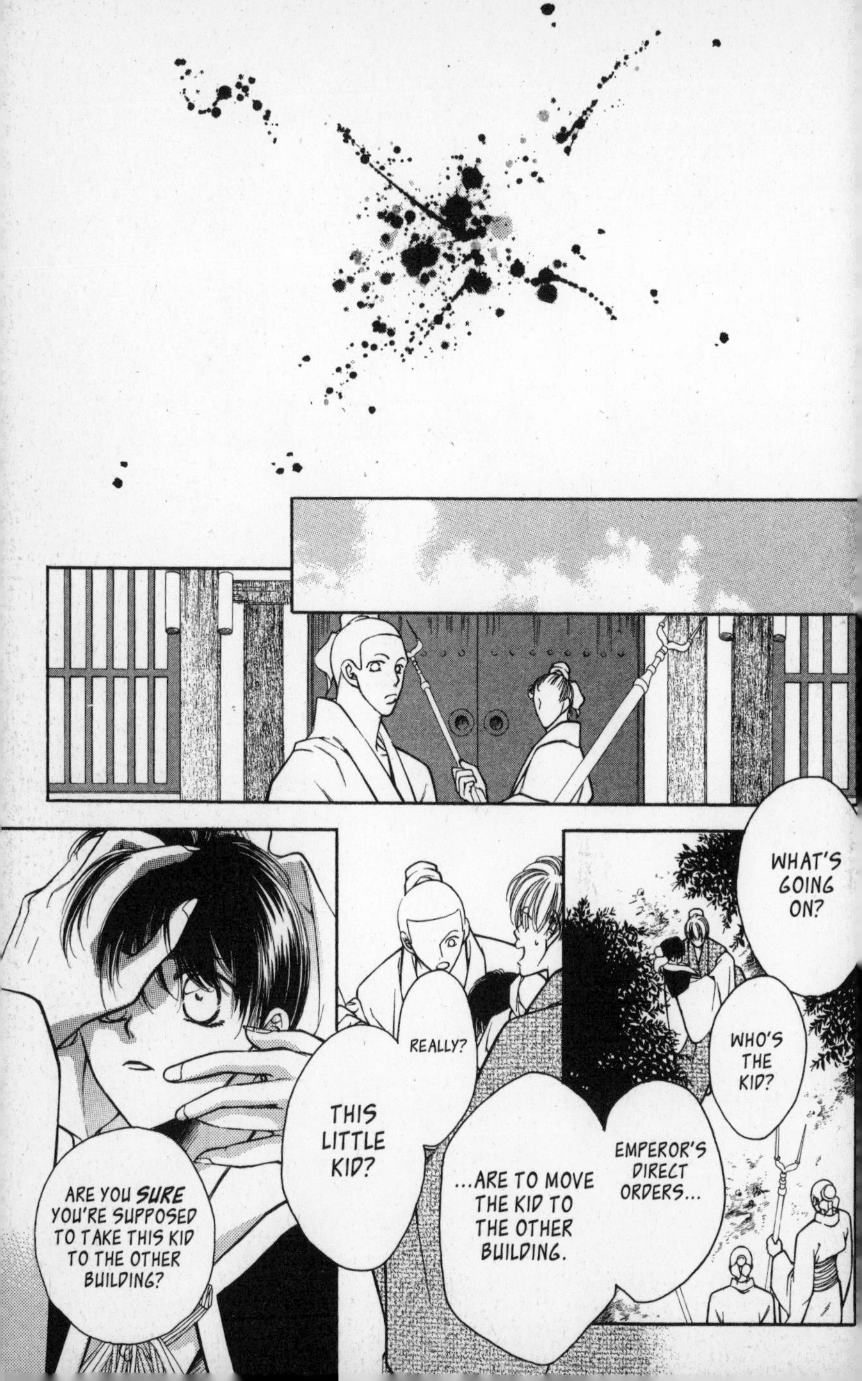
WHAT'S GOING ON?
WHO'S THE KID?
EMPEROR'S DIRECT ORDERS...
...ARE TO MOVE THE KID TO THE OTHER BUILDING.
REALLY?
THIS LITTLE KID?
ARE YOU *SURE* YOU'RE SUPPOSED TO TAKE THIS KID TO THE OTHER BUILDING?

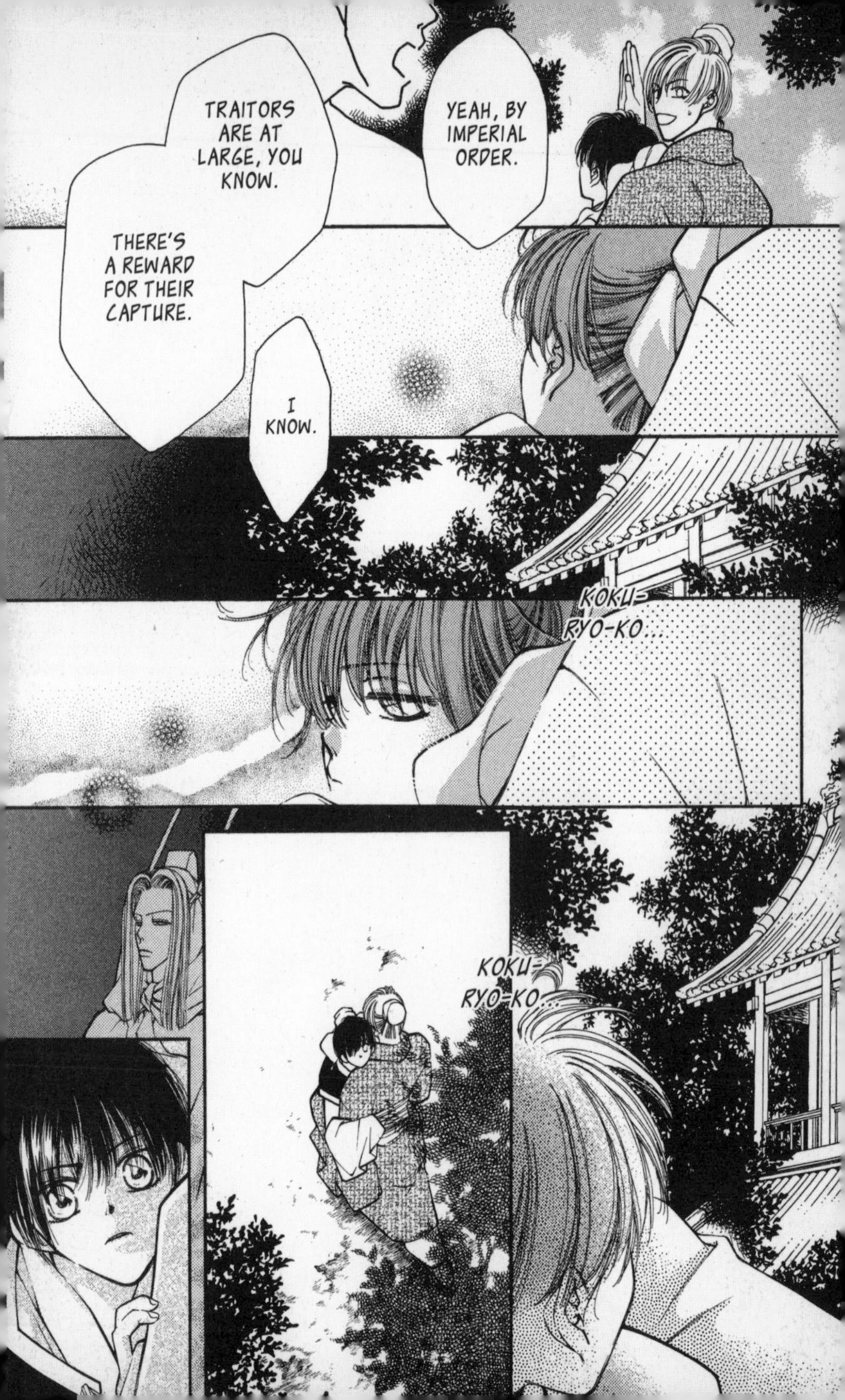
YEAH, BY IMPERIAL ORDER.
TRAITORS ARE AT LARGE, YOU KNOW.
THERE'S A REWARD FOR THEIR CAPTURE.
I KNOW.
KOKU-RYO-KO...
KOKU-RYO-KO...

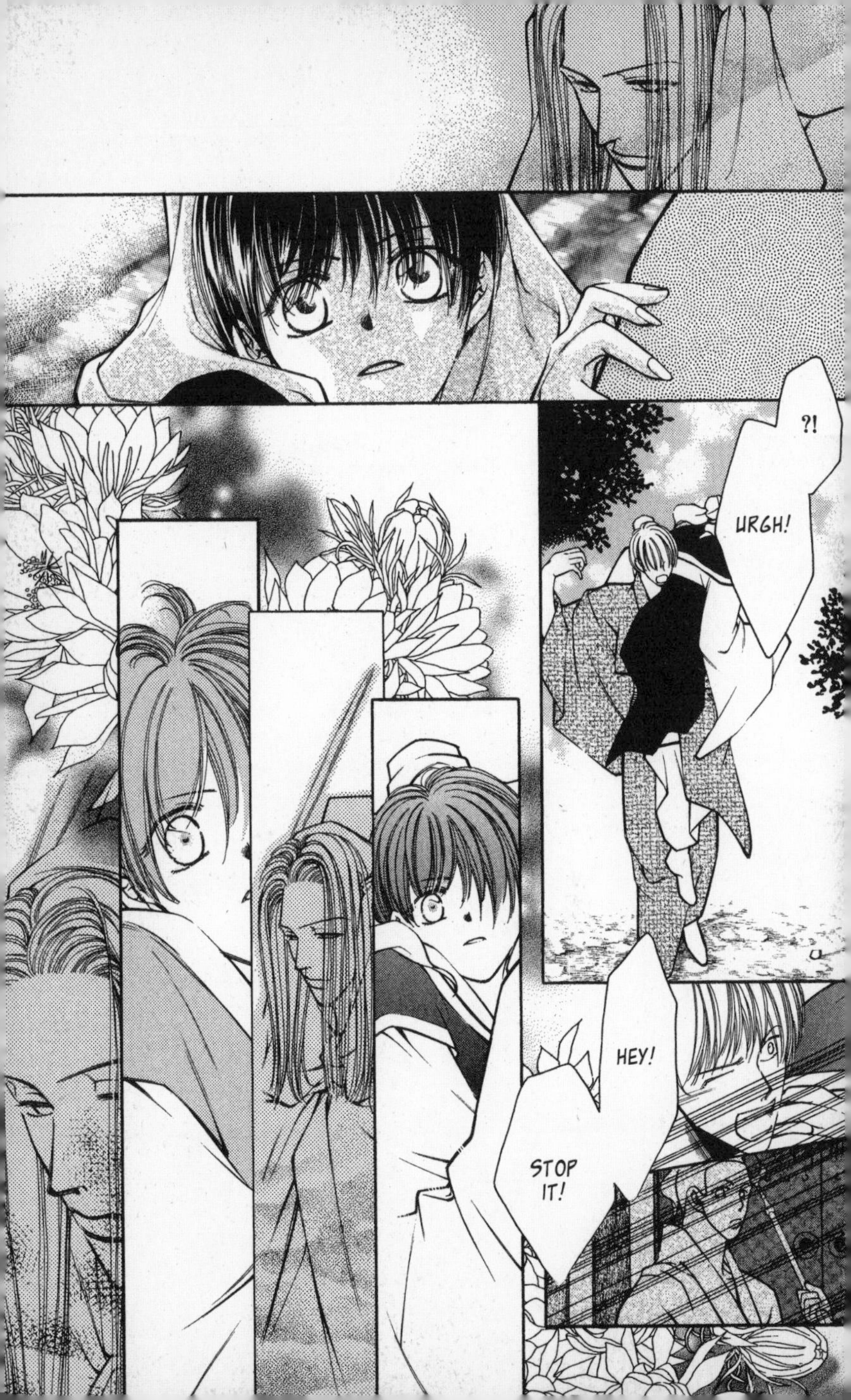
?!
URGH!
HEY!
STOP IT!

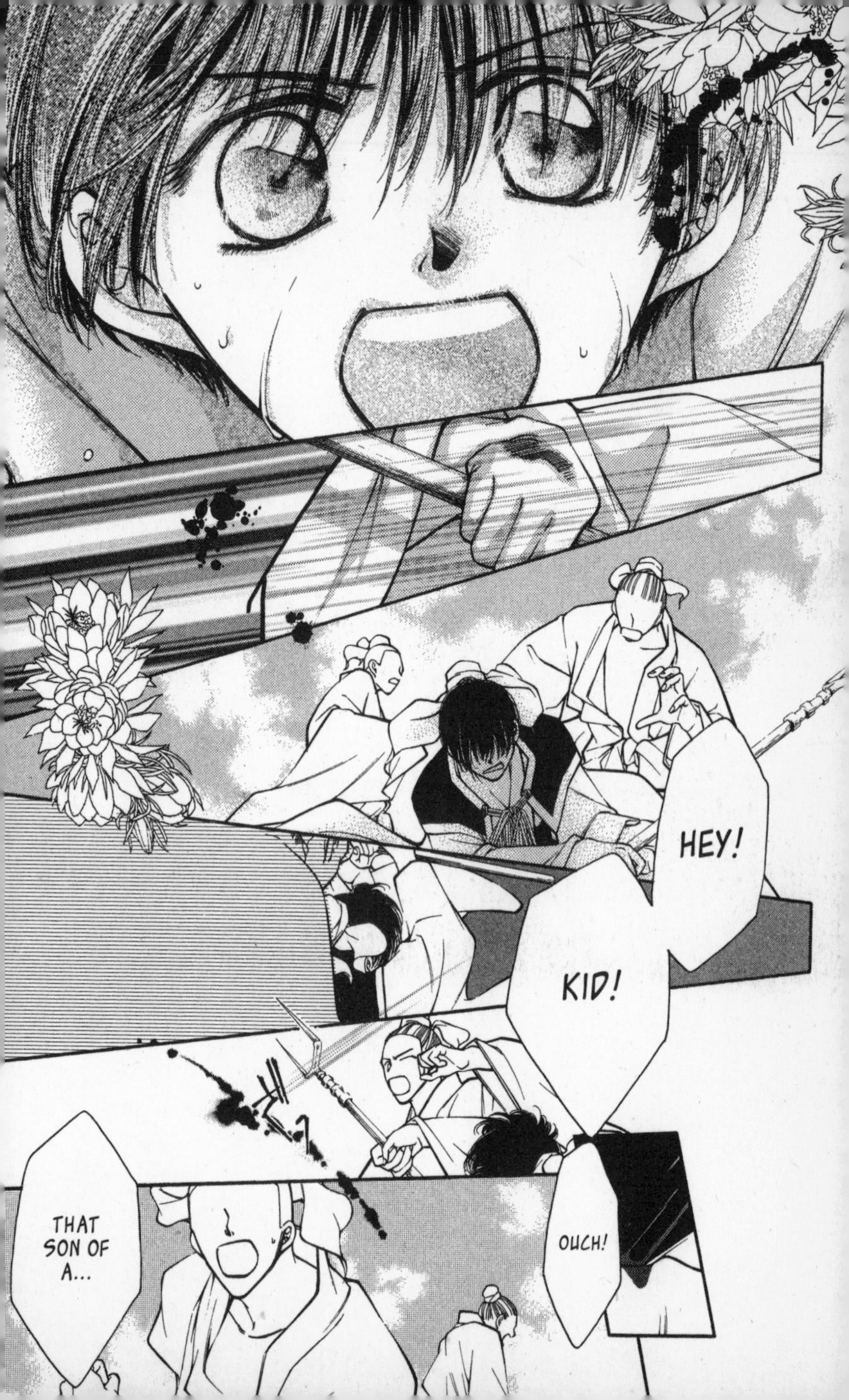
HEY!
KID!
OUCH!
THAT SON OF A...

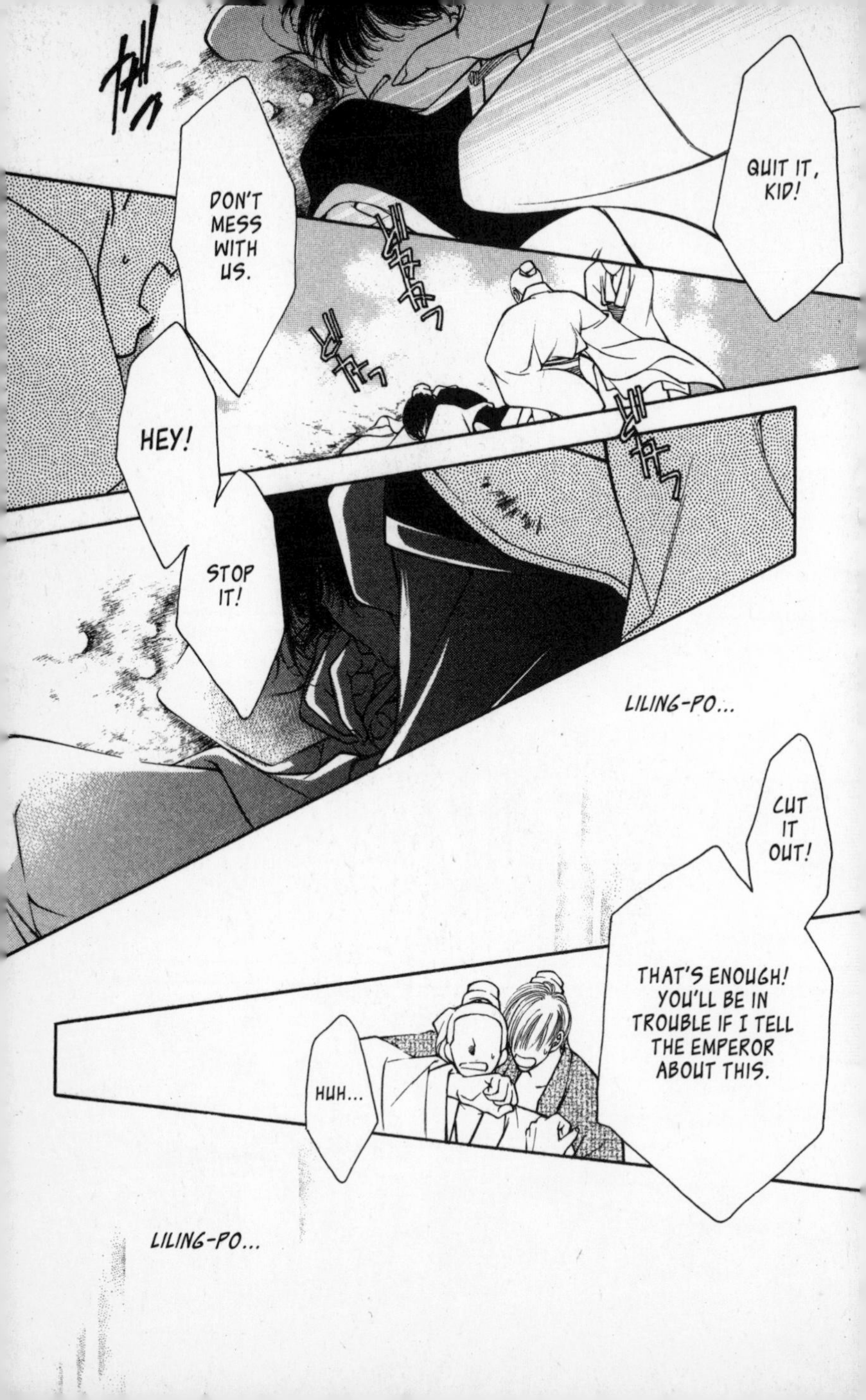
QUIT IT, KID!
DON'T MESS WITH US.
HEY!
STOP IT!
LILING-PO...
CUT IT OUT!
THAT'S ENOUGH! YOU'LL BE IN TROUBLE IF I TELL THE EMPEROR ABOUT THIS.
HUH...
LILING-PO...

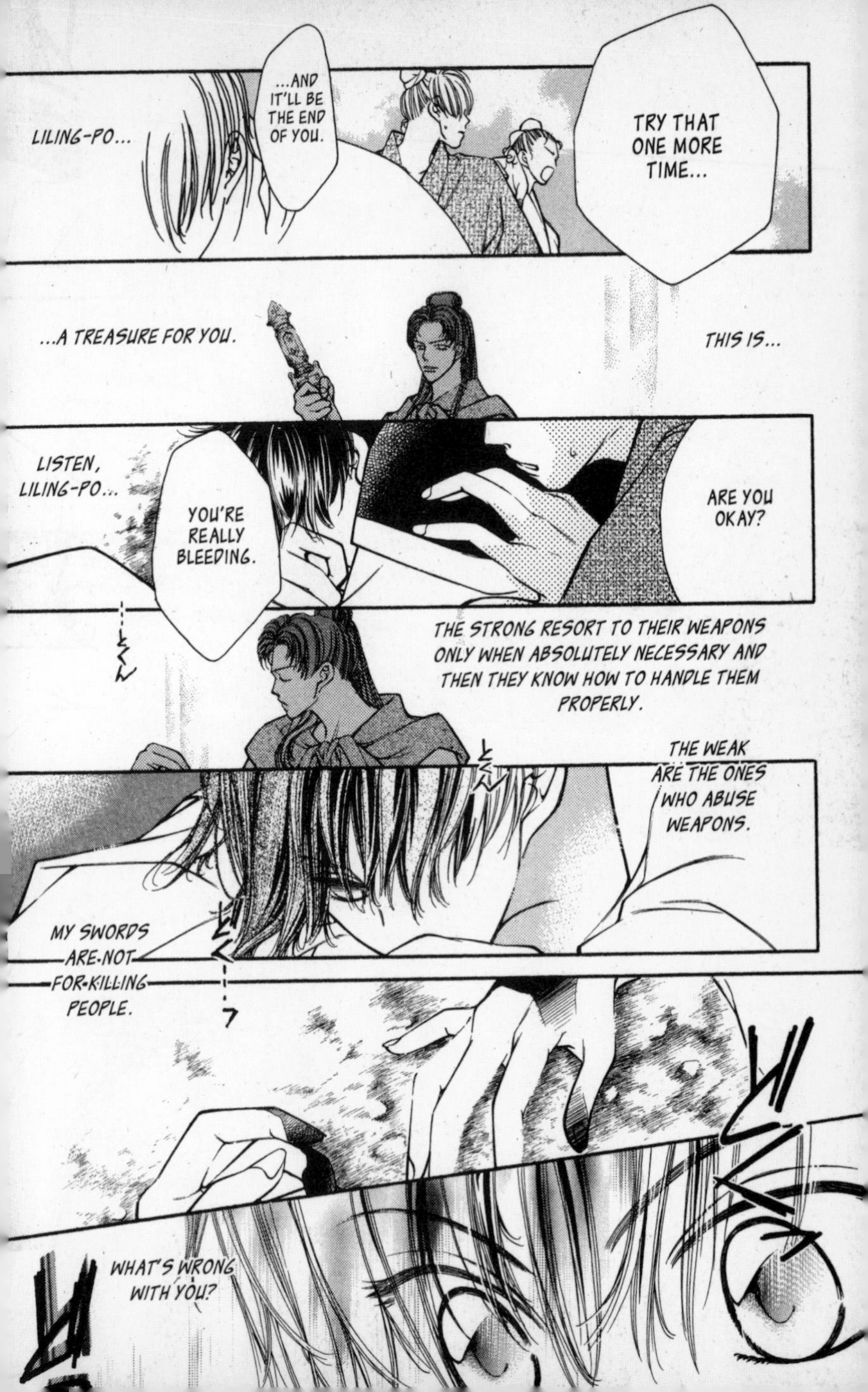
TRY THAT ONE MORE TIME...
...AND IT'LL BE THE END OF YOU.
LILING-PO...
THIS IS...
...A TREASURE FOR YOU.
ARE YOU OKAY?
YOU'RE REALLY BLEEDING.
LISTEN, LILING-PO...
THE STRONG RESORT TO THEIR WEAPONS ONLY WHEN ABSOLUTELY NECESSARY AND THEN THEY KNOW HOW TO HANDLE THEM PROPERLY.
THE WEAK ARE THE ONES WHO ABUSE WEAPONS.
MY SWORDS ARE NOT FOR KILLING PEOPLE.
WHAT'S WRONG WITH YOU?

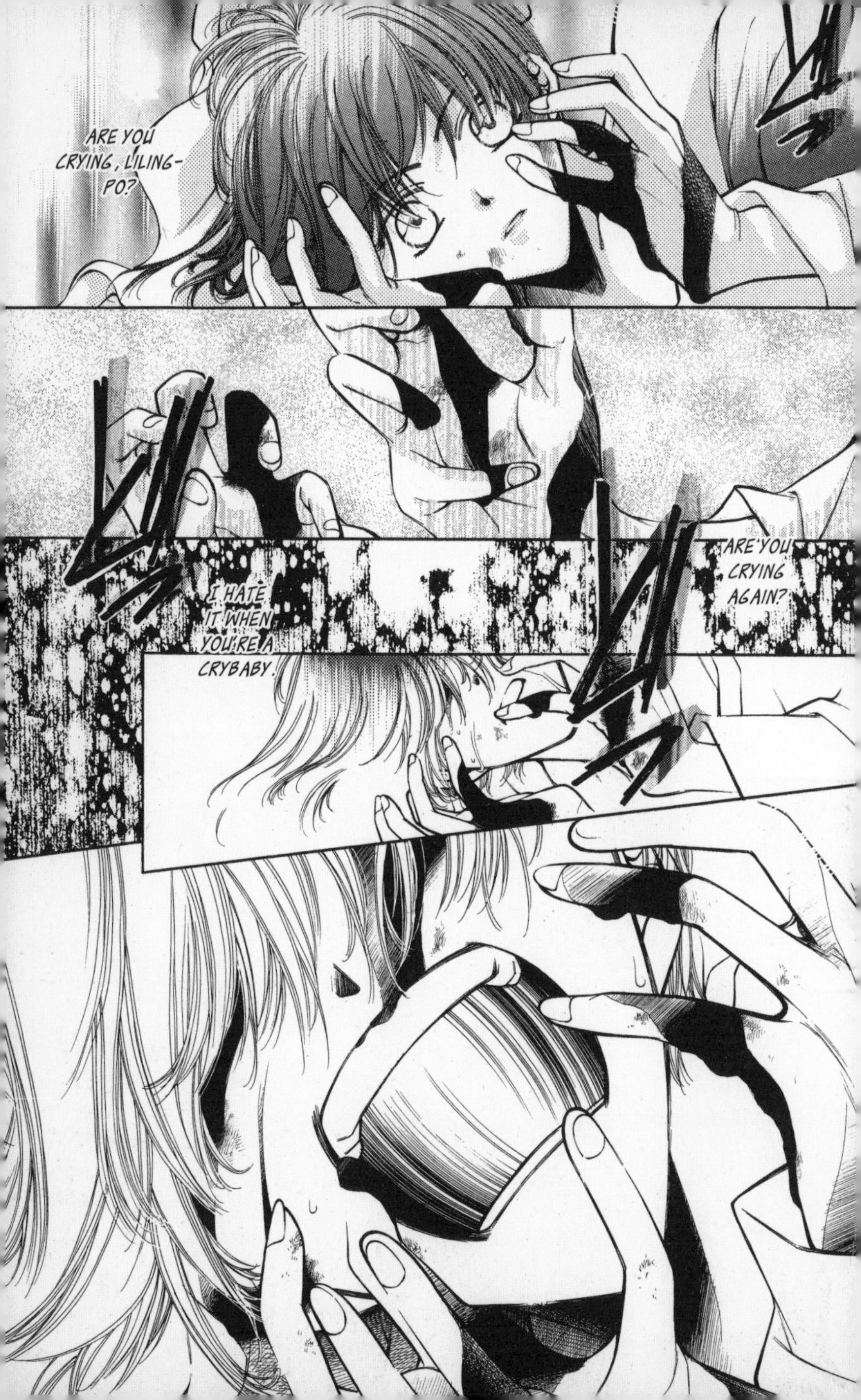
ARE YOU CRYING, LILING-PO?
ARE YOU CRYING AGAIN?
I HATE IT WHEN YOU'RE A CRYBABY!

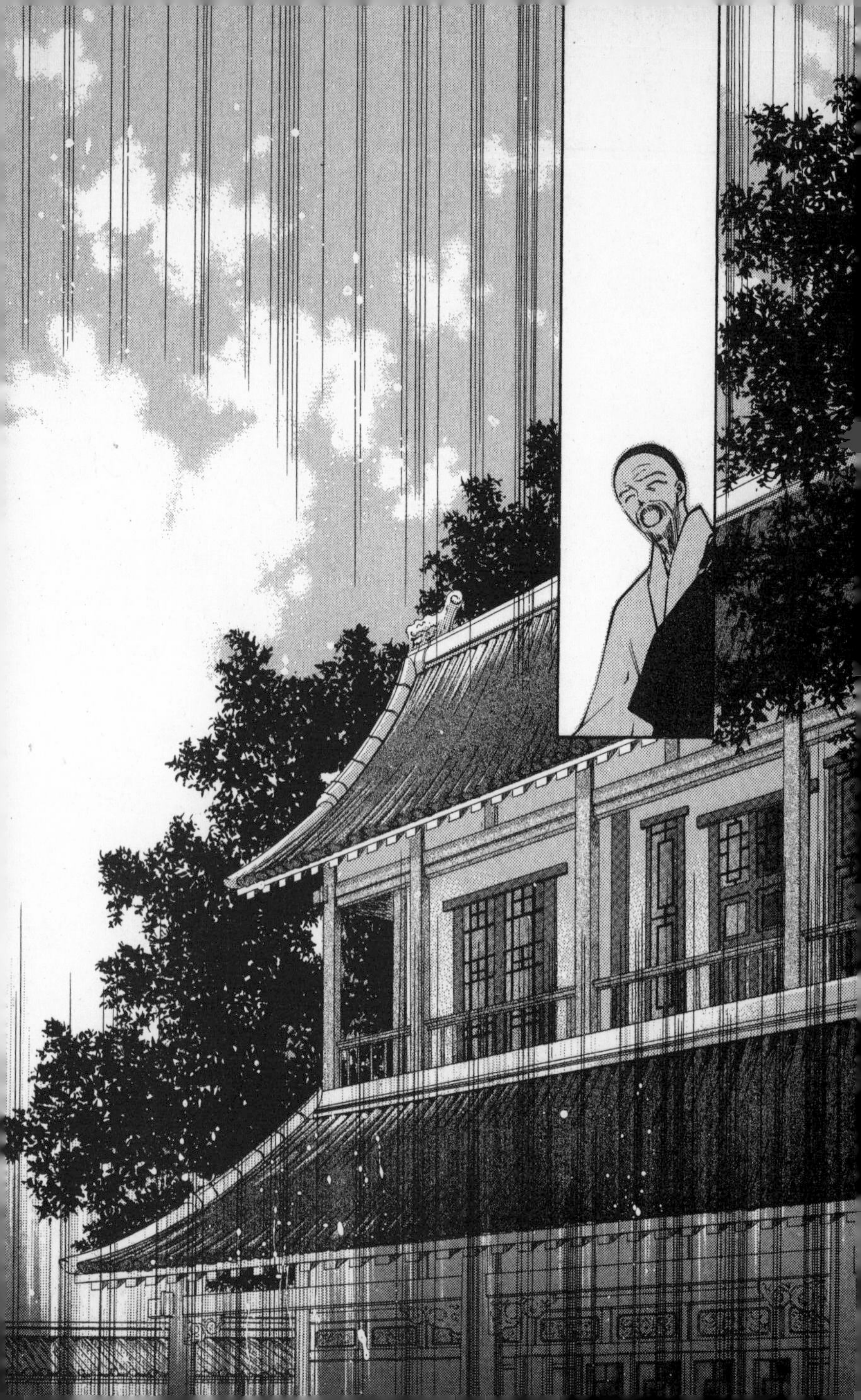

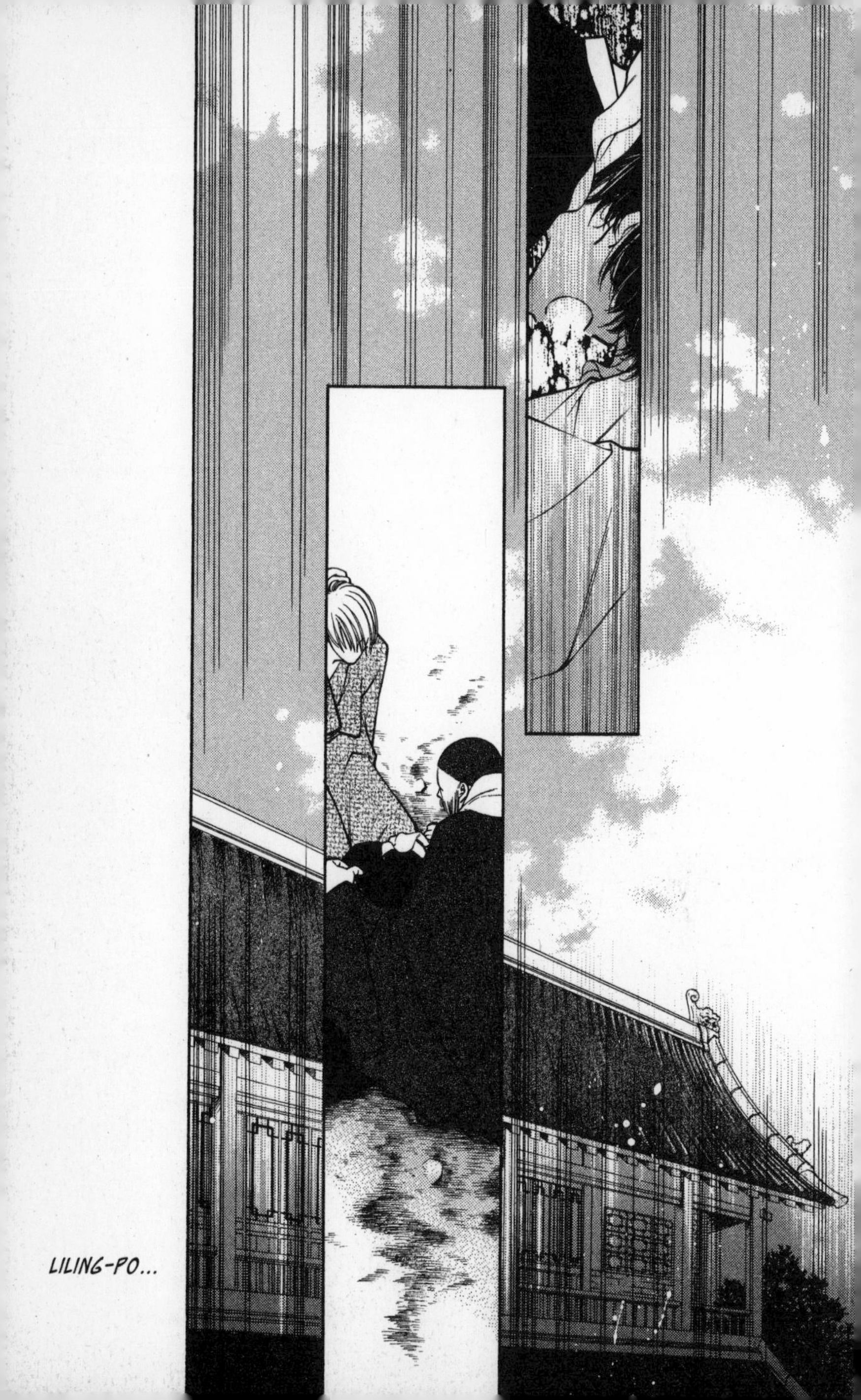
LILING-PO...

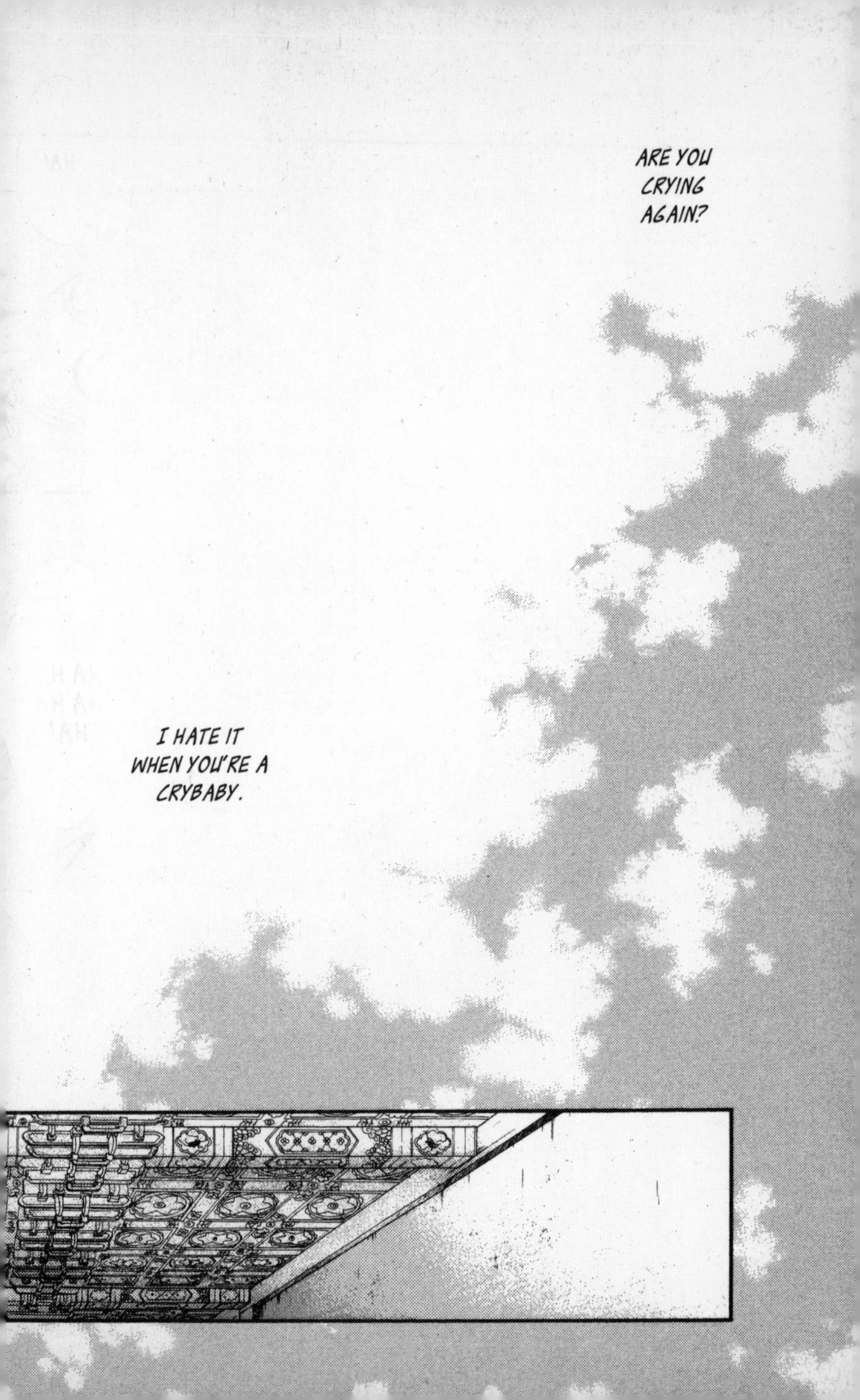
ARE YOU CRYING AGAIN?
I HATE IT WHEN YOU'RE A CRYBABY.

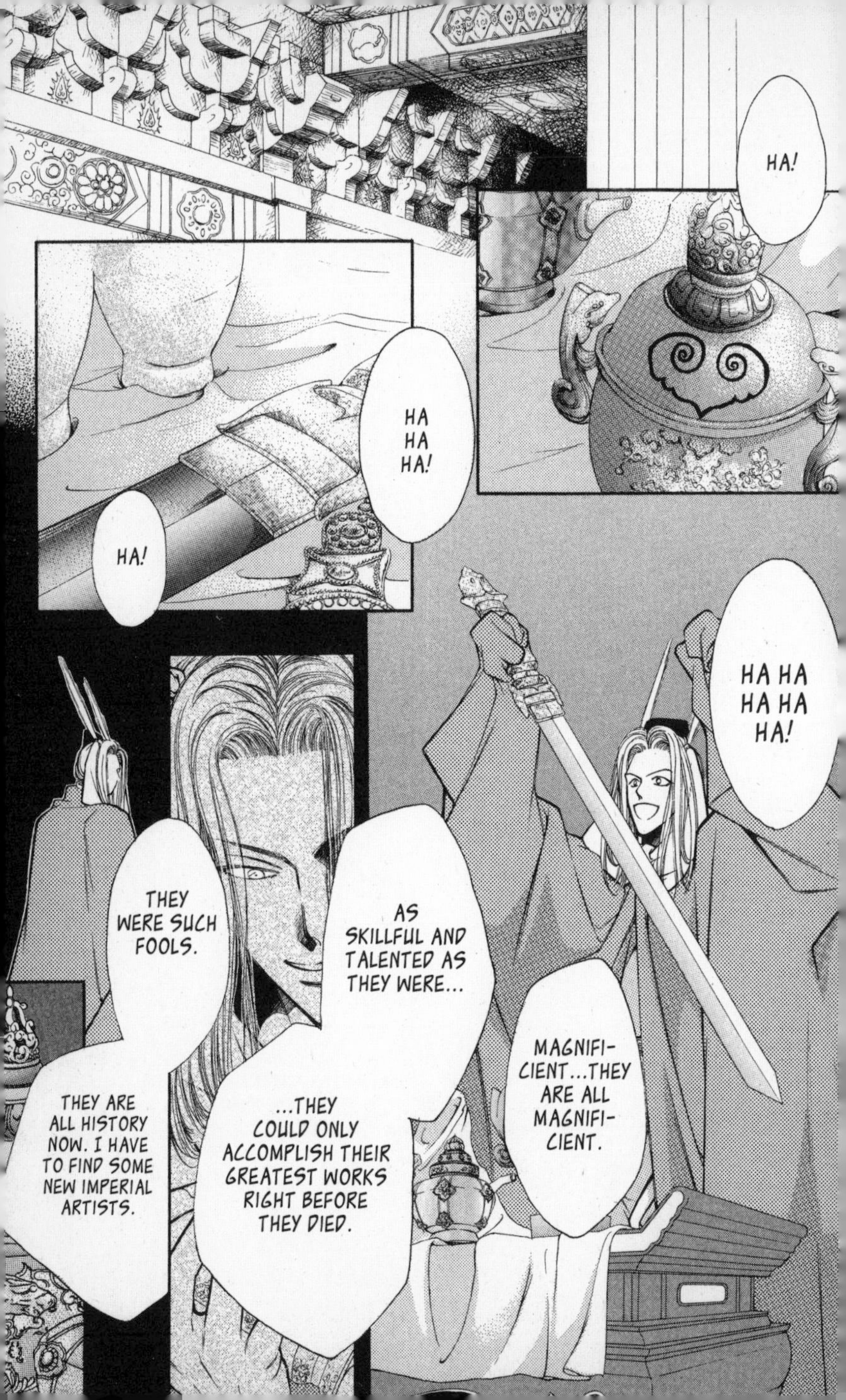
HA!
HA HA HA!
HA!
HA HA HA HA HA!
MAGNIFI-CIENT...THEY ARE ALL MAGNIFI-CIENT.
AS SKILLFUL AND TALENTED AS THEY WERE...
...THEY COULD ONLY ACCOMPLISH THEIR GREATEST WORKS RIGHT BEFORE THEY DIED.
THEY WERE SUCH FOOLS.
THEY ARE ALL HISTORY NOW. I HAVE TO FIND SOME NEW IMPERIAL ARTISTS.

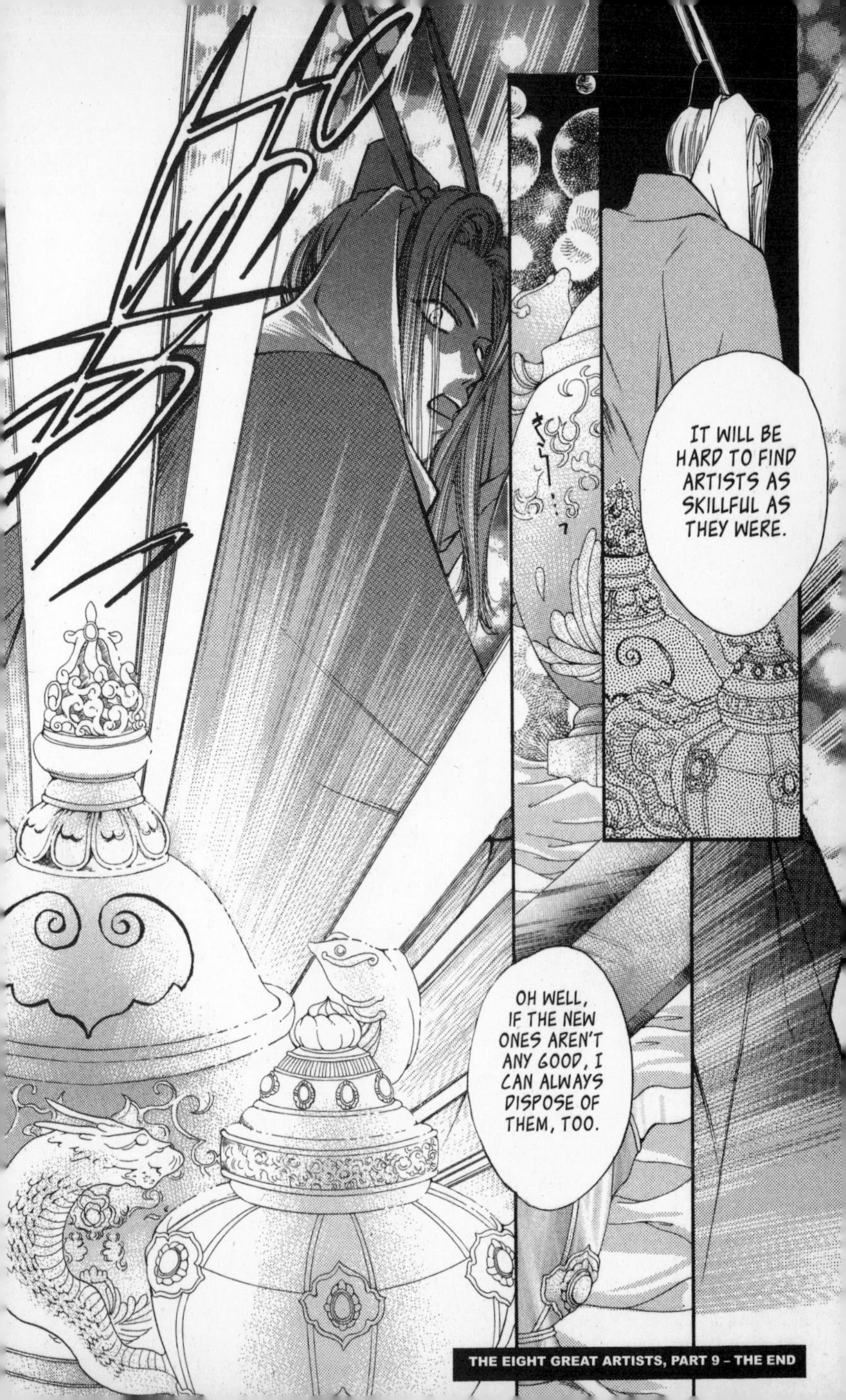
IT WILL BE HARD TO FIND ARTISTS AS SKILLFUL AS THEY WERE.
OH WELL, IF THE NEW ONES AREN'T ANY GOOD, I CAN ALWAYS DISPOSE OF THEM, TOO.

THE EIGHT GREAT ARTISTS, PART 9 – THE END

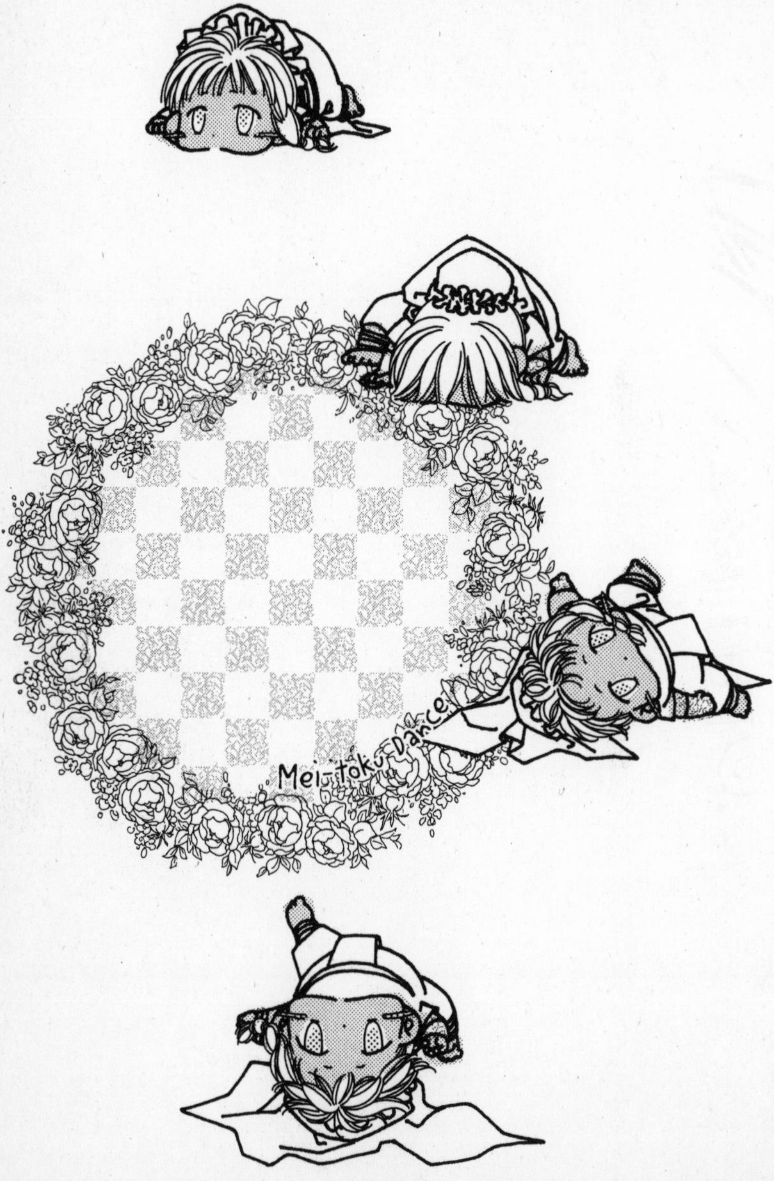
Mei-toku-Dance

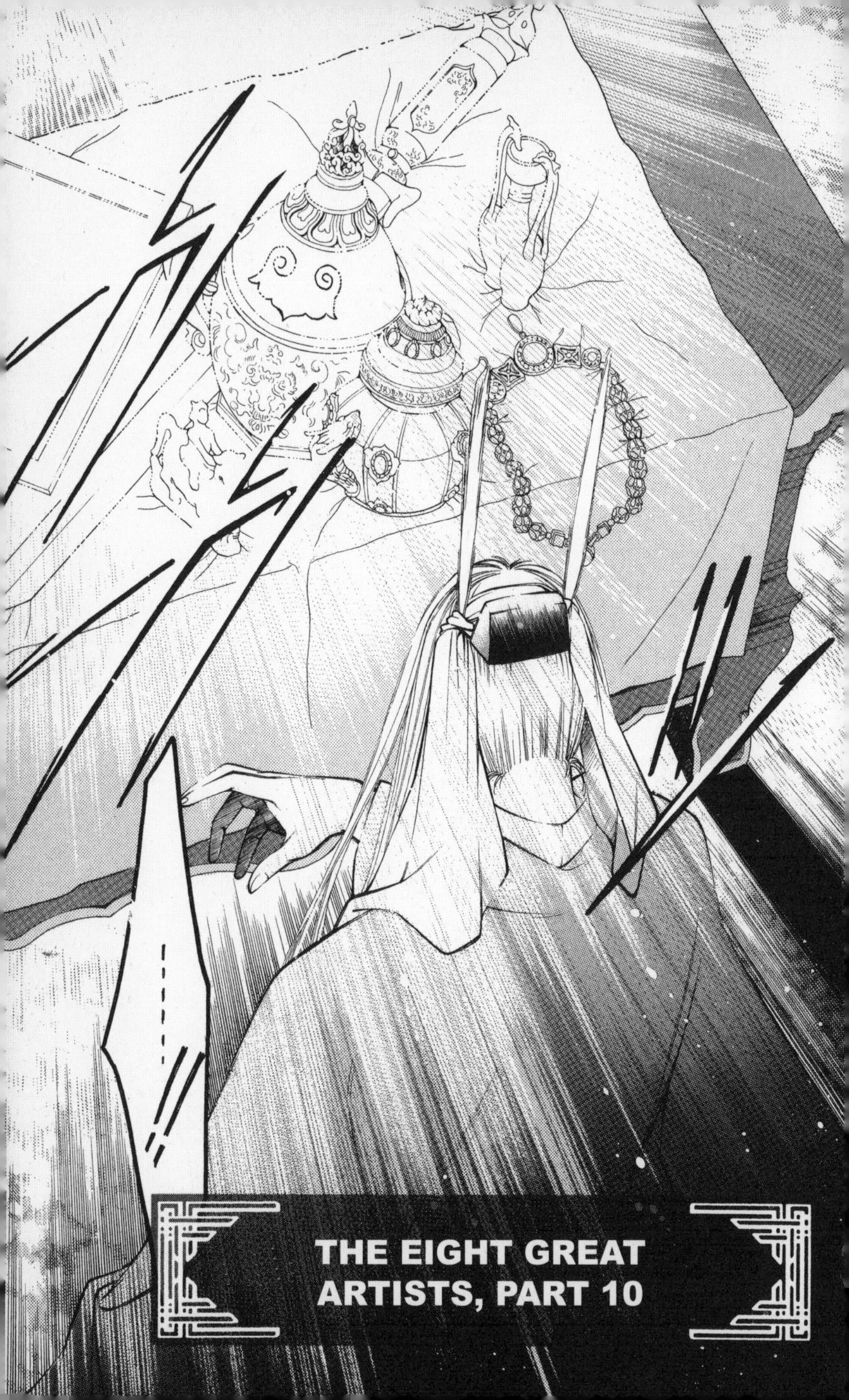

THE EIGHT GREAT ARTISTS, PART 10

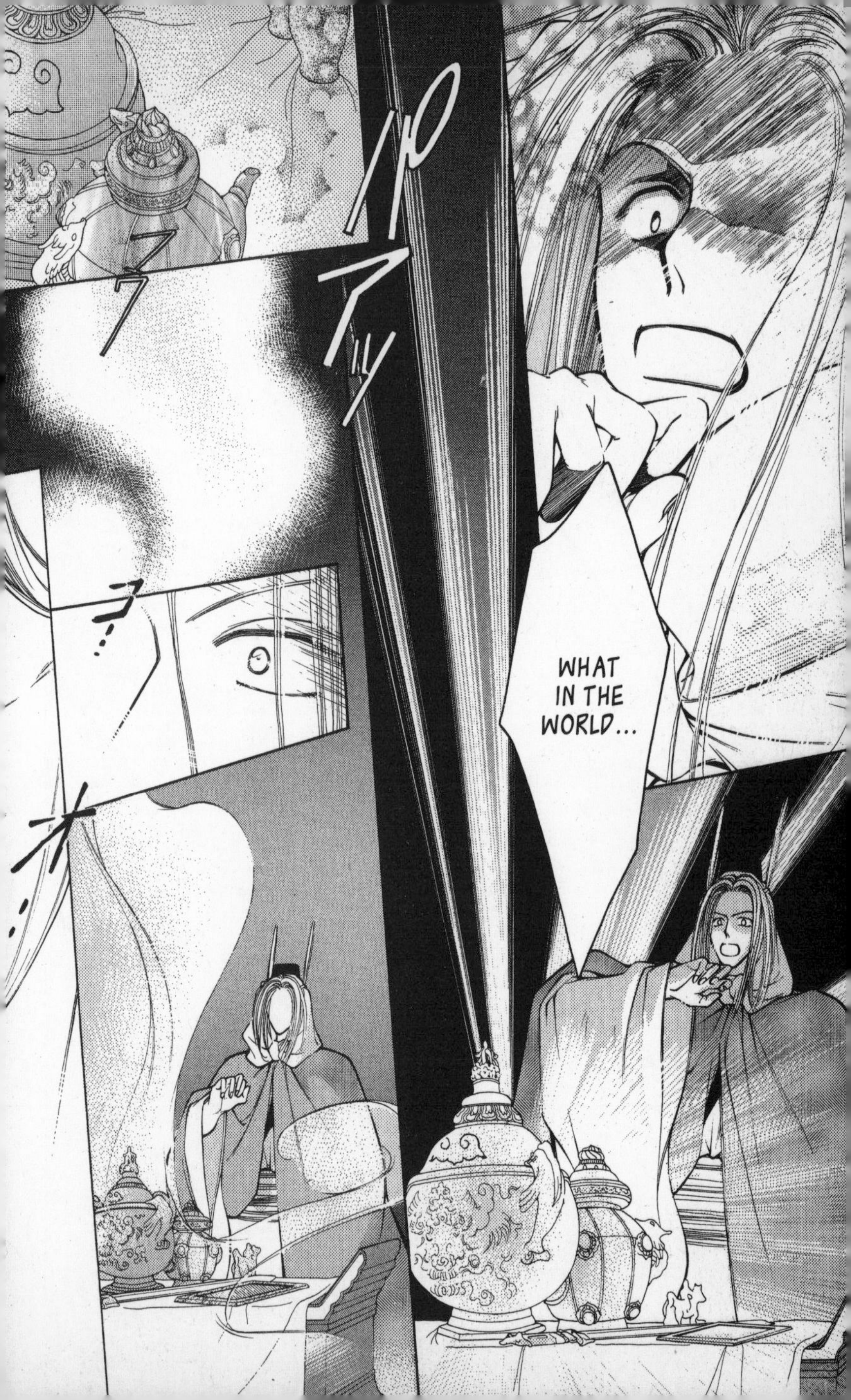
WHAT IN THE WORLD...

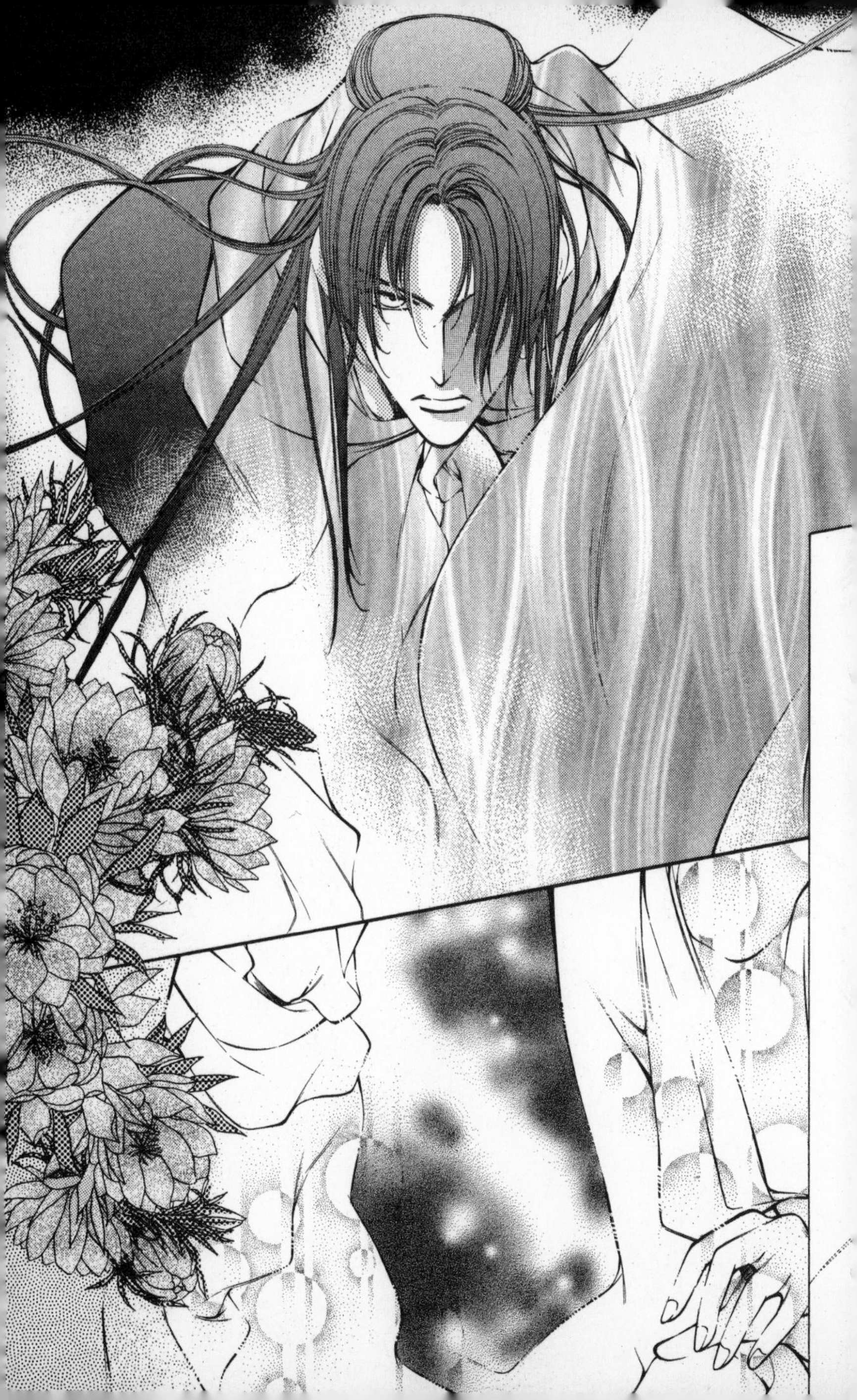

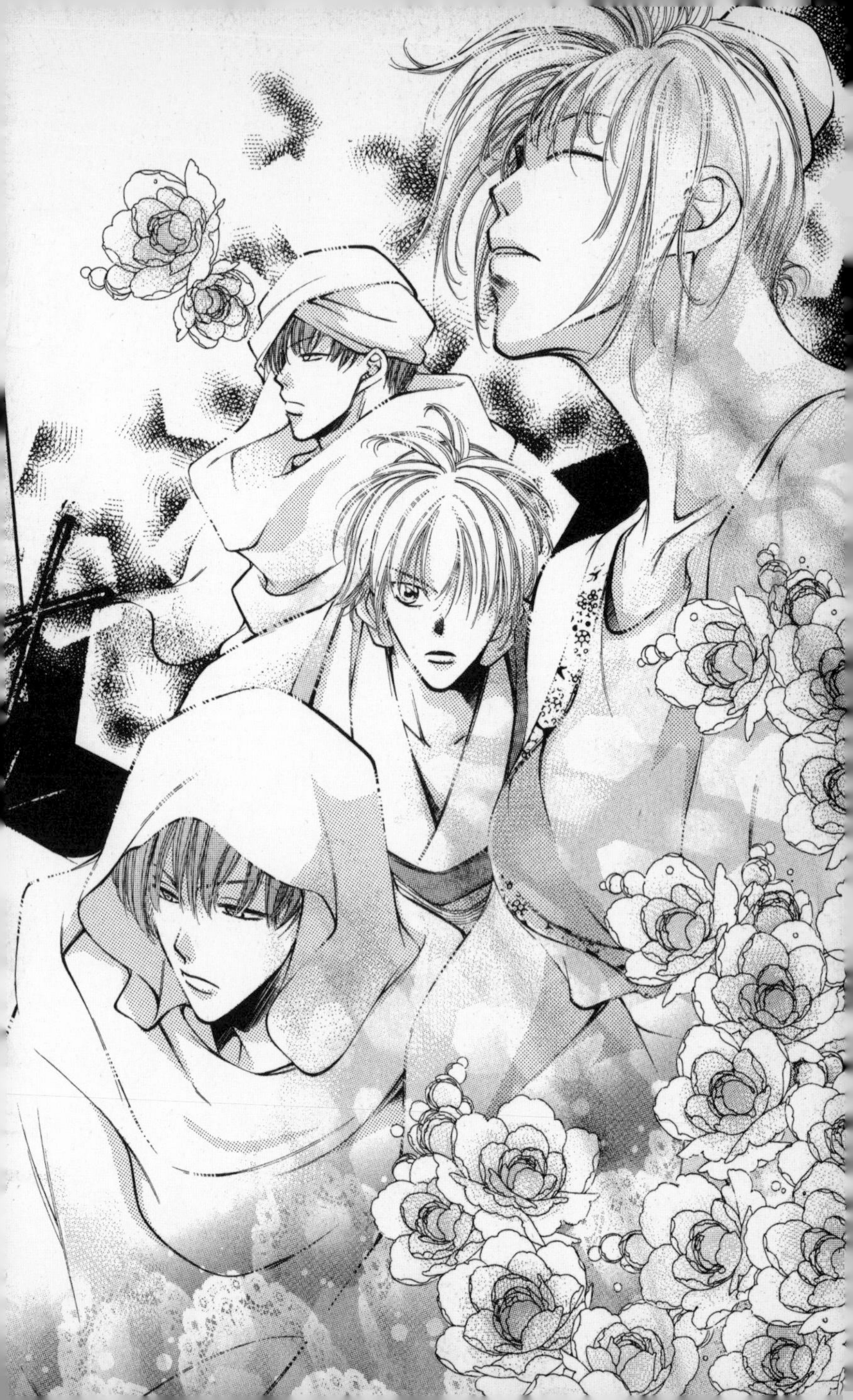

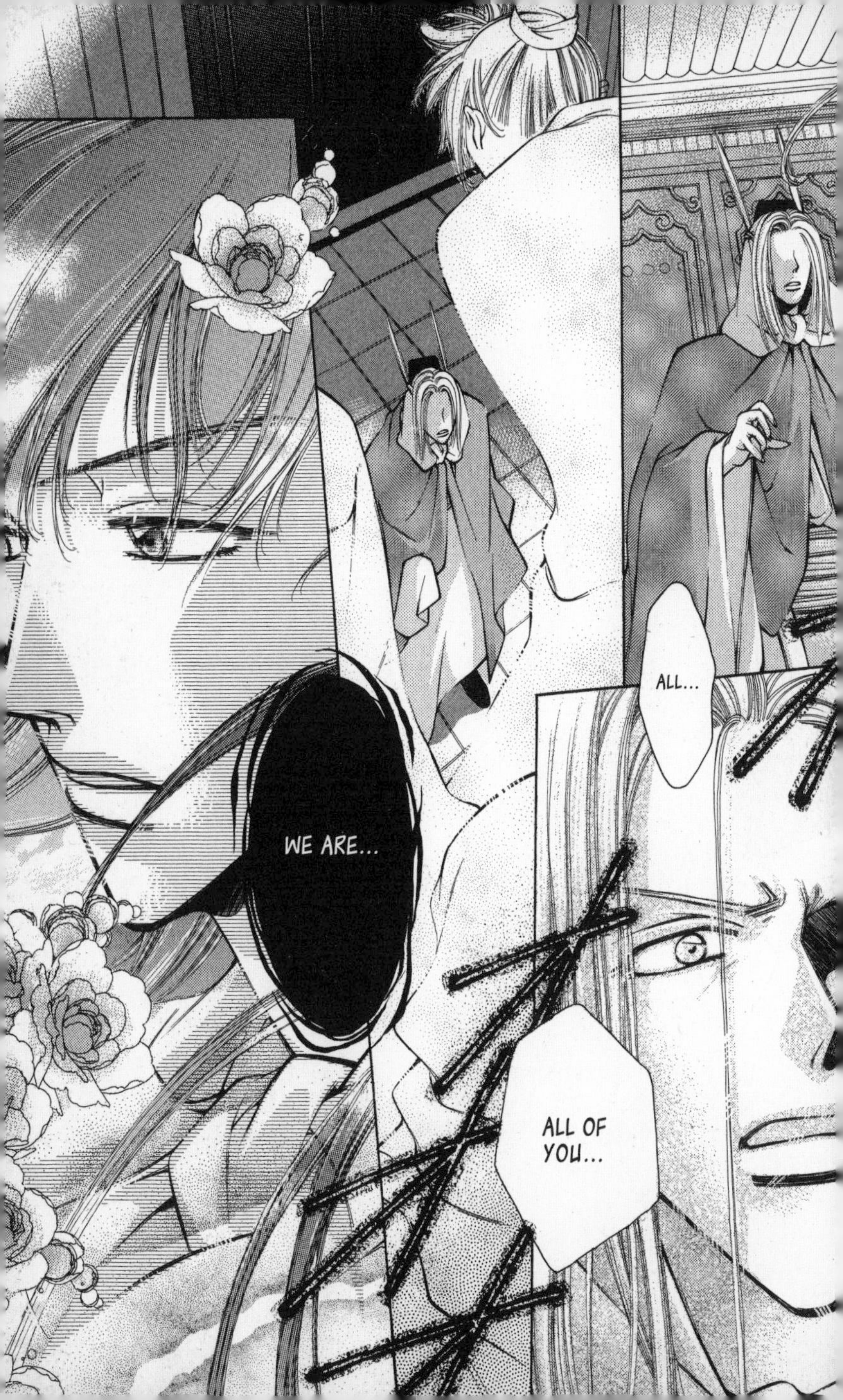
ALL...
WE ARE...
ALL OF YOU...

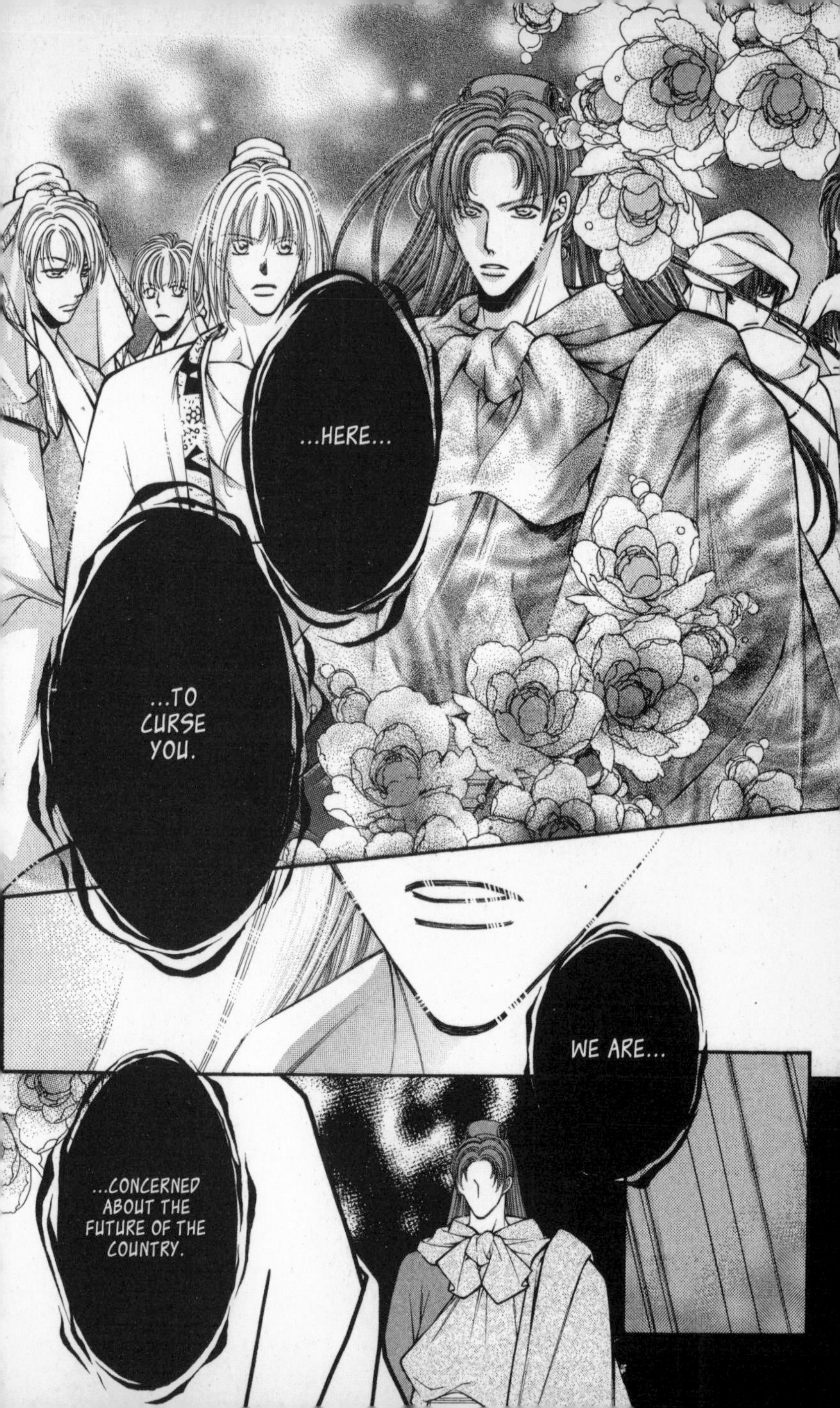
...HERE...
...TO CURSE YOU.
WE ARE...
...CONCERNED ABOUT THE FUTURE OF THE COUNTRY.

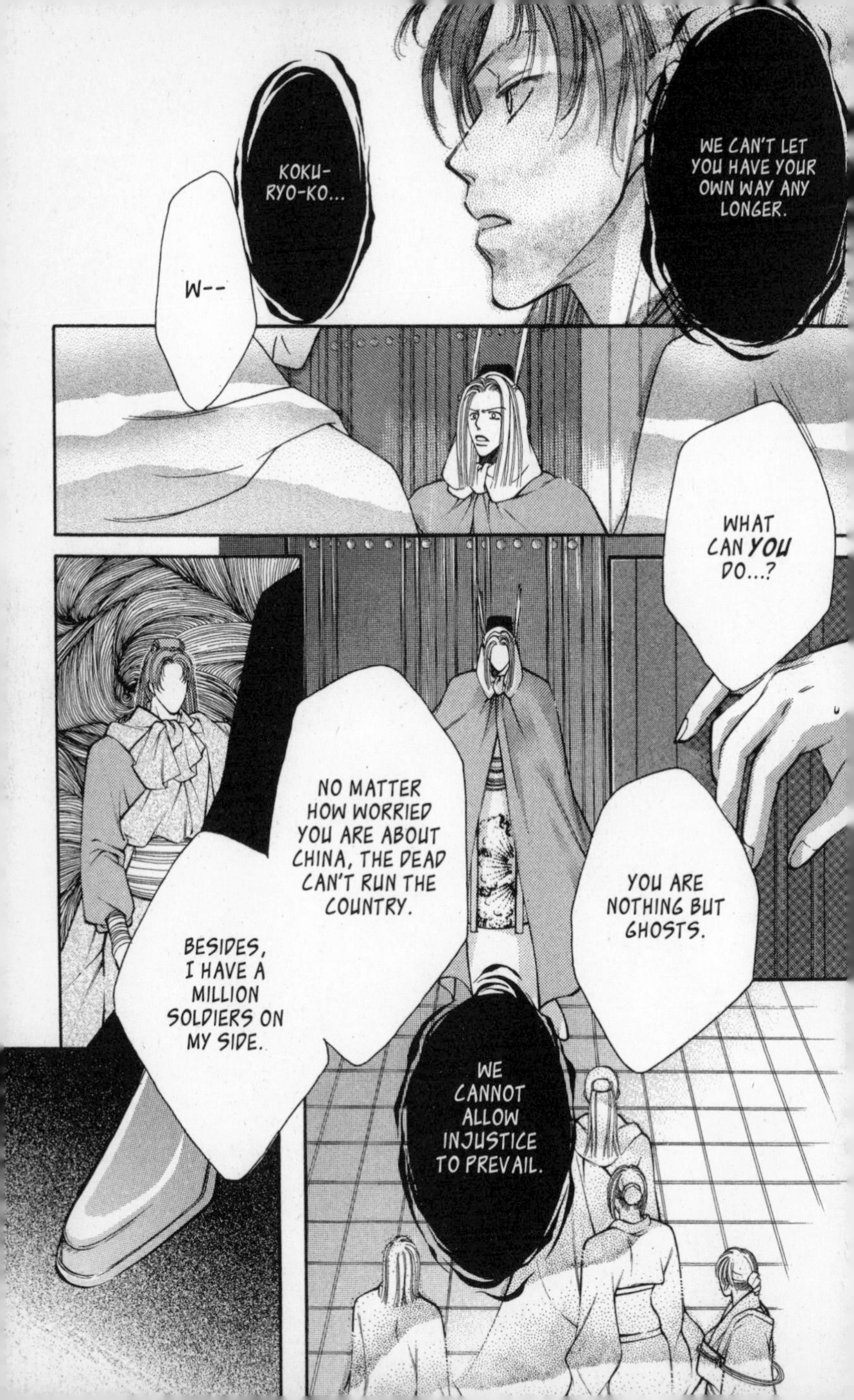
WE CAN'T LET YOU HAVE YOUR OWN WAY ANY LONGER.
KOKU-RYO-KO...
W--
WHAT CAN *YOU* DO...?
YOU ARE NOTHING BUT GHOSTS.
NO MATTER HOW WORRIED YOU ARE ABOUT CHINA, THE DEAD CAN'T RUN THE COUNTRY.
BESIDES, I HAVE A MILLION SOLDIERS ON MY SIDE.
WE CANNOT ALLOW INJUSTICE TO PREVAIL.

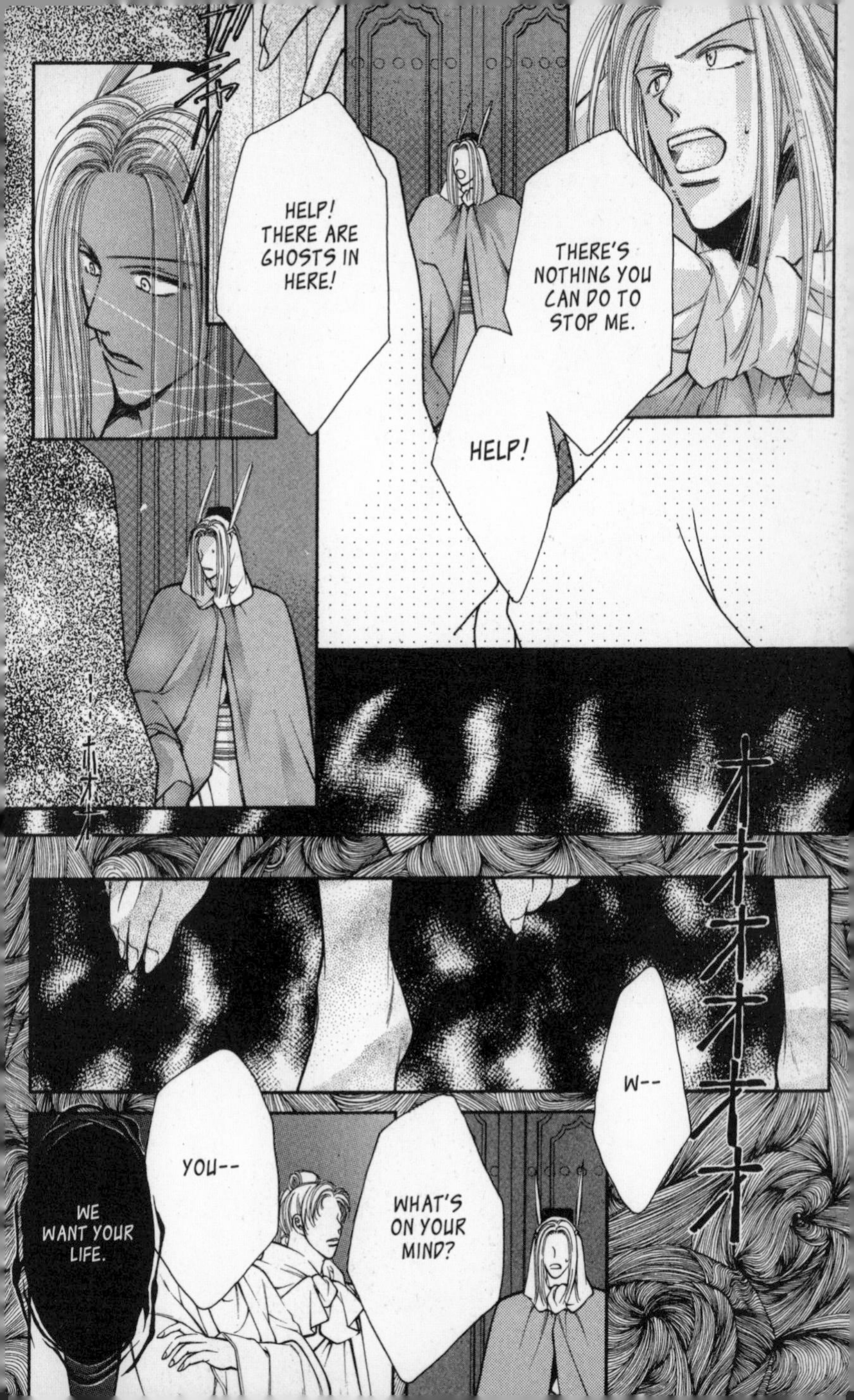
THERE'S NOTHING YOU CAN DO TO STOP ME.
HELP! THERE ARE GHOSTS IN HERE!
HELP!
W--
WHAT'S ON YOUR MIND?
YOU--
WE WANT YOUR LIFE.

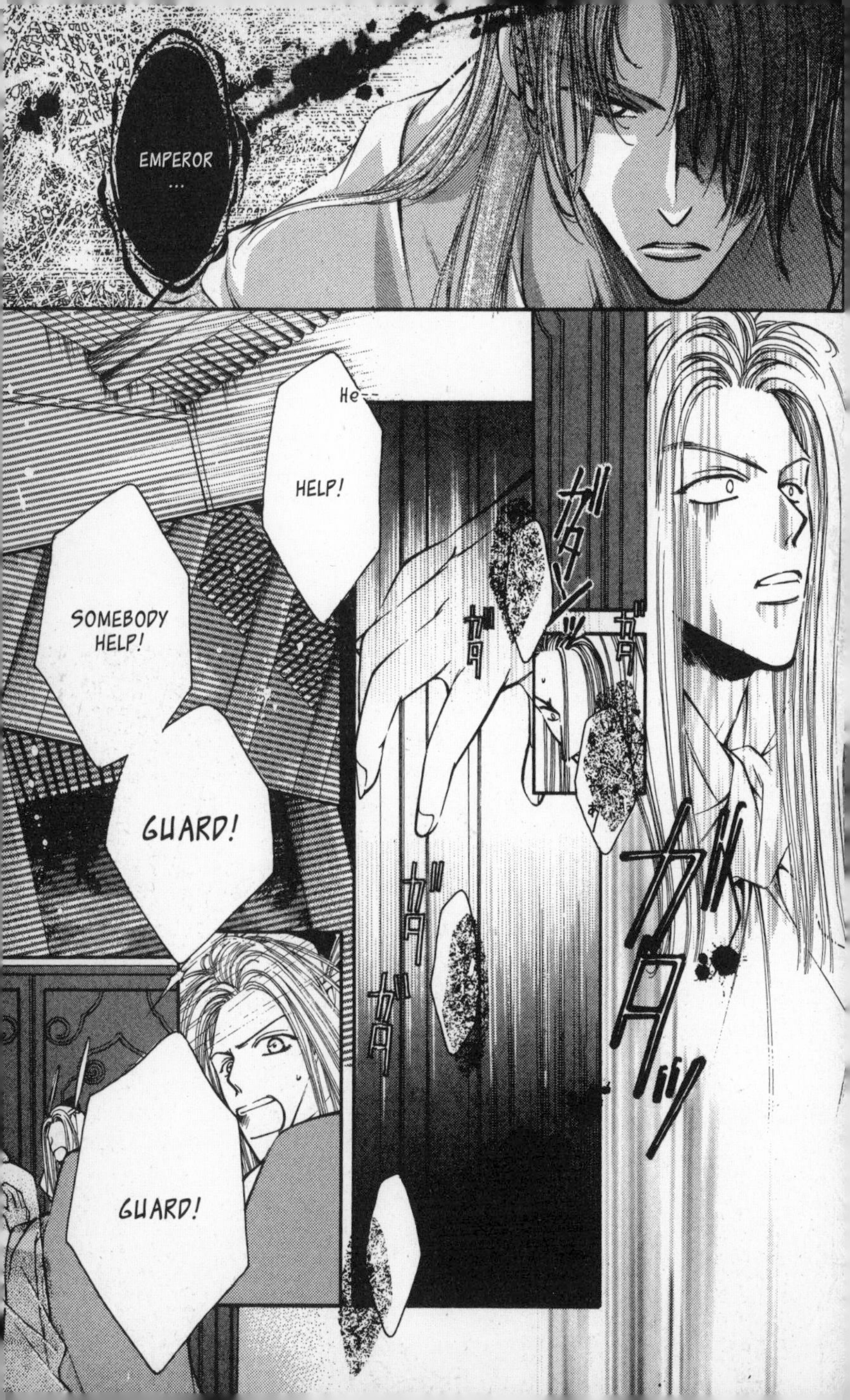

EMPEROR ...
He--
HELP!
SOMEBODY HELP!
GUARD!
GUARD!

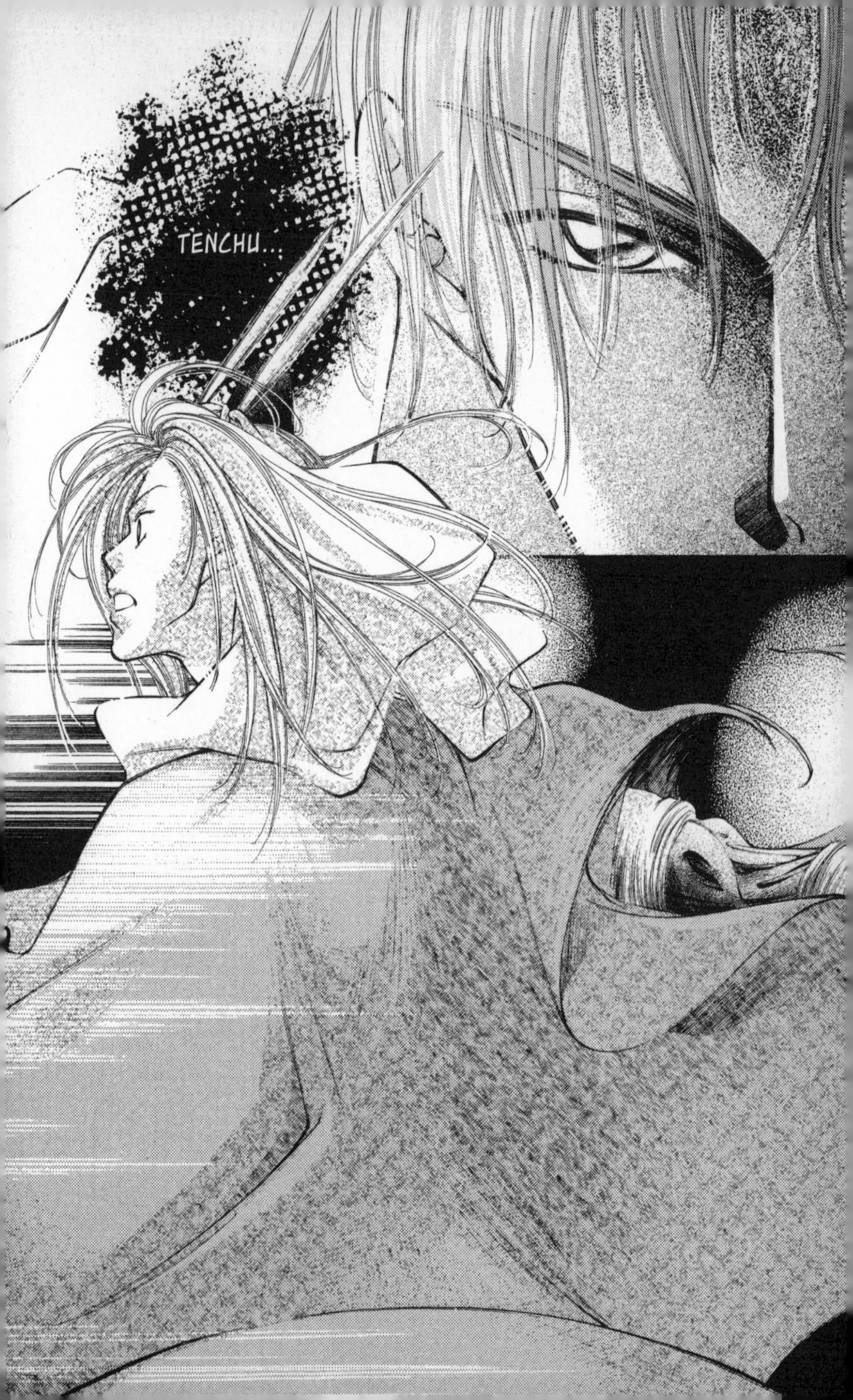
TENCHU...

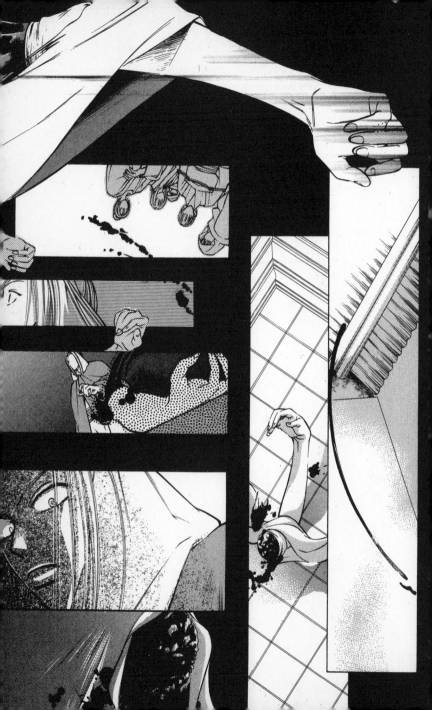

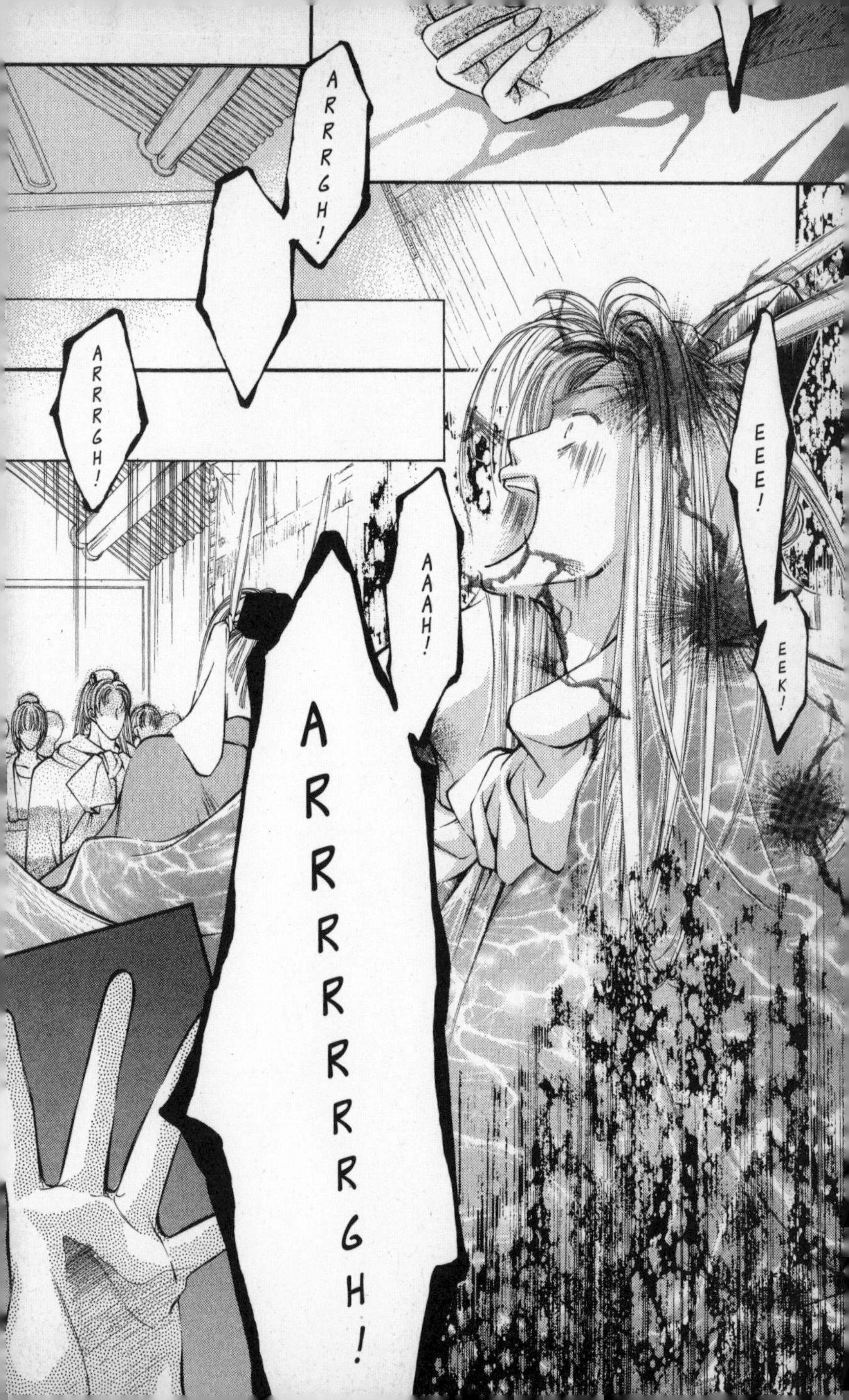
EEE!
EEK!
ARRRGH!
AAAAH!
ARRRGH!
ARRRRRRRGH!

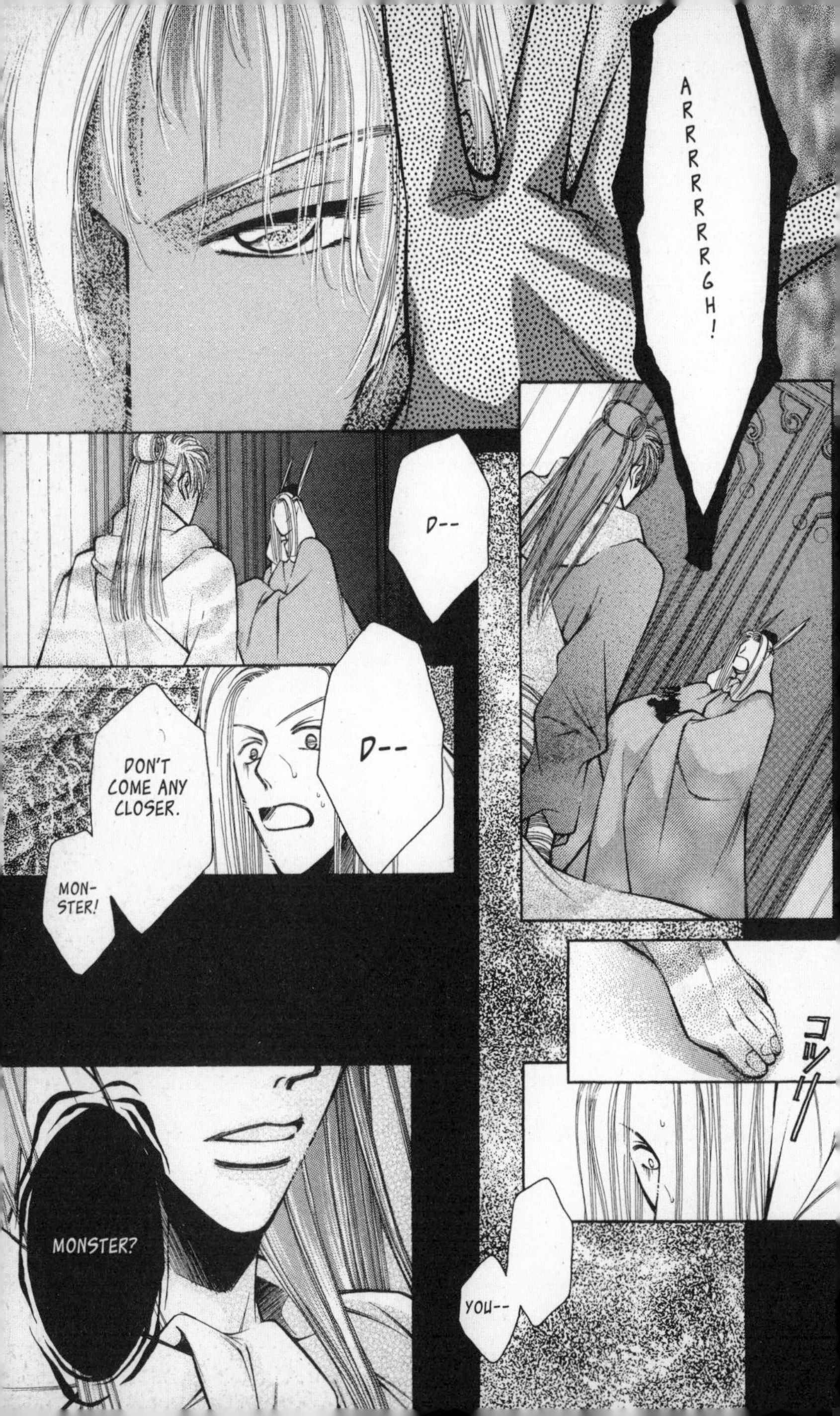
ARRRRRRRGH!
D--
D--
DON'T COME ANY CLOSER.
MONSTER!
MONSTER?
コツン
YOU--

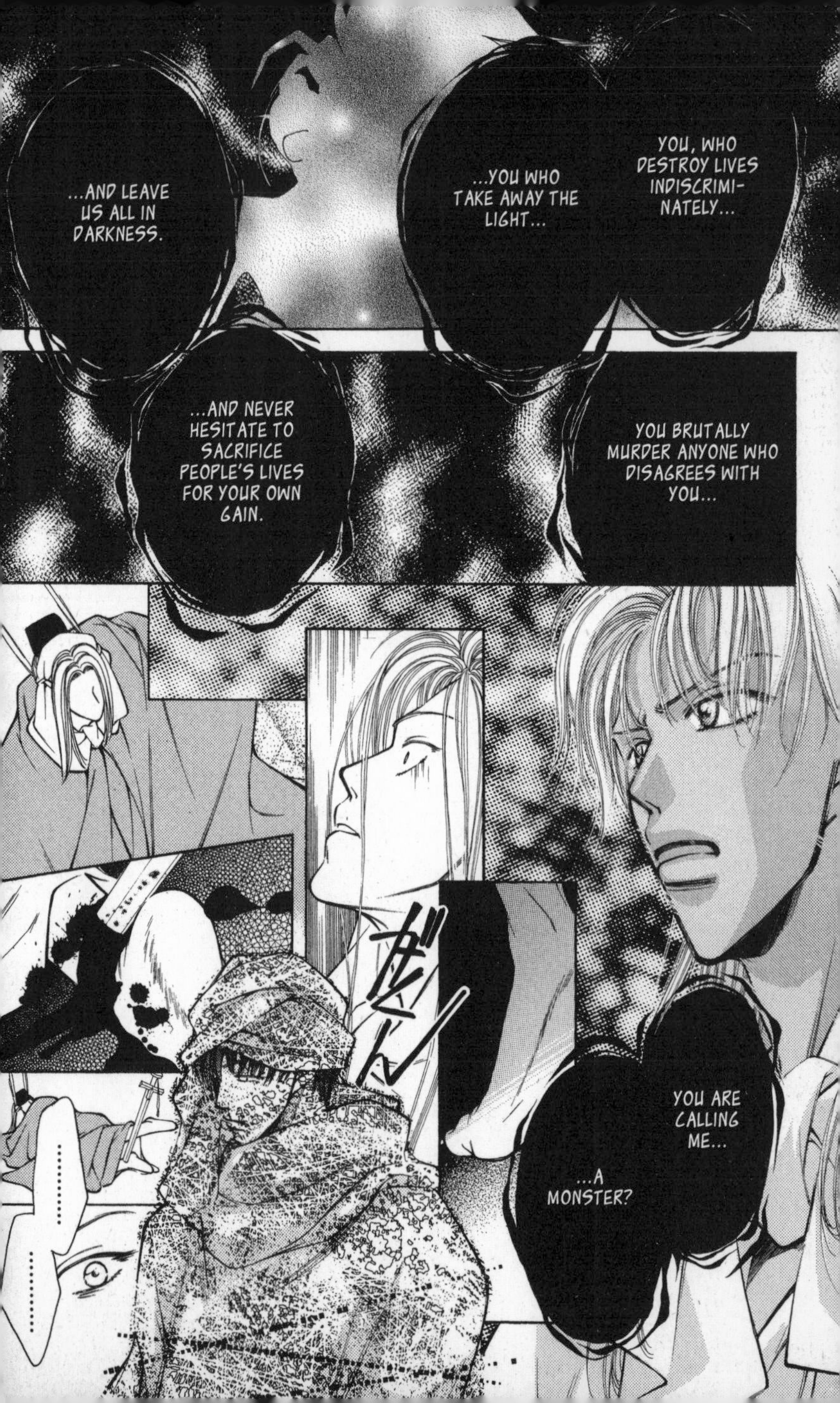
YOU, WHO DESTROY LIVES INDISCRIMINATELY...
...YOU WHO TAKE AWAY THE LIGHT...
...AND LEAVE US ALL IN DARKNESS.
YOU BRUTALLY MURDER ANYONE WHO DISAGREES WITH YOU...
...AND NEVER HESITATE TO SACRIFICE PEOPLE'S LIVES FOR YOUR OWN GAIN.
YOU ARE CALLING ME...
...A MONSTER?

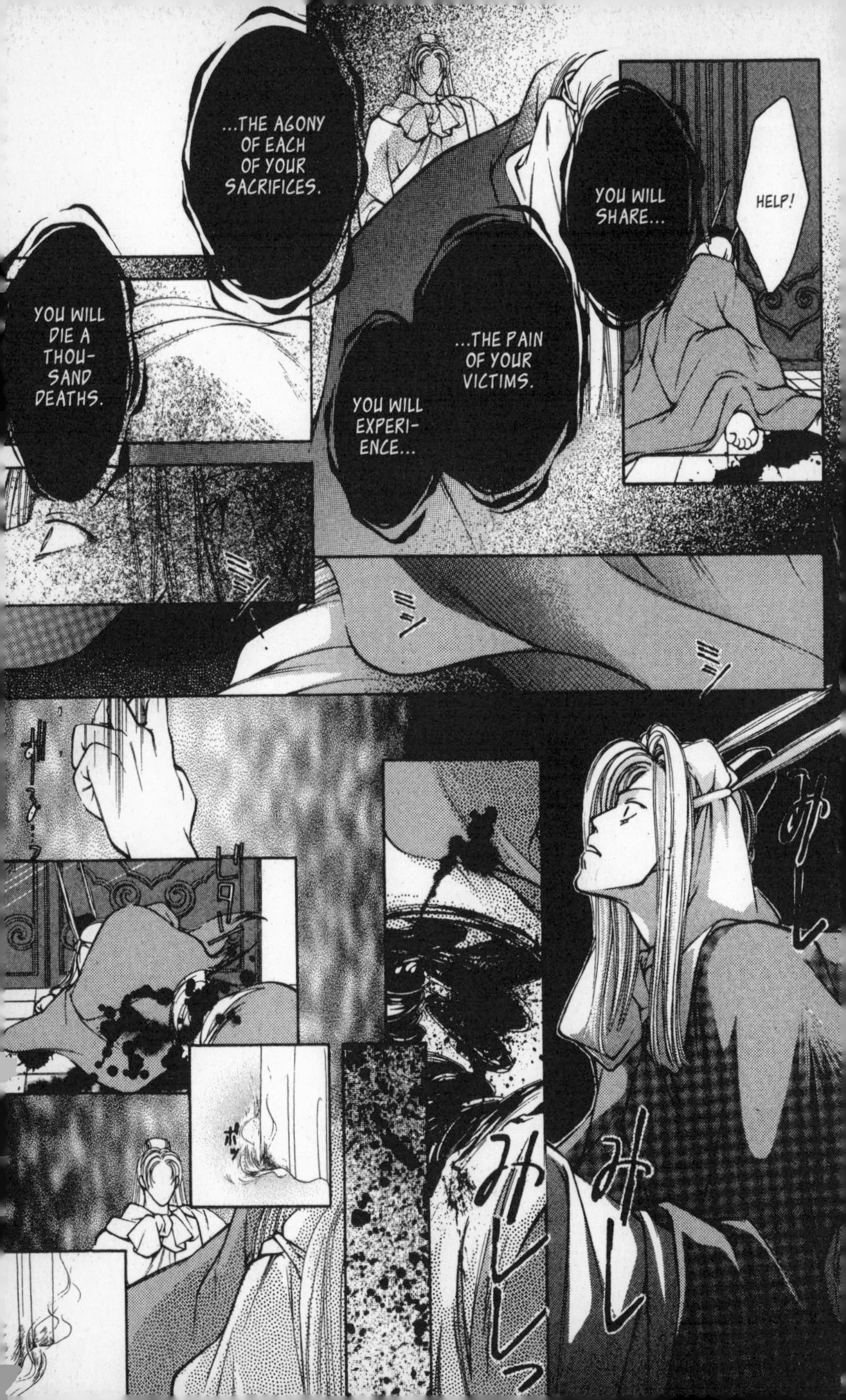
HELP!
YOU WILL SHARE...
...THE PAIN OF YOUR VICTIMS.
YOU WILL EXPERIENCE...
...THE AGONY OF EACH OF YOUR SACRIFICES.
YOU WILL DIE A THOUSAND DEATHS.

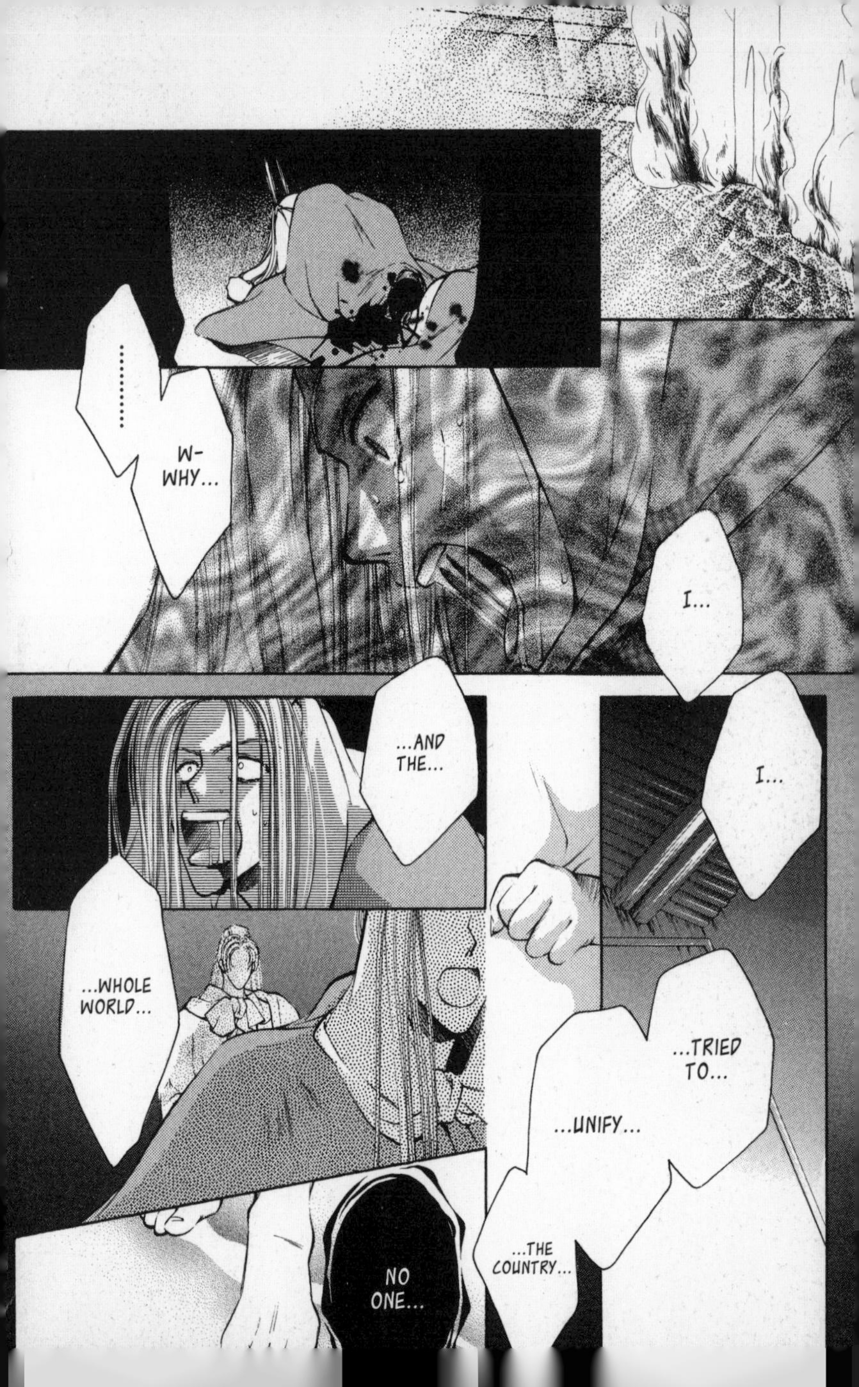
......
W-
WHY...
I...
I...
...TRIED
TO...
...UNIFY...
...THE
COUNTRY...
...AND
THE...
...WHOLE
WORLD...
NO
ONE...

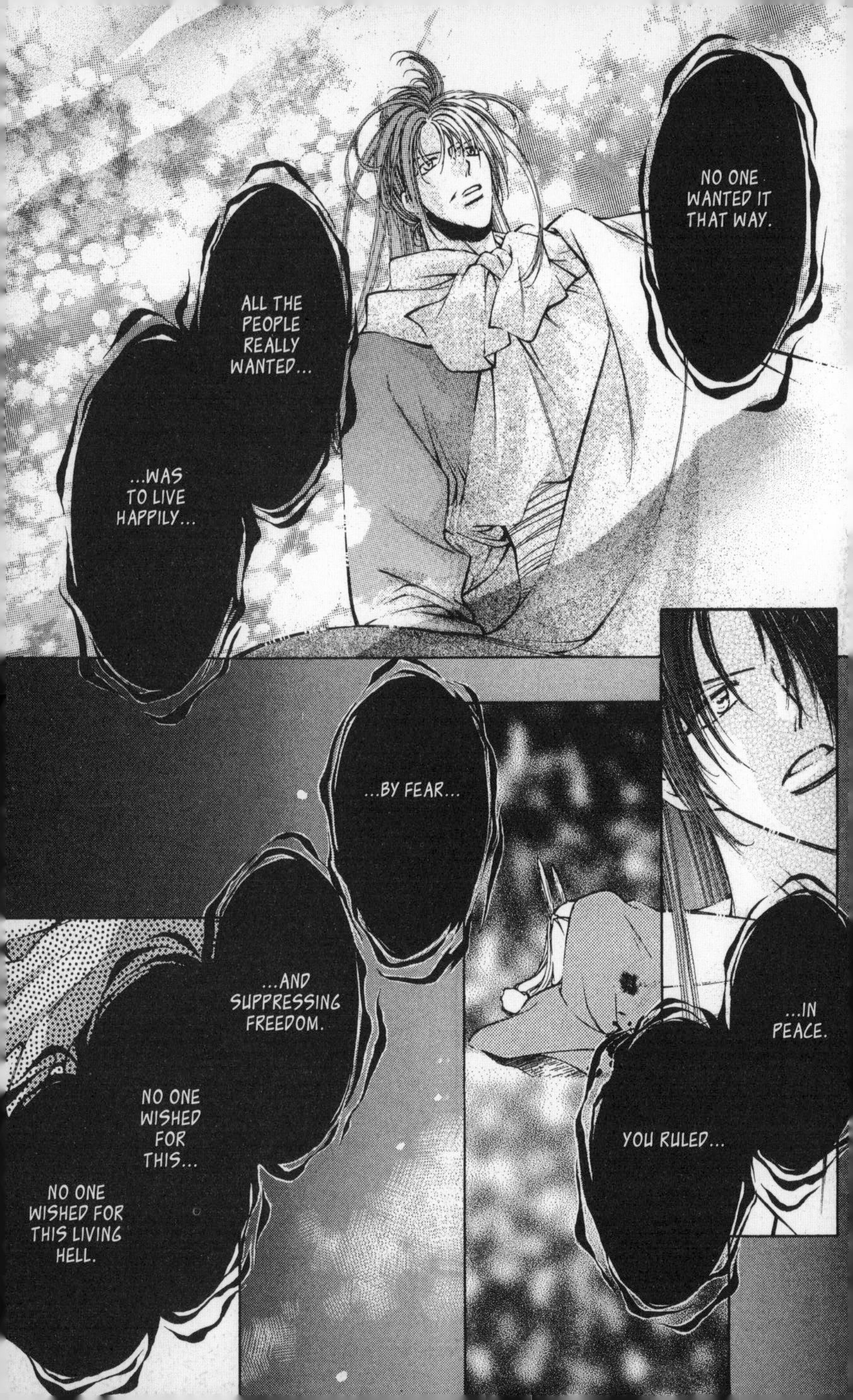
NO ONE WANTED IT THAT WAY.
ALL THE PEOPLE REALLY WANTED...
...WAS TO LIVE HAPPILY...
...IN PEACE.
YOU RULED...
...BY FEAR...
...AND SUPPRESSING FREEDOM.
NO ONE WISHED FOR THIS...
NO ONE WISHED FOR THIS LIVING HELL.

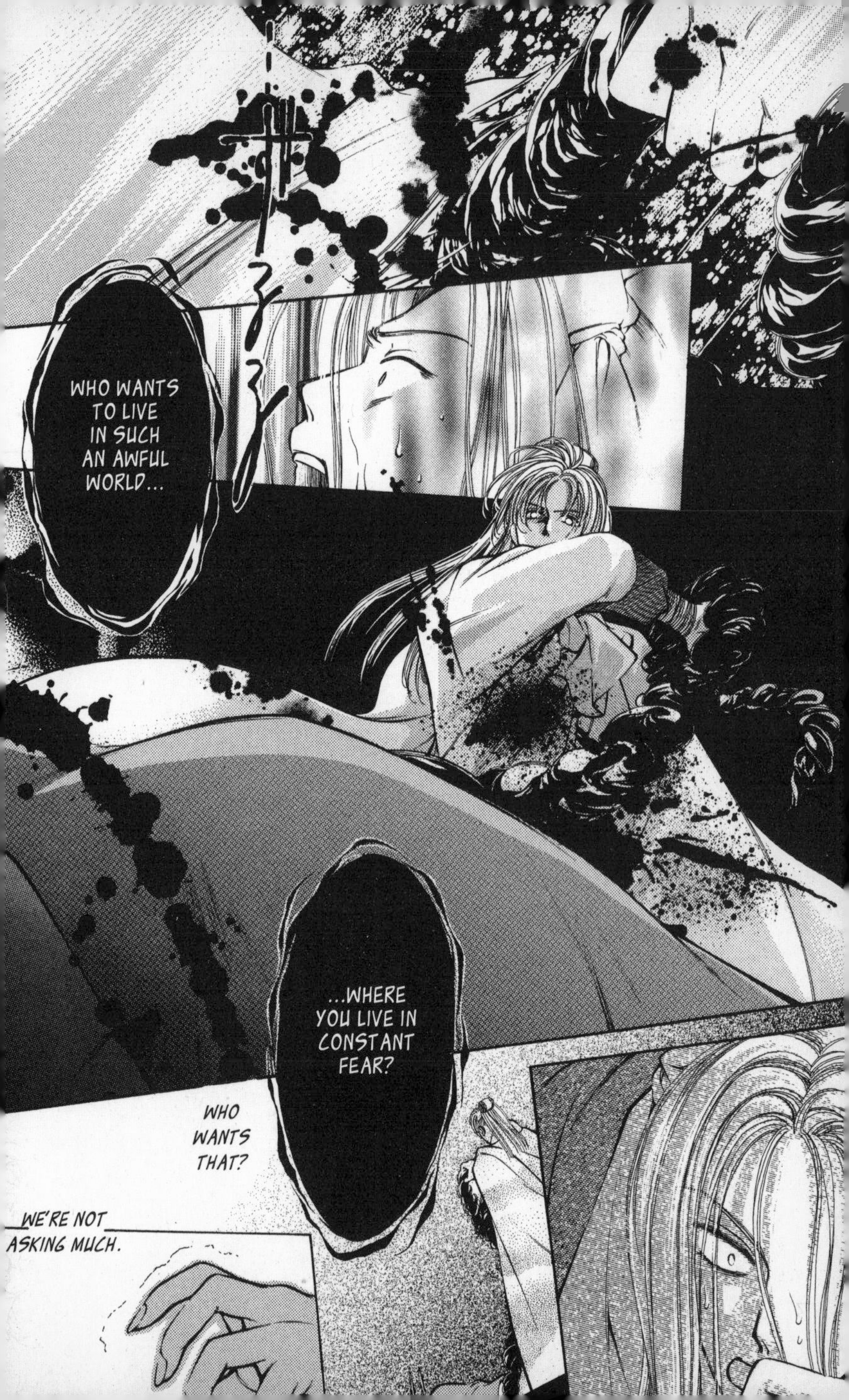
WHO WANTS TO LIVE IN SUCH AN AWFUL WORLD...
...WHERE YOU LIVE IN CONSTANT FEAR?
WHO WANTS THAT?
WE'RE NOT ASKING MUCH.

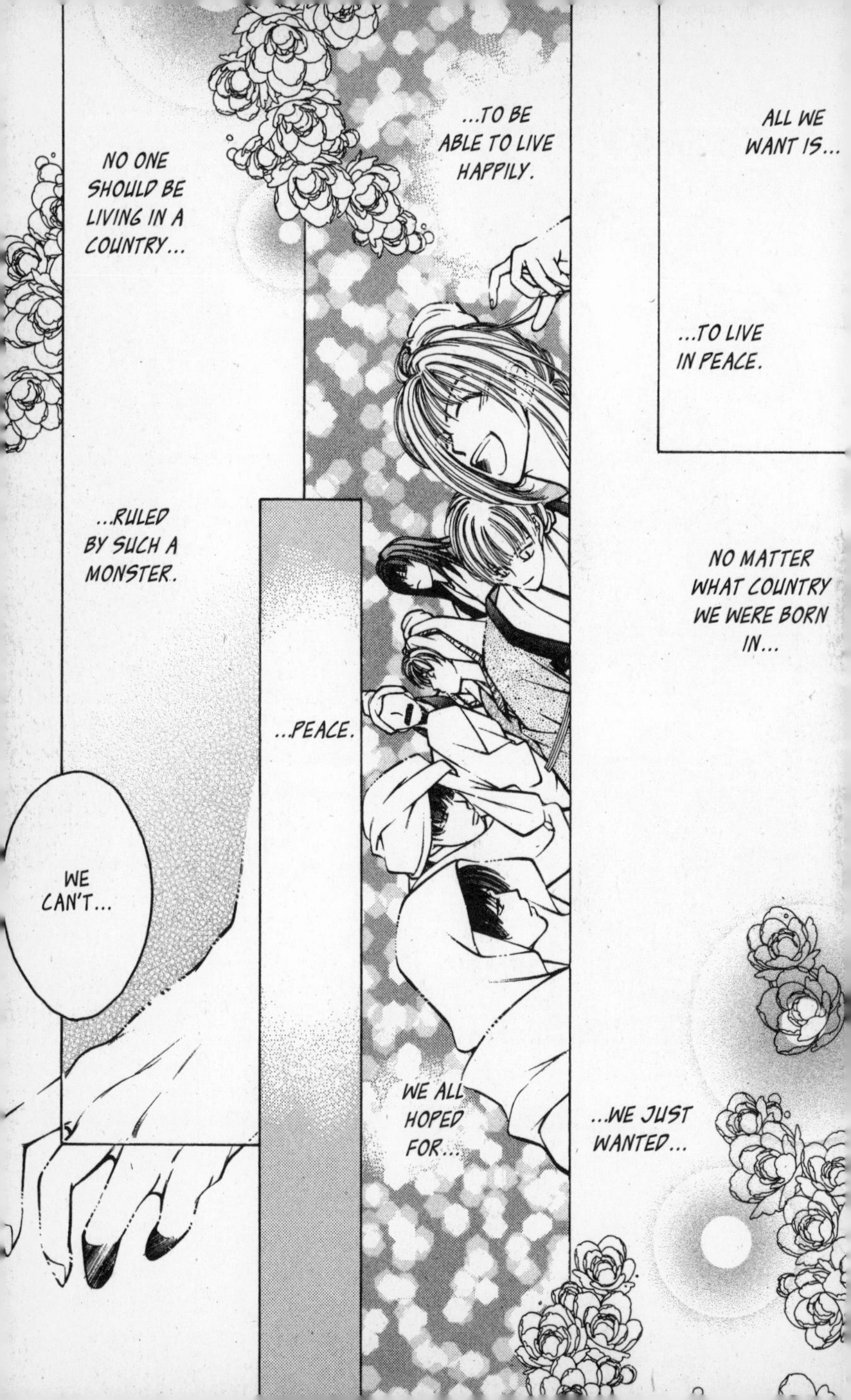

ALL WE WANT IS...
...TO LIVE IN PEACE.
NO MATTER WHAT COUNTRY WE WERE BORN IN...
...WE JUST WANTED...
...TO BE ABLE TO LIVE HAPPILY.
WE ALL HOPED FOR...
...PEACE.
NO ONE SHOULD BE LIVING IN A COUNTRY...
...RULED BY SUCH A MONSTER.
WE CAN'T...

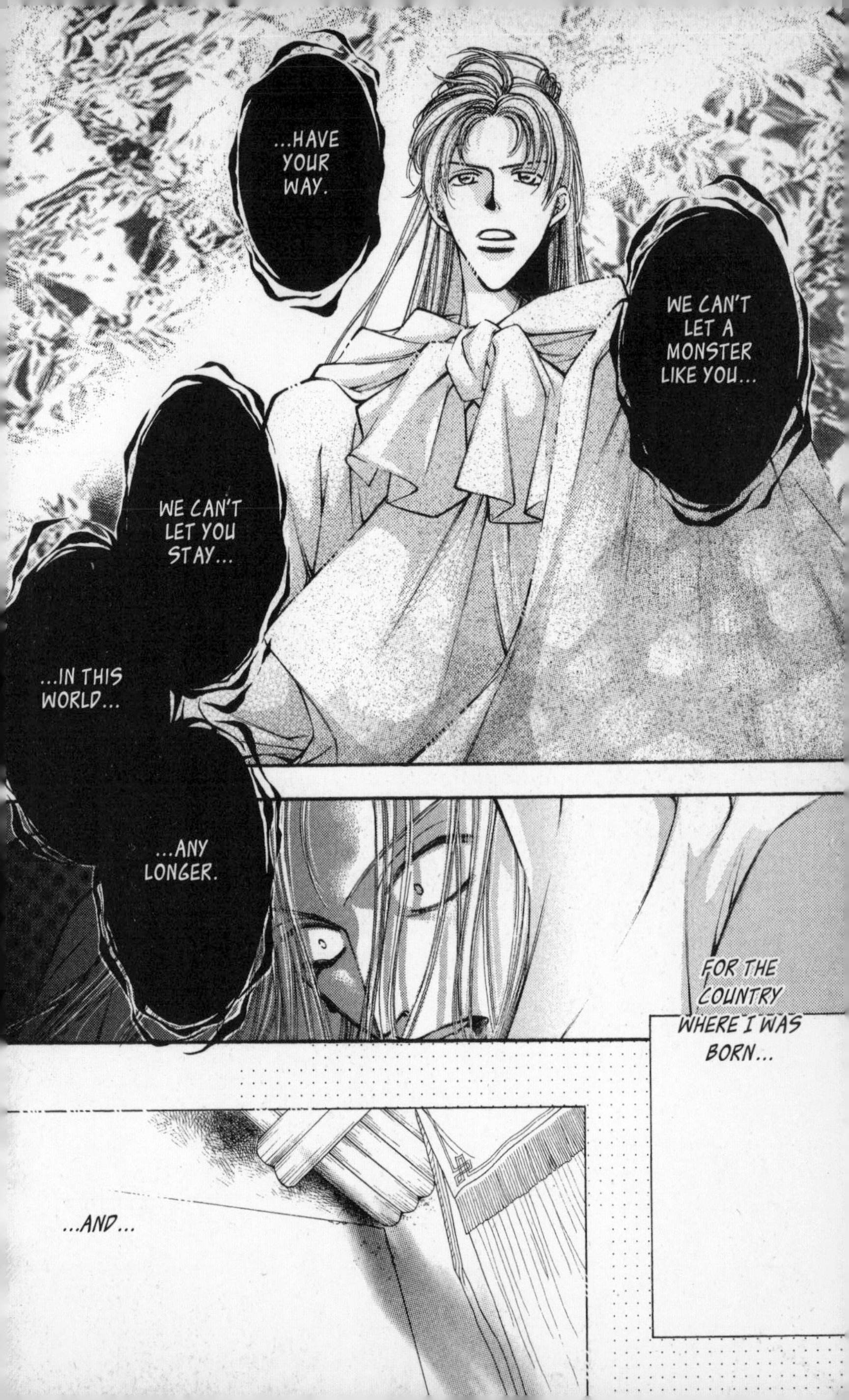
WE CAN'T LET A MONSTER LIKE YOU...
...HAVE YOUR WAY.
WE CAN'T LET YOU STAY...
...IN THIS WORLD...
...ANY LONGER.
FOR THE COUNTRY WHERE I WAS BORN...
...AND...

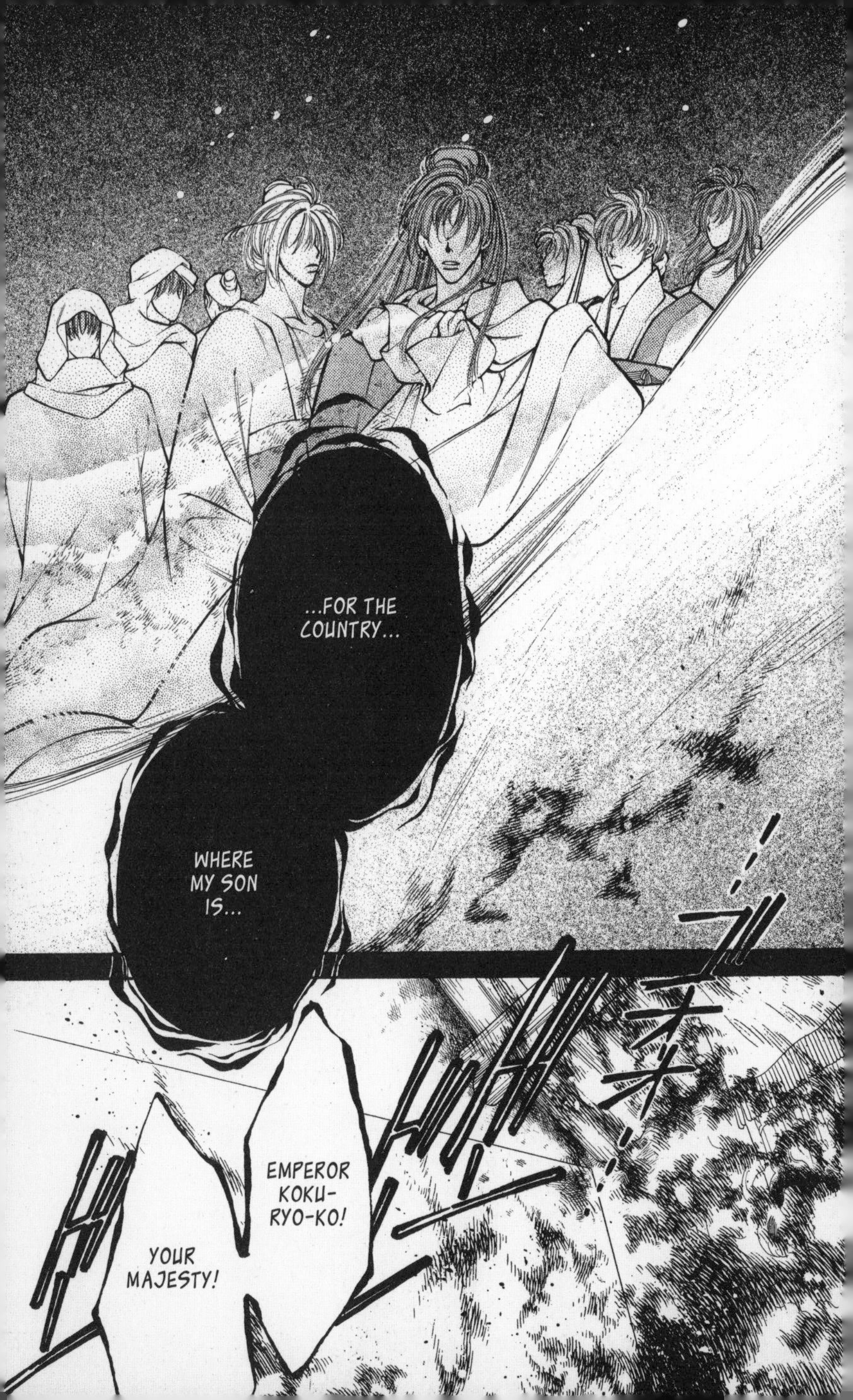
...FOR THE COUNTRY...
WHERE MY SON IS...
EMPEROR KOKU-RYO-KO!
YOUR MAJESTY!

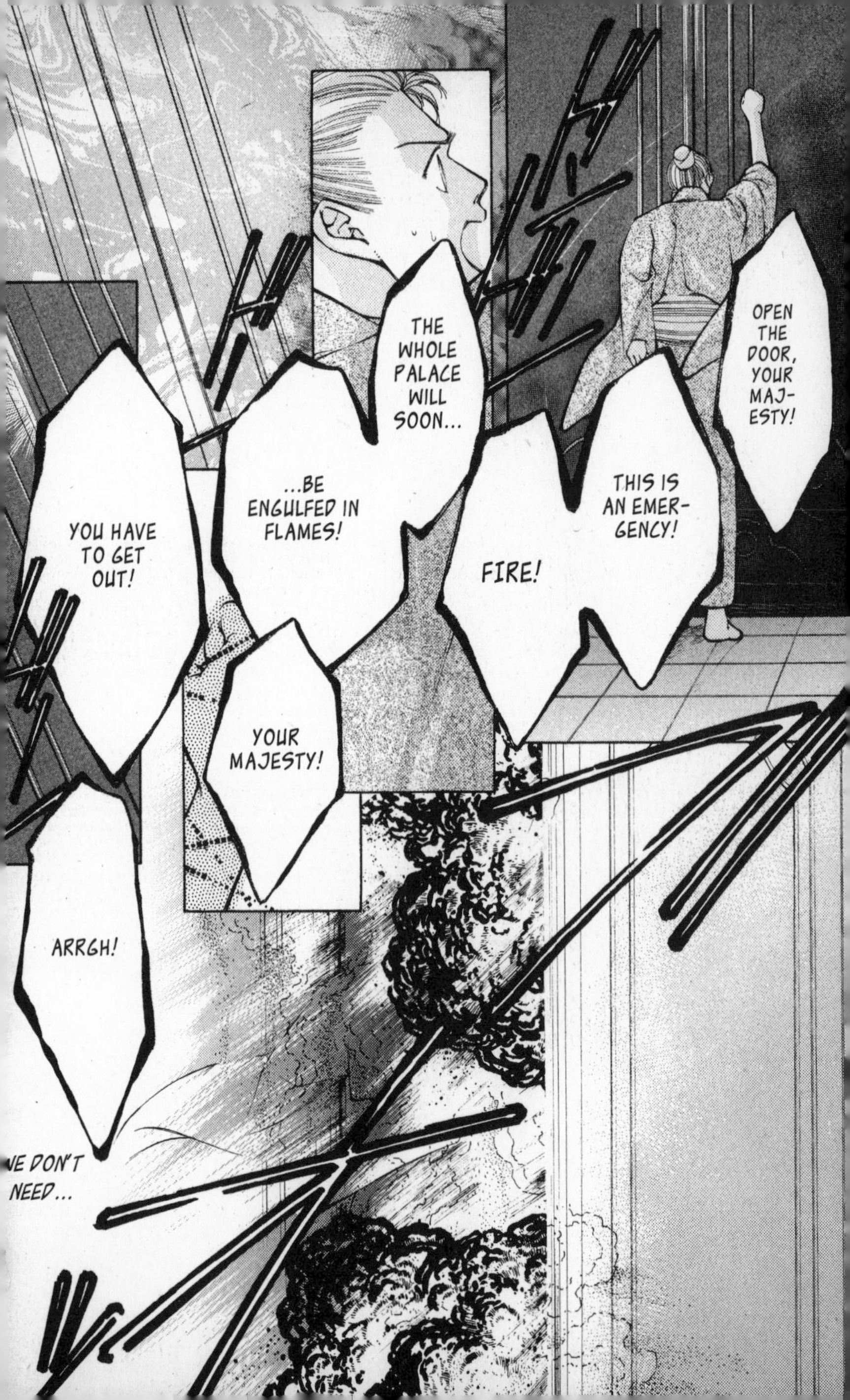
OPEN THE DOOR, YOUR MAJESTY!
THIS IS AN EMERGENCY!
FIRE!
THE WHOLE PALACE WILL SOON...
...BE ENGULFED IN FLAMES!
YOU HAVE TO GET OUT!
YOUR MAJESTY!
ARRGH!
WE DON'T NEED...

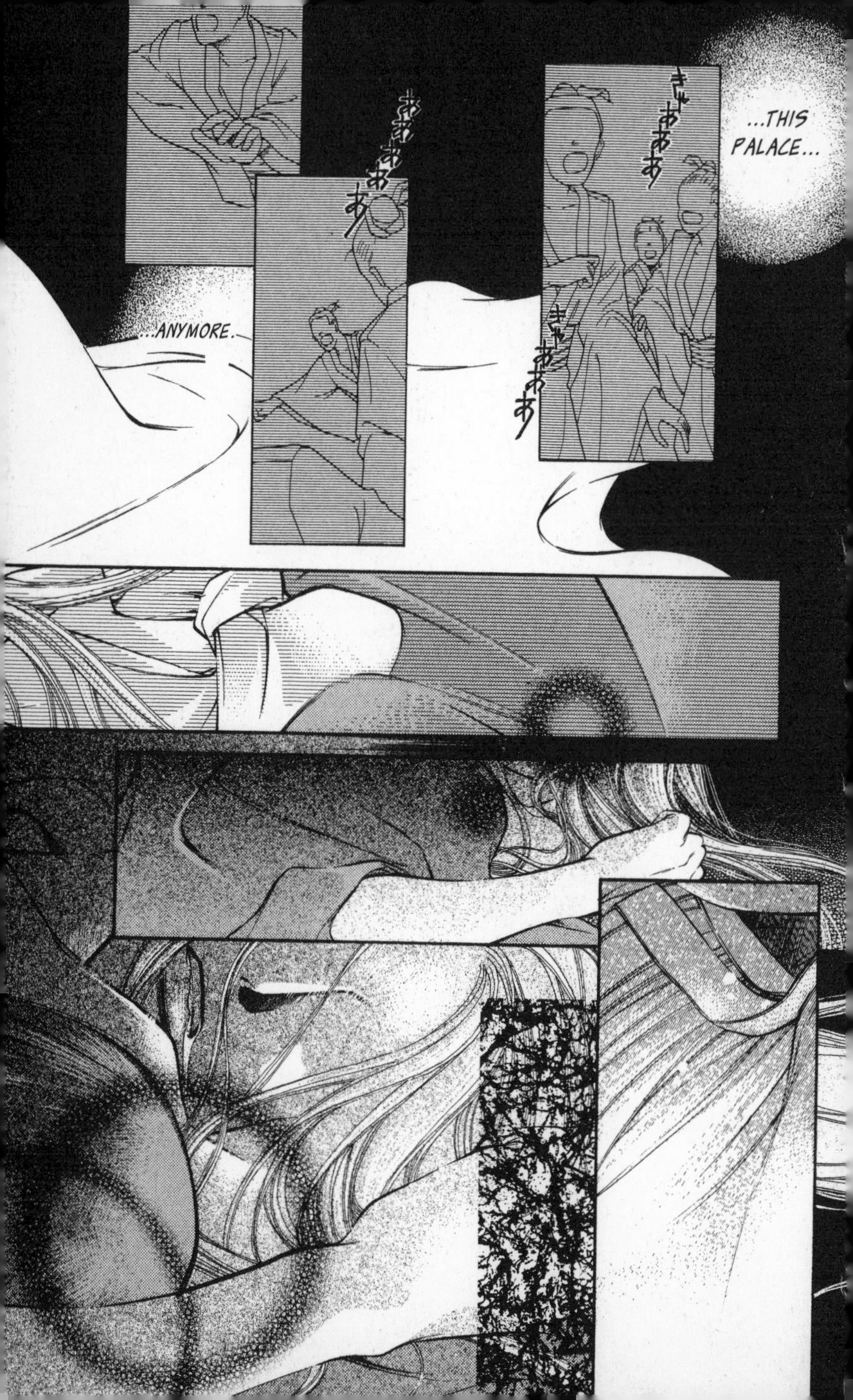
...THIS PALACE...
きゃあああ
きゃあああ
...ANYMORE.

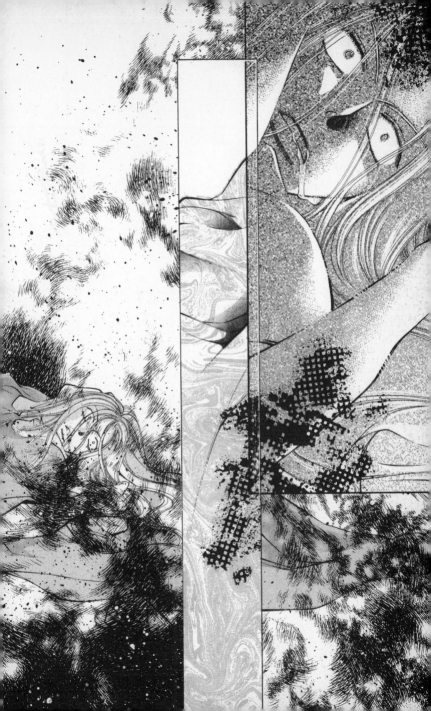

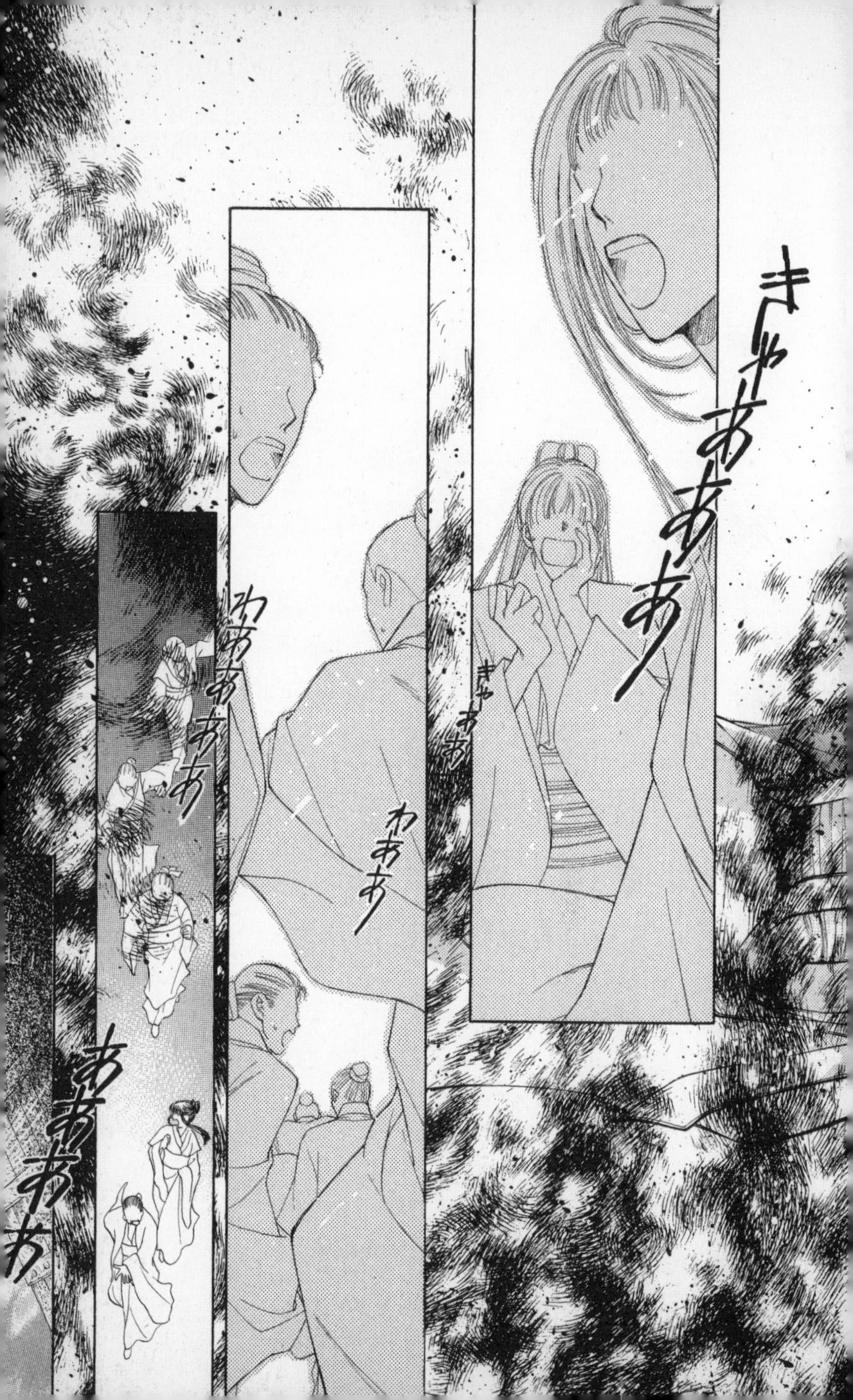
きゃあああ
きゃああ
わああ
わああああ
ああああ

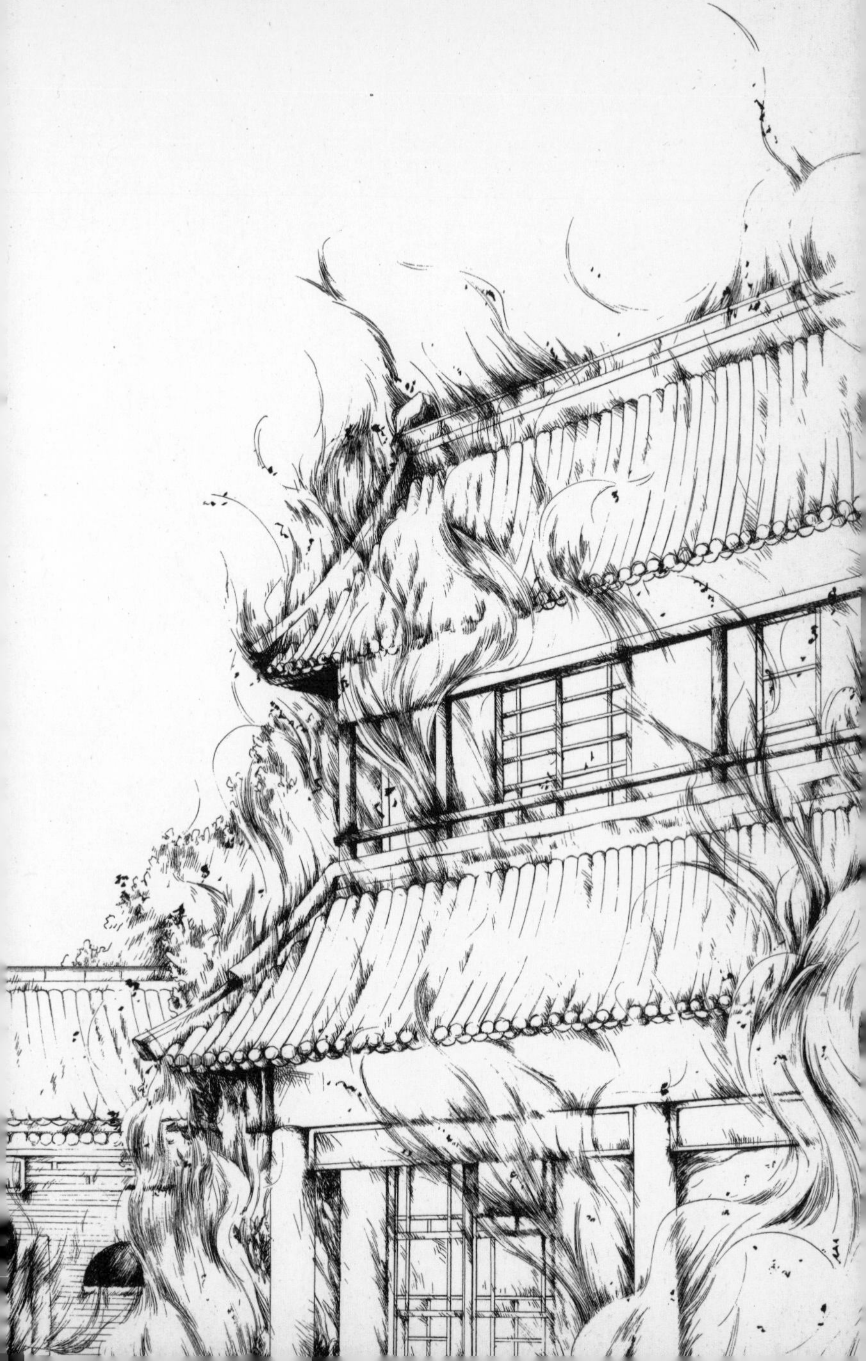

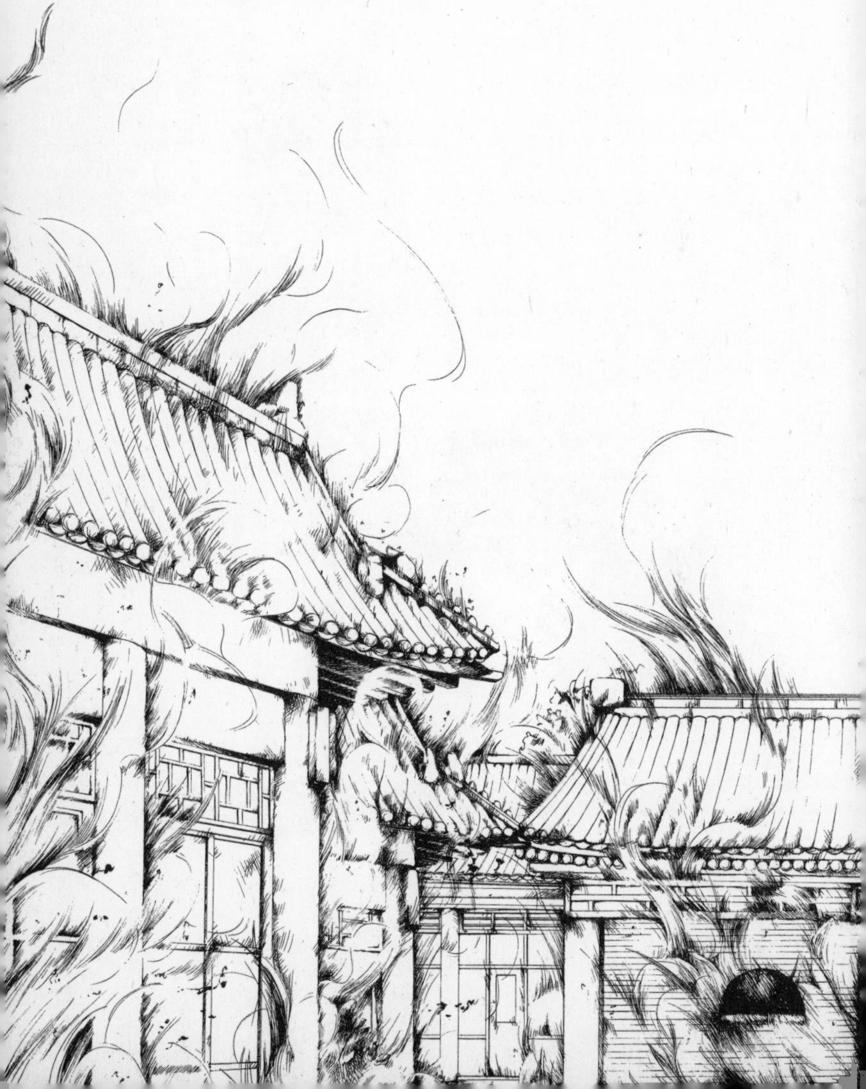

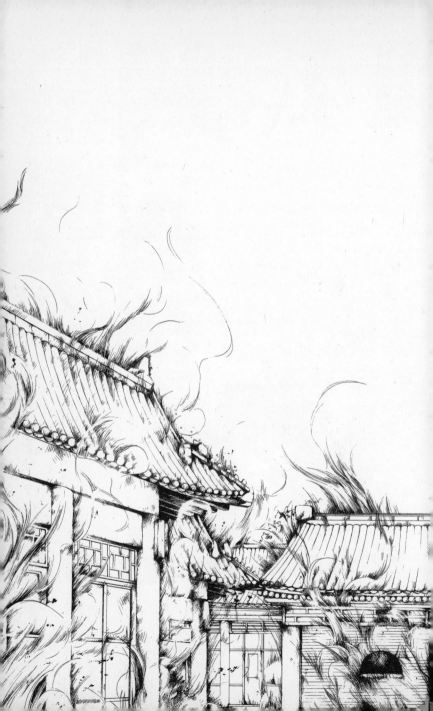

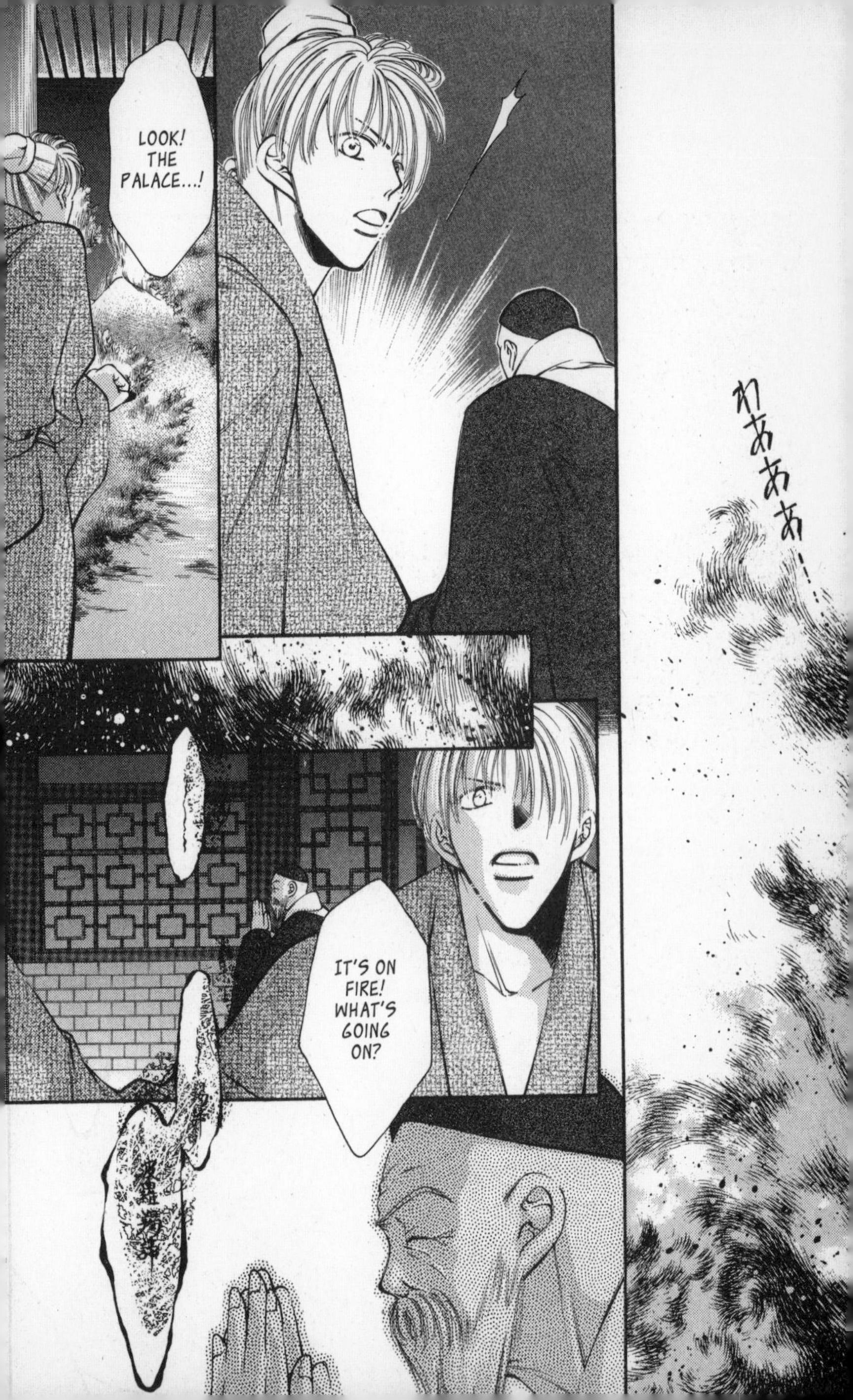
わあああ…
LOOK! THE PALACE...!
IT'S ON FIRE! WHAT'S GOING ON?

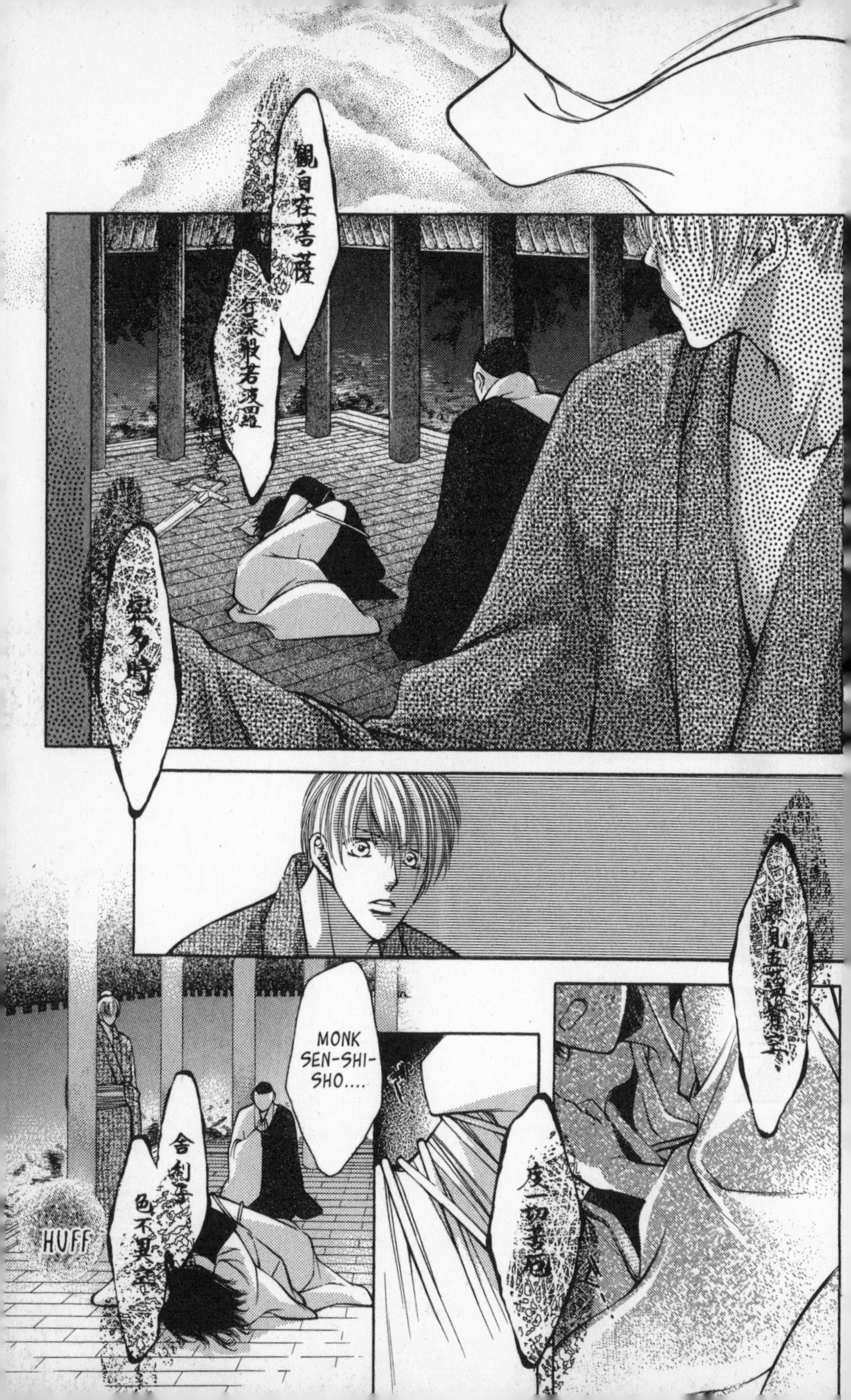

觀自在菩薩
行深般若波羅
蜜多時
照見五蘊皆空
度一切苦厄
MONK SEN-SHI-SHO....
舍利子
色不異空
HUFF

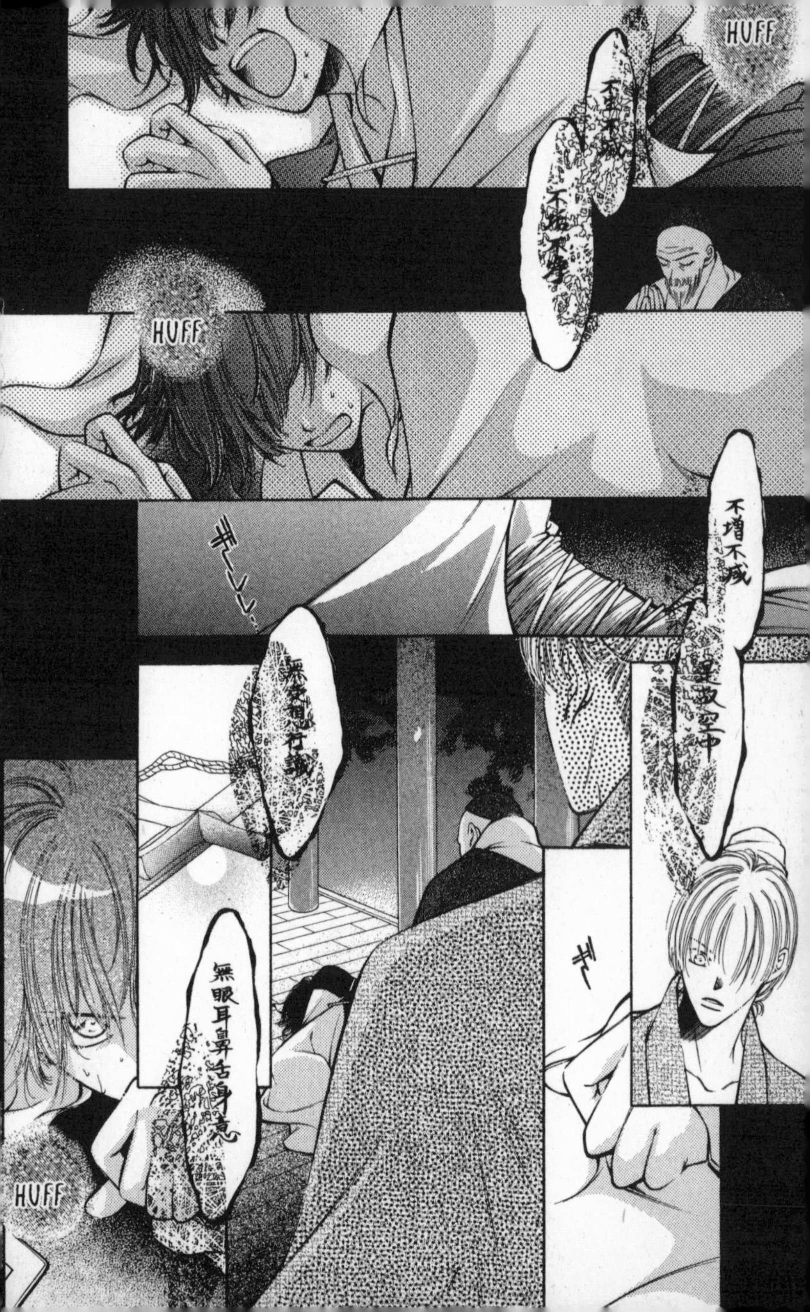
HUFF
不生不滅
不垢不淨
HUFF
不增不減
是故空中
無受想行識
無眼耳鼻舌身意
HUFF

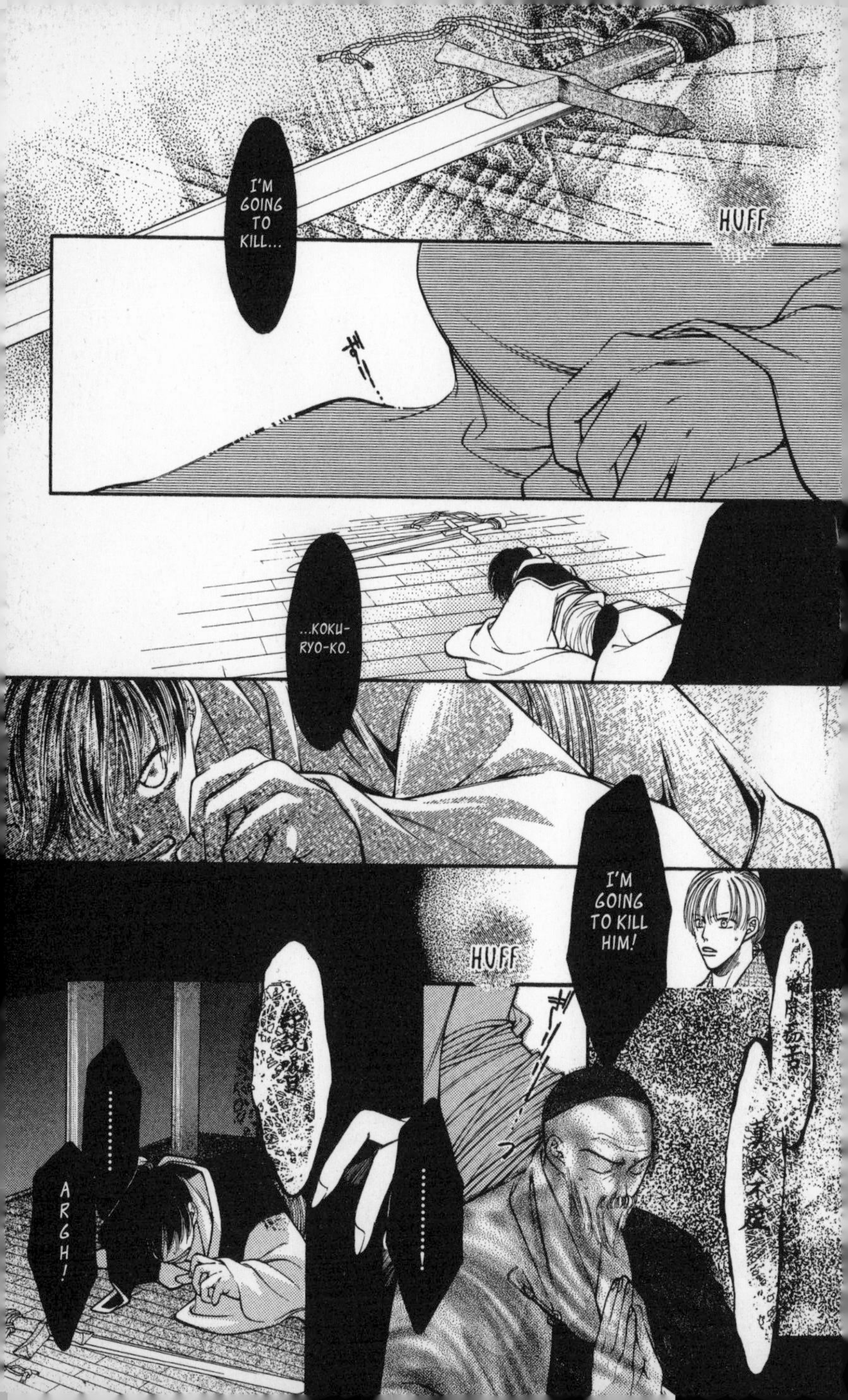
HUFF
I'M GOING TO KILL...
...KOKU-RYO-KO.
I'M GOING TO KILL HIM!
HUFF
......!
......
ARGH!

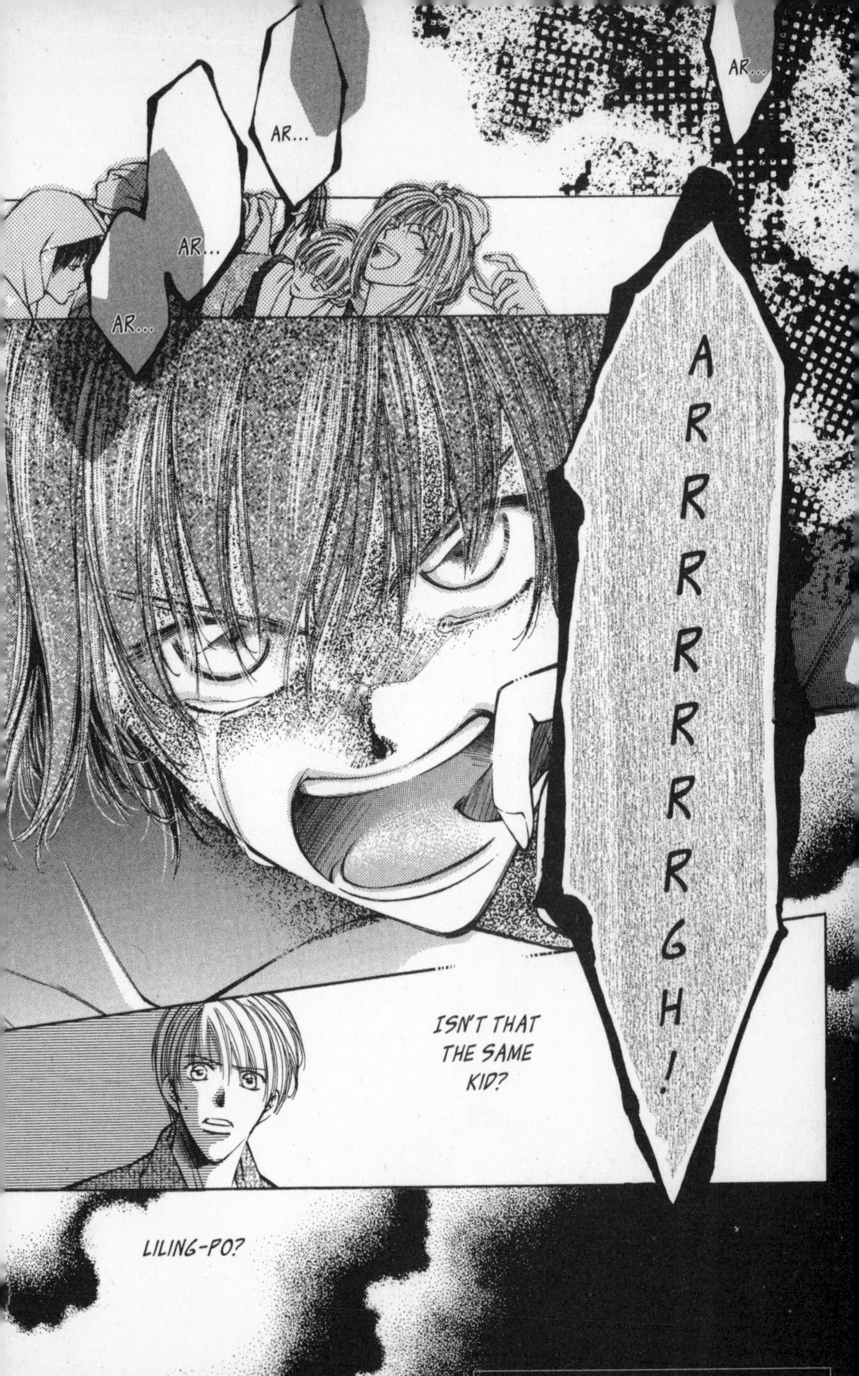
AR...
AR...
AR...
AR...
ARRRRRRGH!
ISN'T THAT THE SAME KID?
LILING-PO?
THE EIGHT GREAT ARTISTS, PART 10 – THE END

Huh...

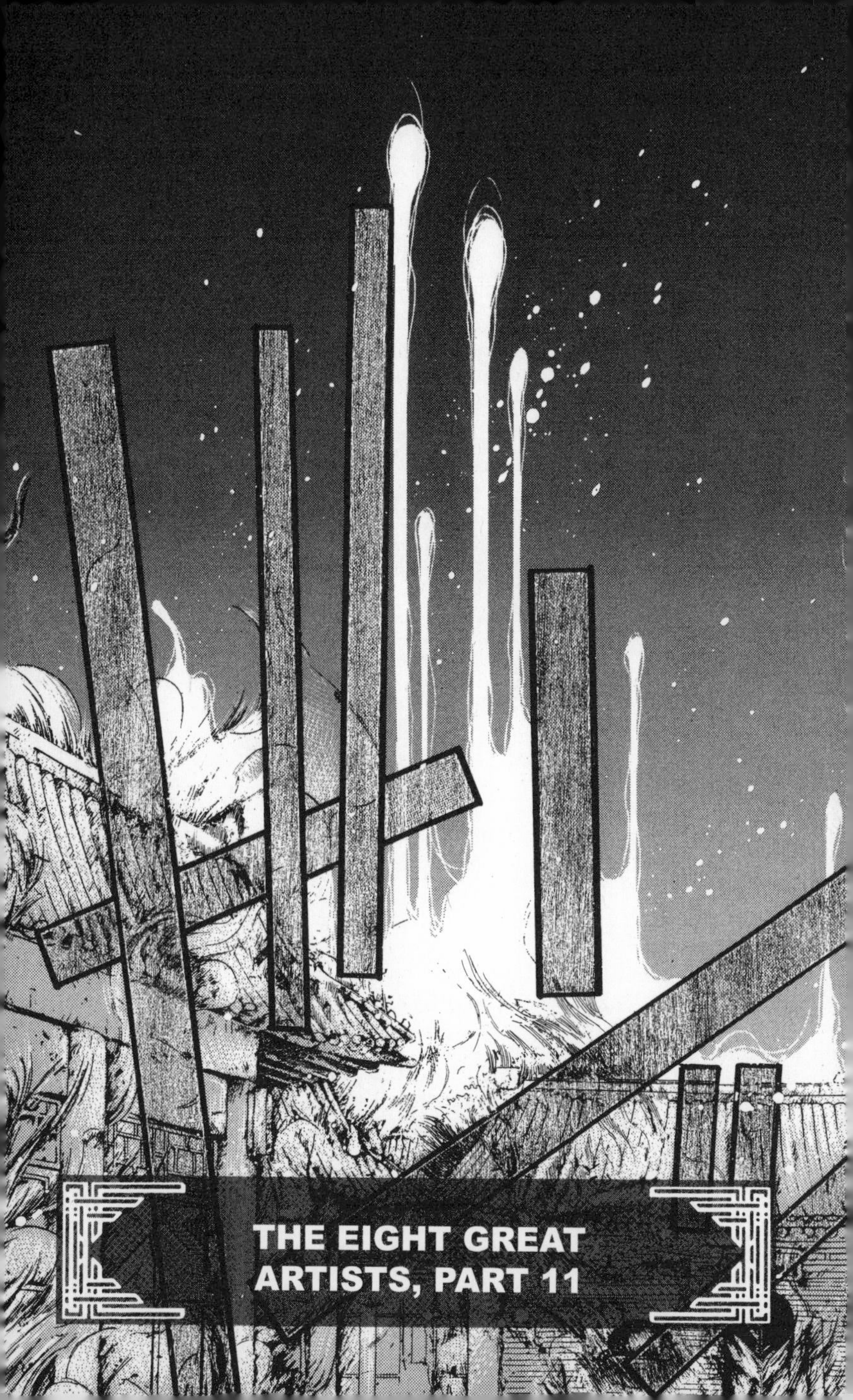
THE EIGHT GREAT
ARTISTS, PART 11

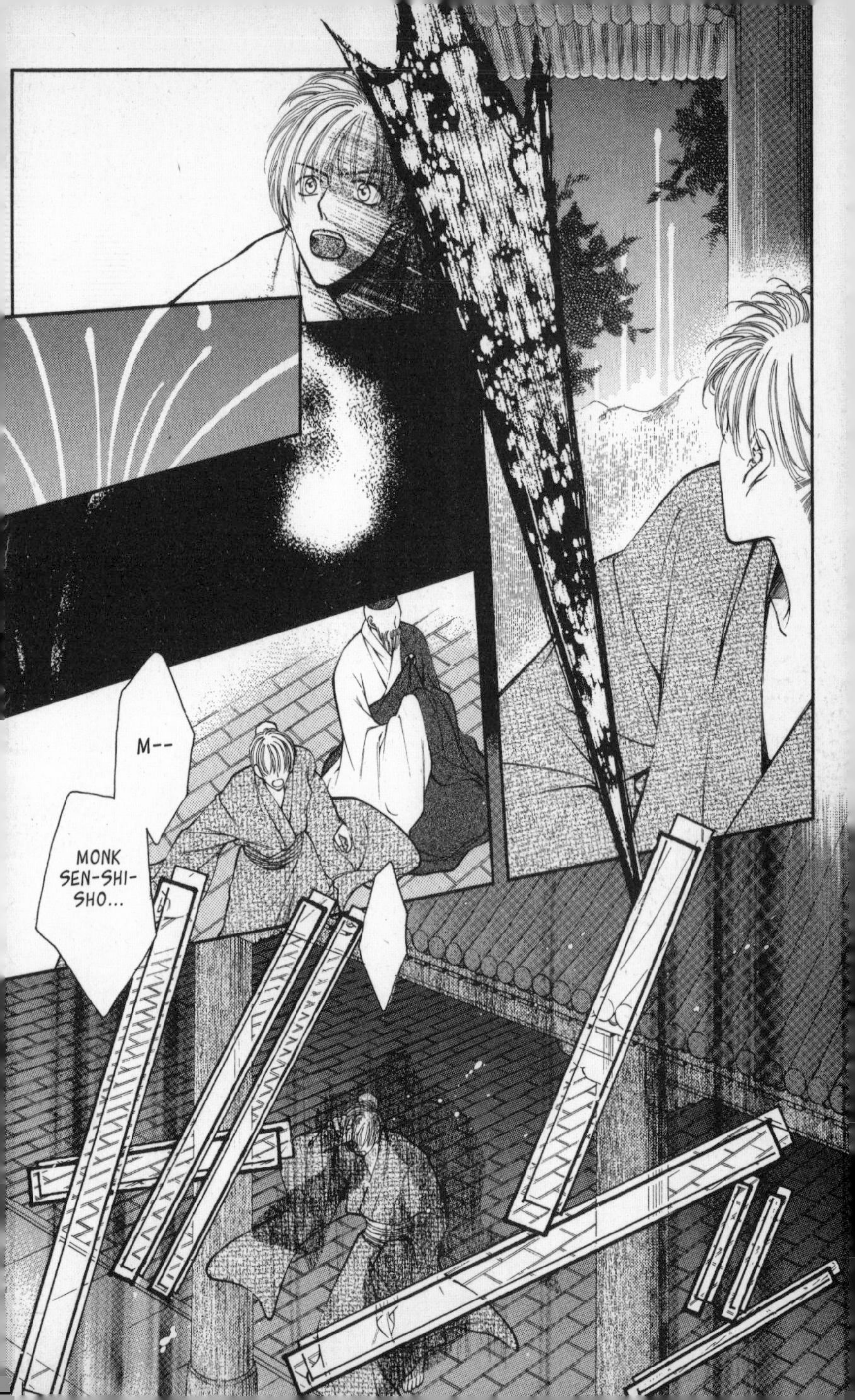
M--
MONK SEN-SHI-SHO...

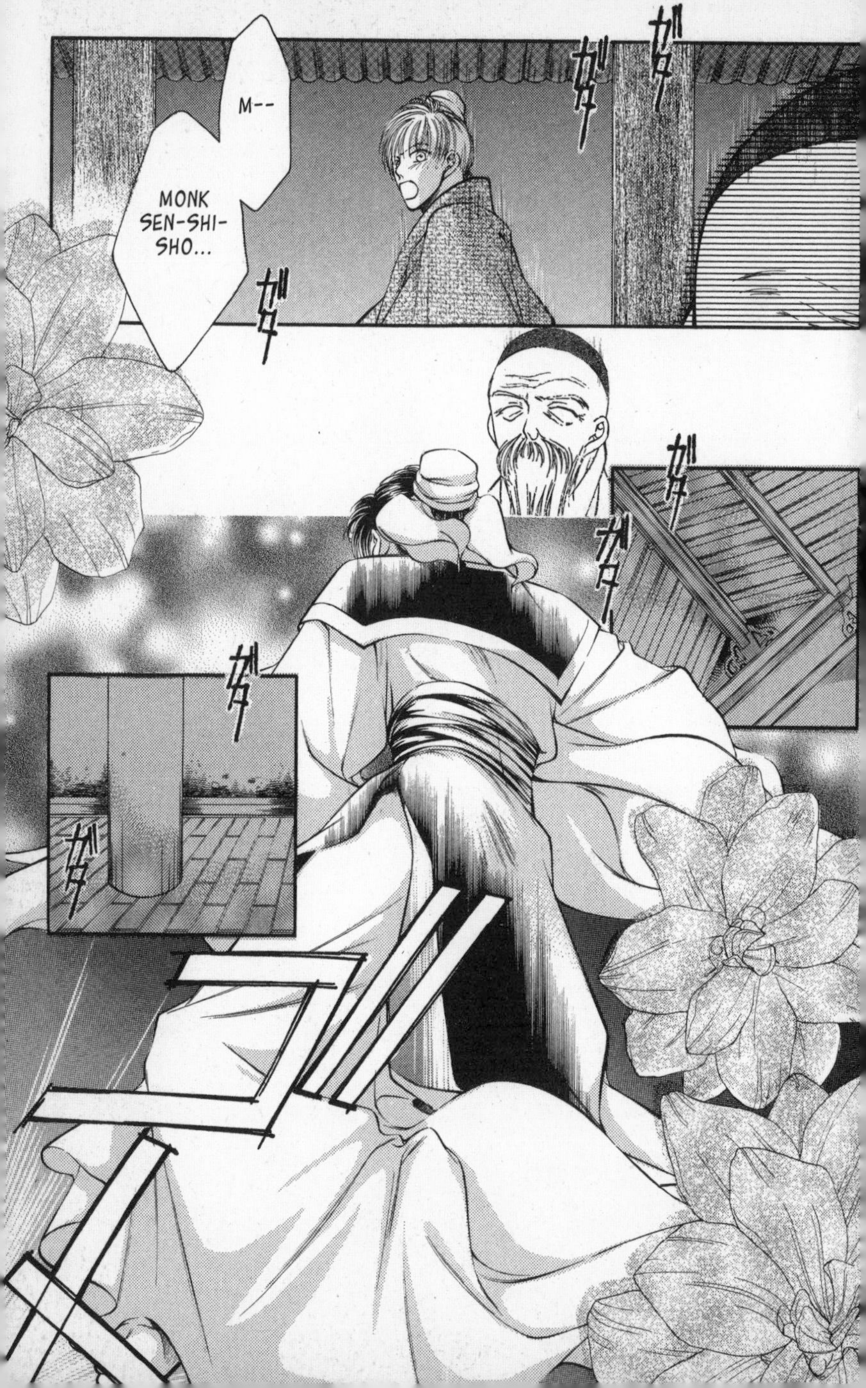
ガタ
ガタ
M--
MONK SEN-SHI-SHO...
ガタ
ガタ
ガタ
ガタ
ガタ

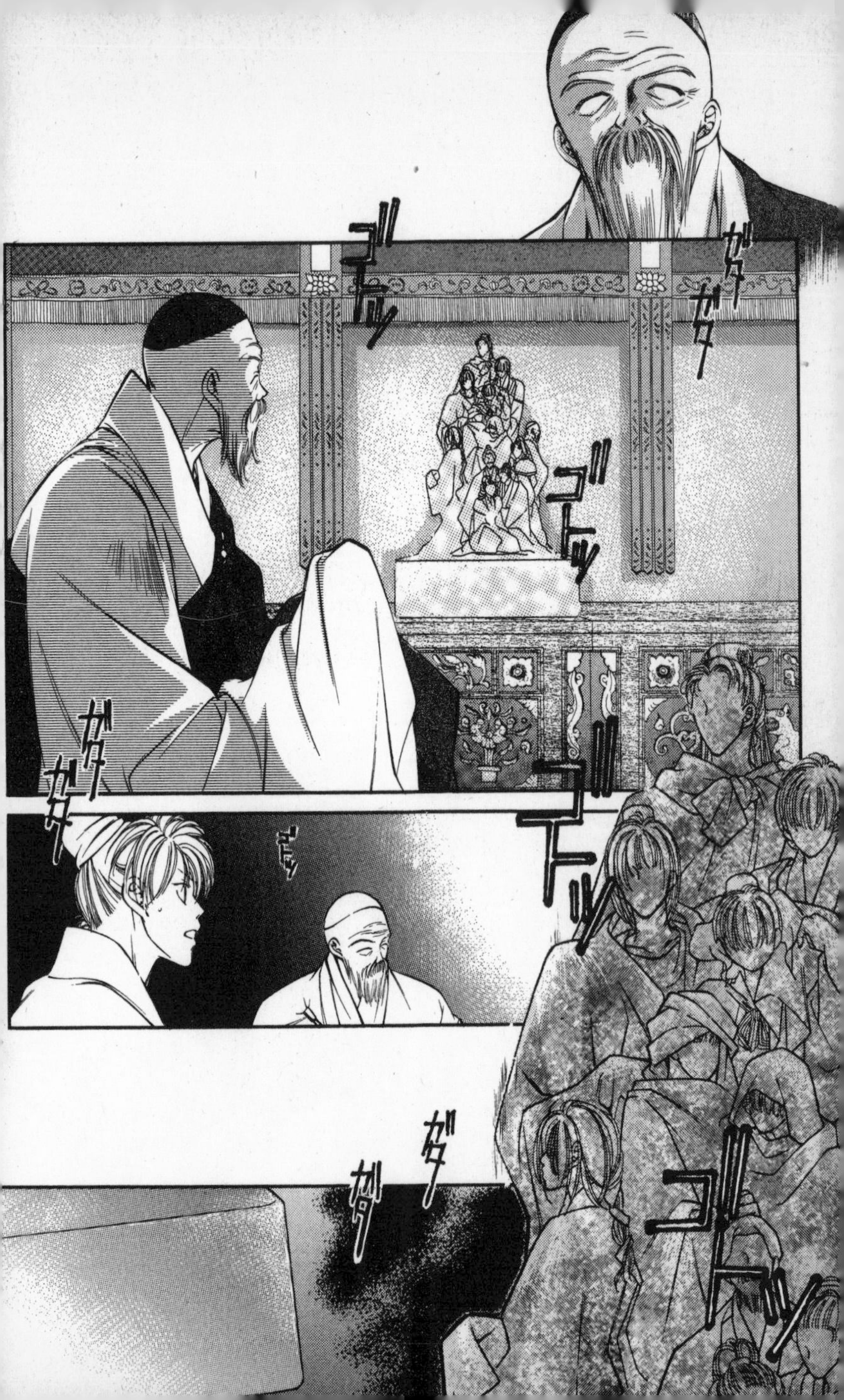
ガタガタ
ゴトッ
ゴトッ
ガタガタ
ゴトッ
ゴトッ
ゴトッ
ガタ
ガタ

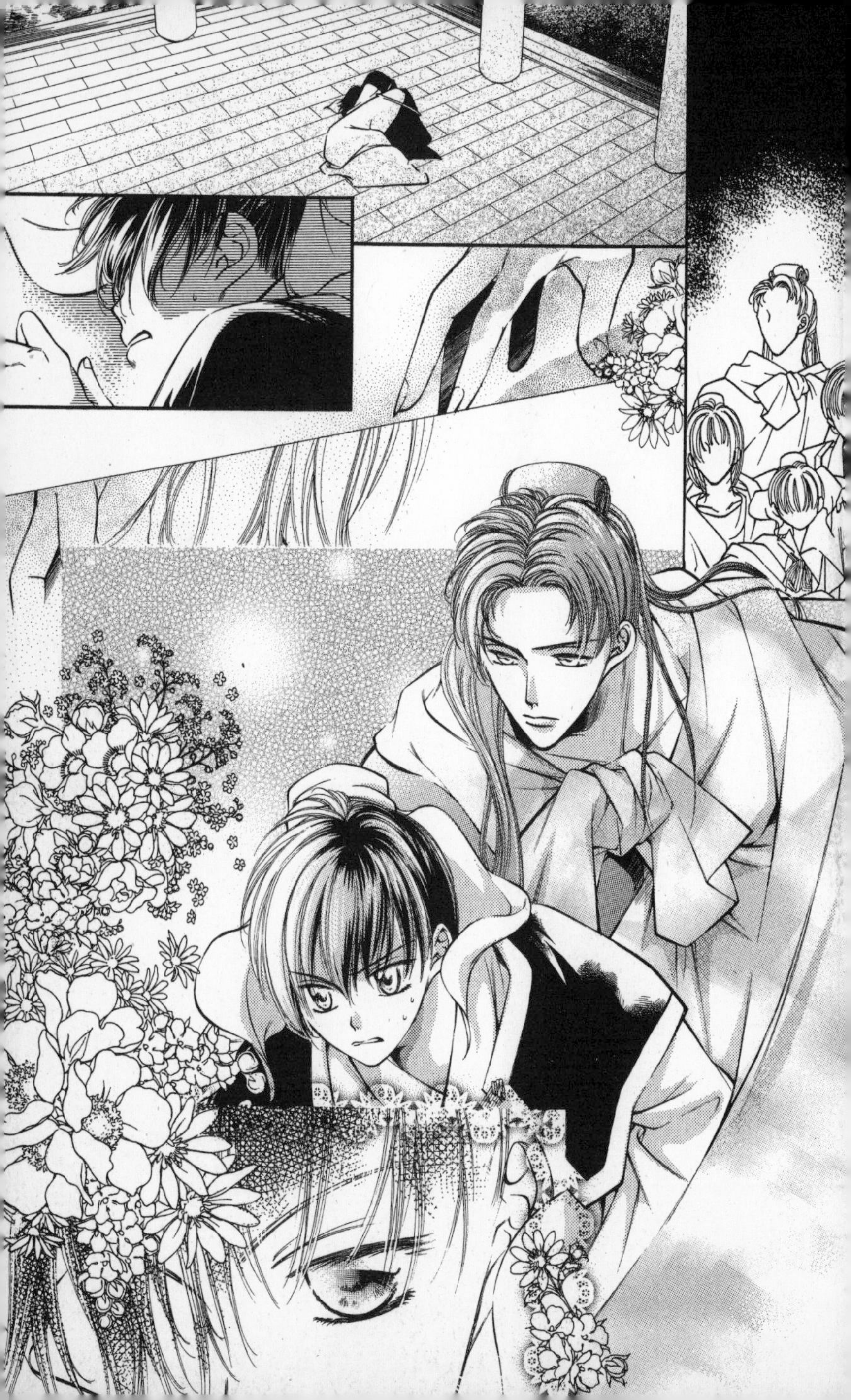

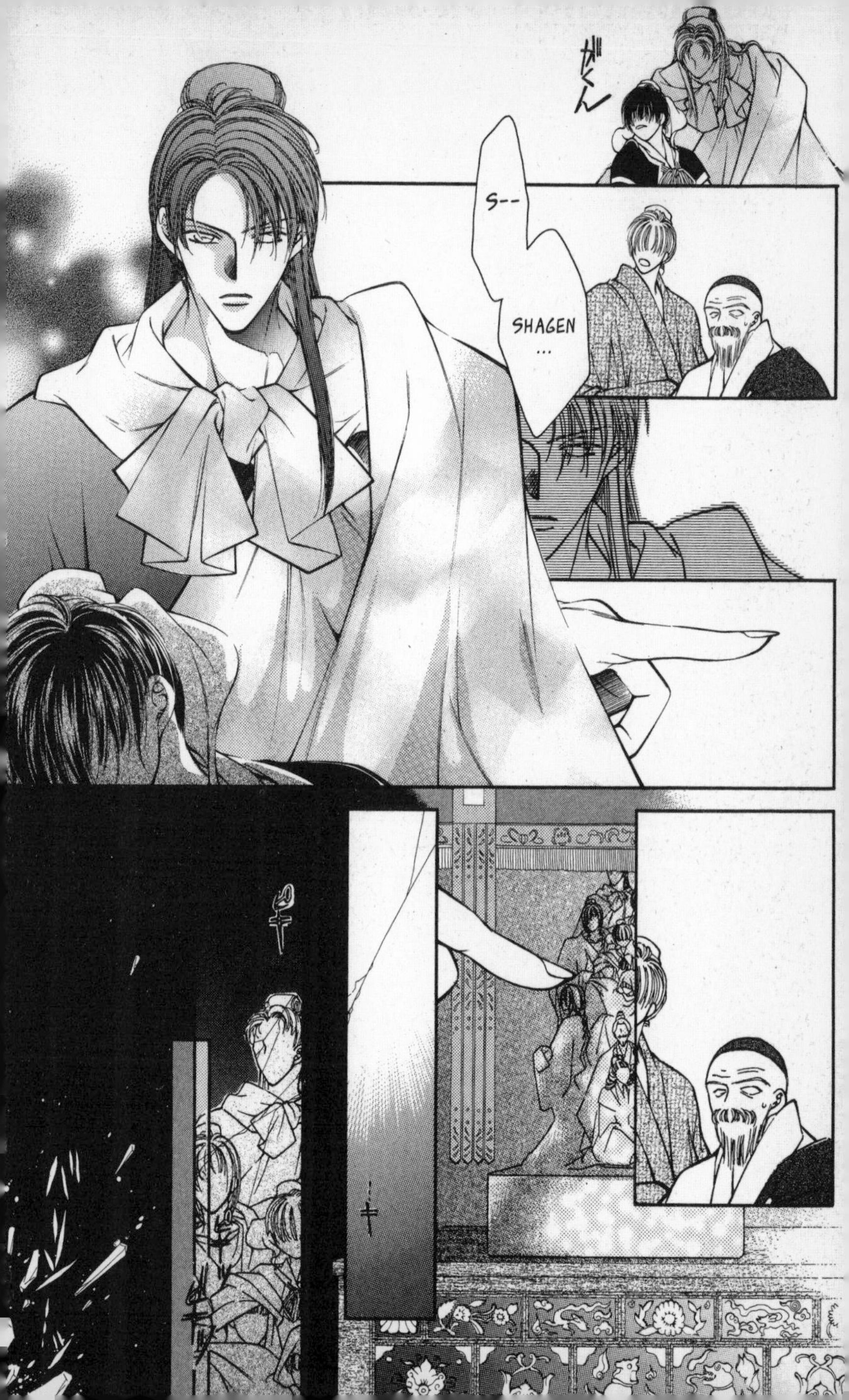
がくん
S--
SHAGEN
...

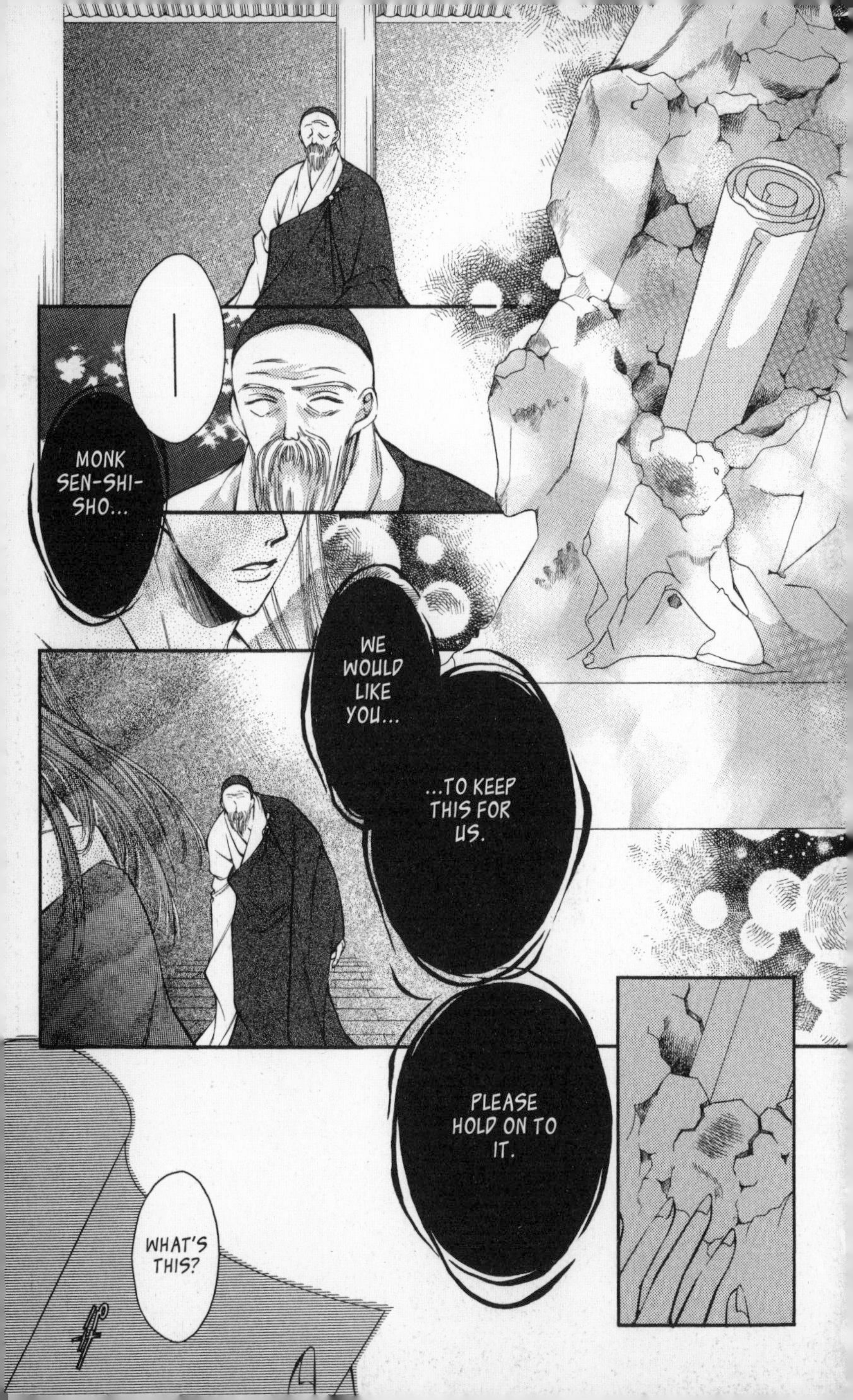

MONK SEN-SHI-SHO...
WE WOULD LIKE YOU...
...TO KEEP THIS FOR US.
PLEASE HOLD ON TO IT.
WHAT'S THIS?

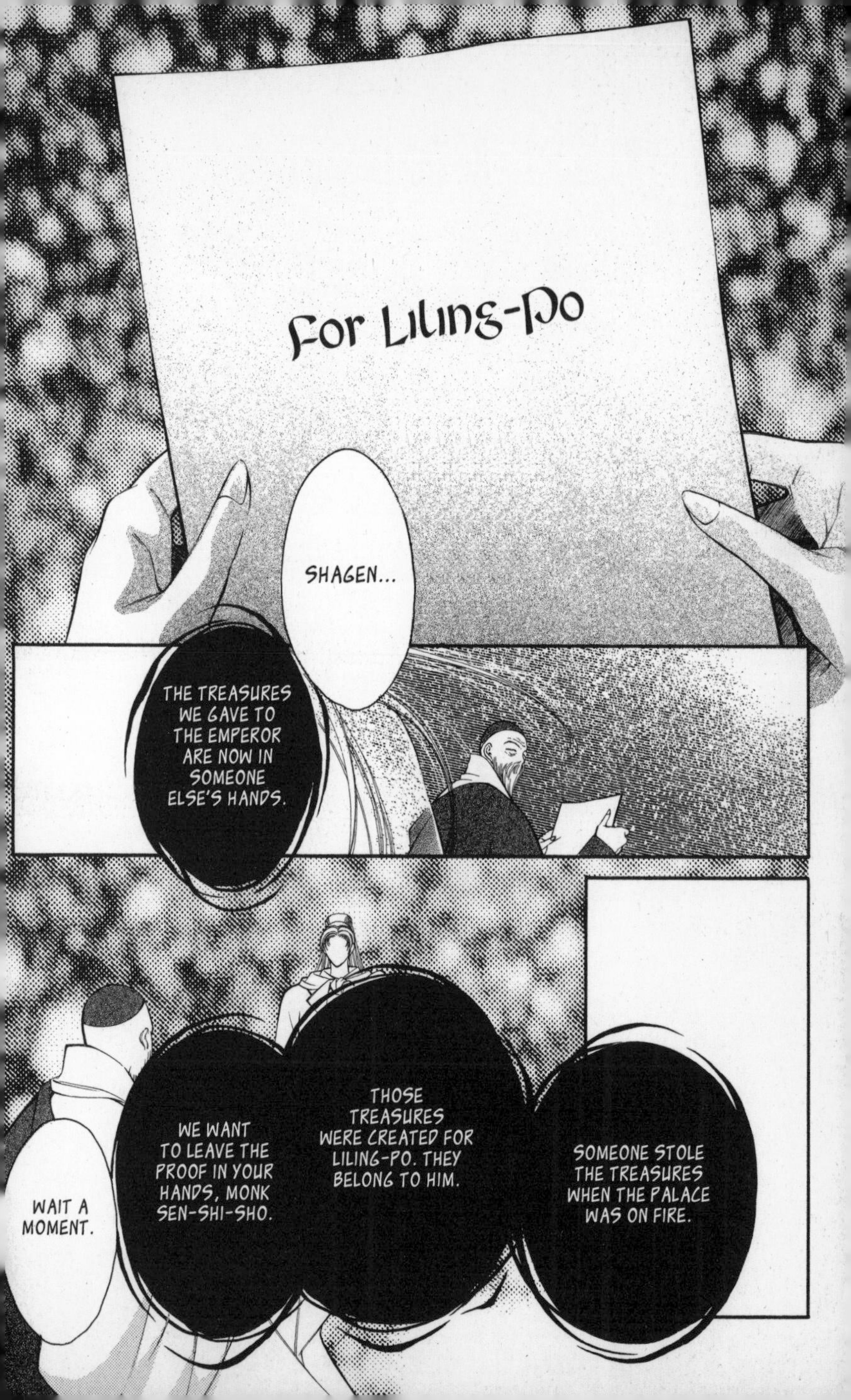
For Liling-Po
SHAGEN...
THE TREASURES WE GAVE TO THE EMPEROR ARE NOW IN SOMEONE ELSE'S HANDS.
SOMEONE STOLE THE TREASURES WHEN THE PALACE WAS ON FIRE.
THOSE TREASURES WERE CREATED FOR LILING-PO. THEY BELONG TO HIM.
WE WANT TO LEAVE THE PROOF IN YOUR HANDS, MONK SEN-SHI-SHO.
WAIT A MOMENT.

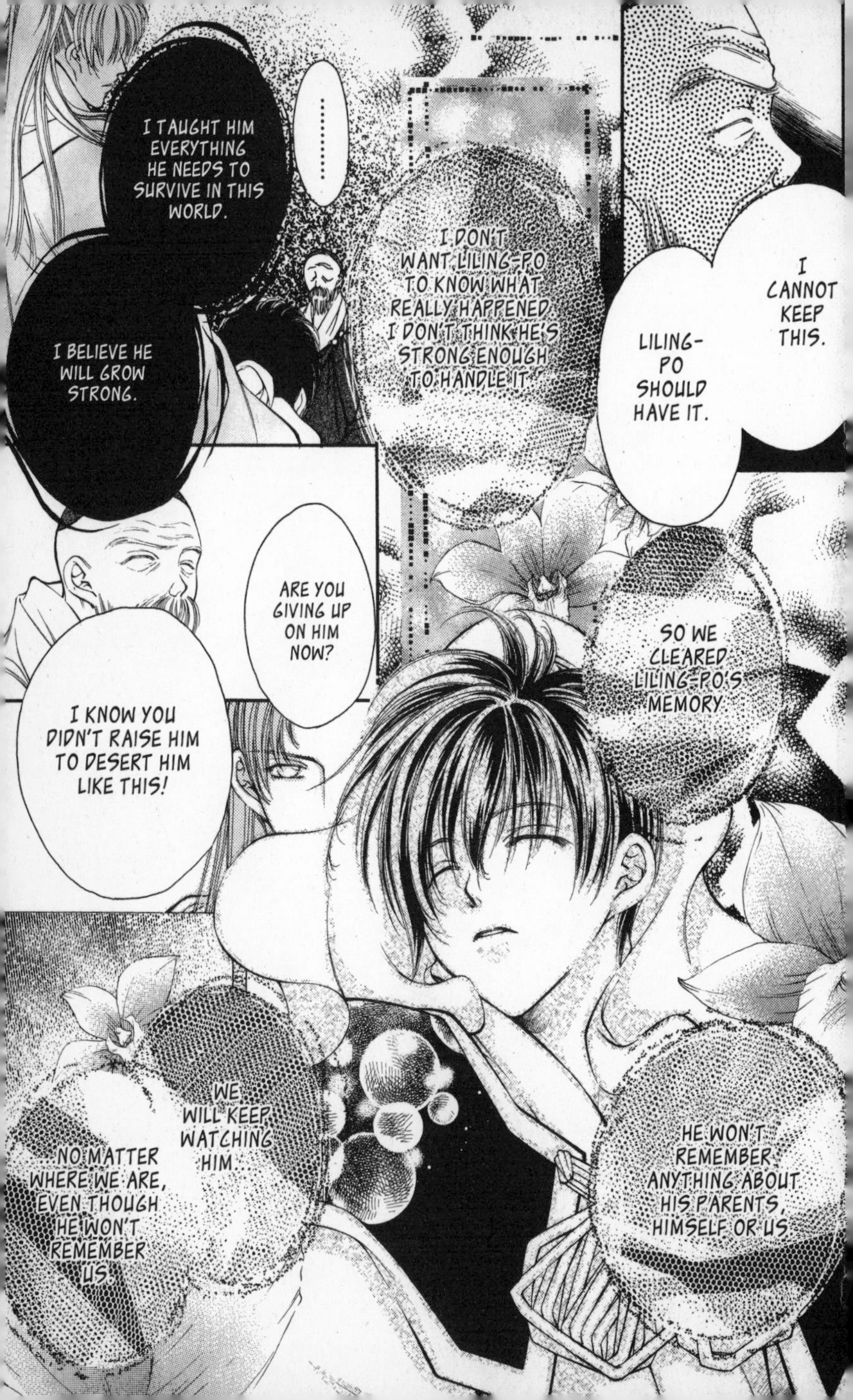
I CANNOT KEEP THIS.
LILING-PO SHOULD HAVE IT.
I DON'T WANT LILING-PO TO KNOW WHAT REALLY HAPPENED. I DON'T THINK HE'S STRONG ENOUGH TO HANDLE IT.
......
I TAUGHT HIM EVERYTHING HE NEEDS TO SURVIVE IN THIS WORLD.
I BELIEVE HE WILL GROW STRONG.
ARE YOU GIVING UP ON HIM NOW?
I KNOW YOU DIDN'T RAISE HIM TO DESERT HIM LIKE THIS!
SO WE CLEARED LILING-PO'S MEMORY.
HE WON'T REMEMBER ANYTHING ABOUT HIS PARENTS, HIMSELF OR US.
WE WILL KEEP WATCHING HIM.
NO MATTER WHERE WE ARE, EVEN THOUGH HE WON'T REMEMBER US.

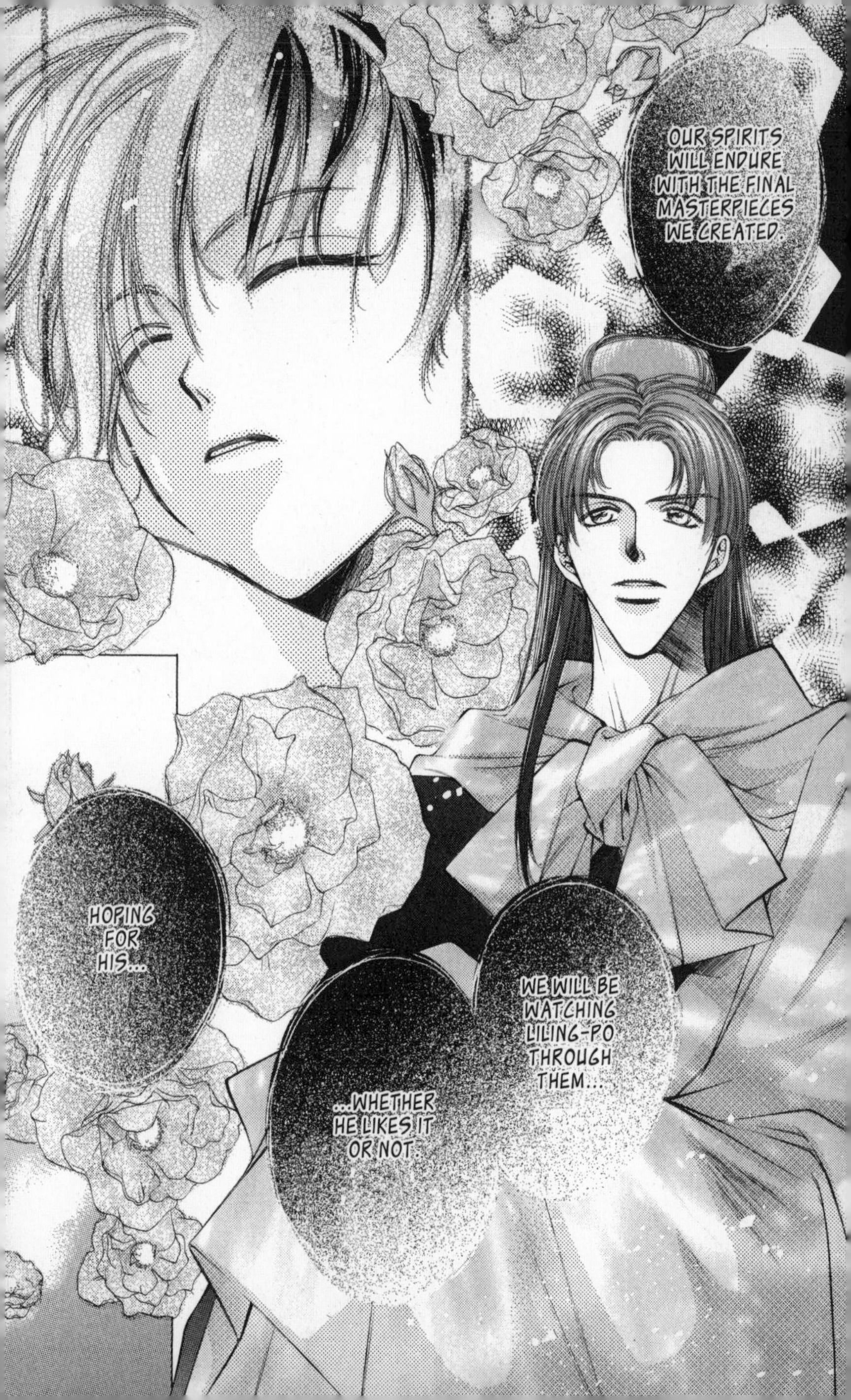
OUR SPIRITS WILL ENDURE WITH THE FINAL MASTERPIECES WE CREATED.
WE WILL BE WATCHING LILING-PO THROUGH THEM...
...WHETHER HE LIKES IT OR NOT.
HOPING FOR HIS...

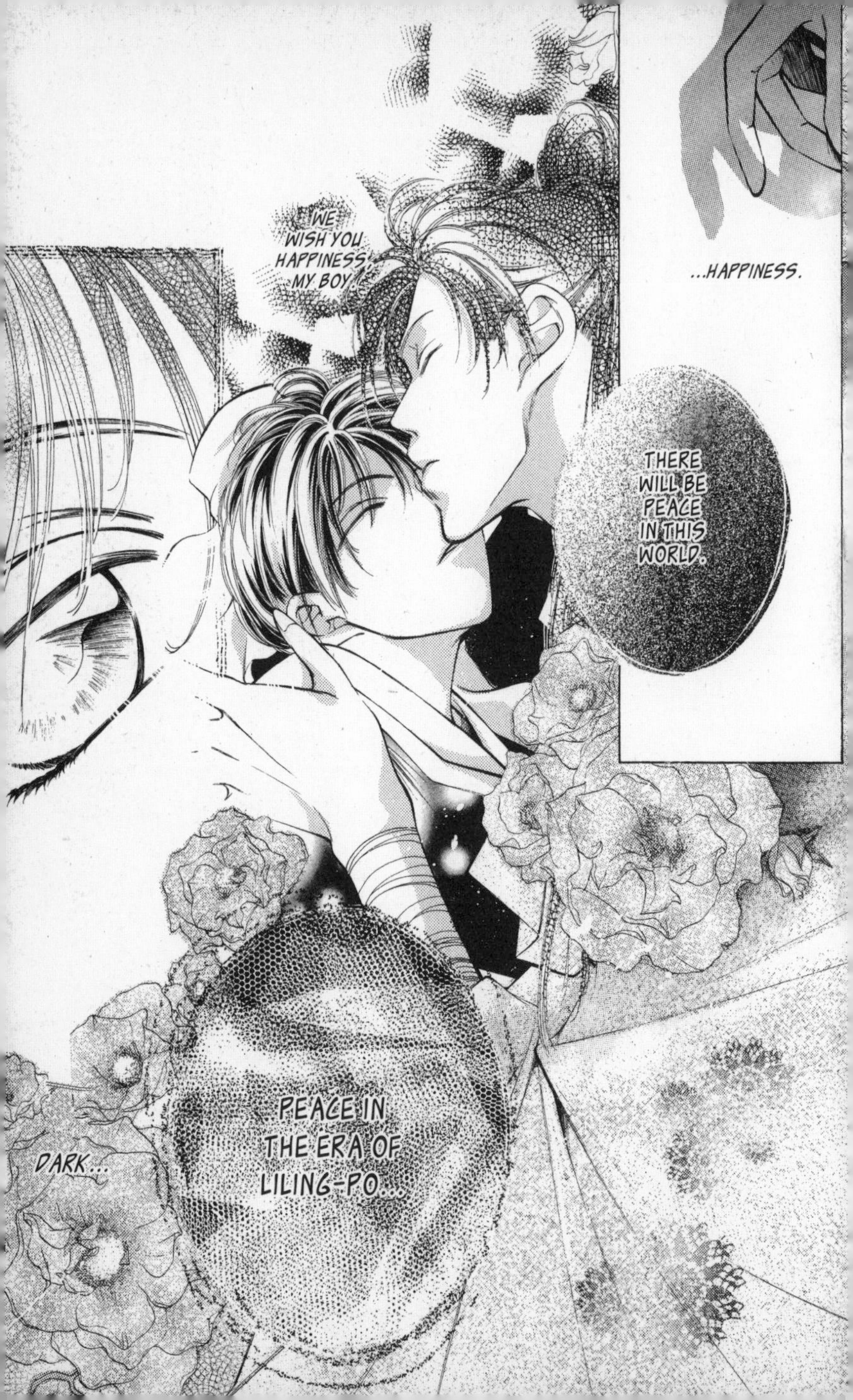
...HAPPINESS.
WE WISH YOU HAPPINESS, MY BOY.
THERE WILL BE PEACE IN THIS WORLD.
PEACE IN THE ERA OF LILING-PO...
DARK...

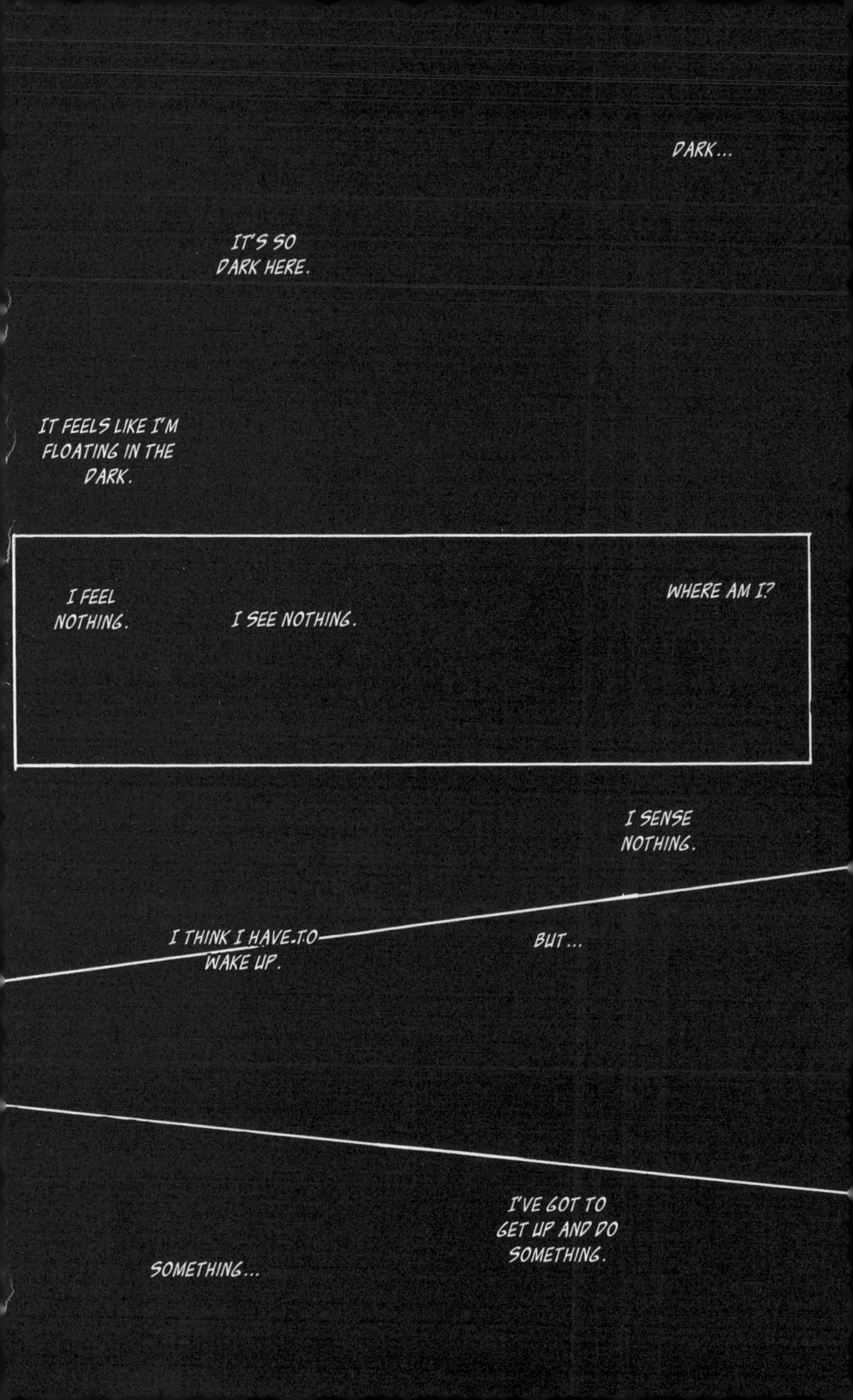
DARK...
IT'S SO DARK HERE.
IT FEELS LIKE I'M FLOATING IN THE DARK.
WHERE AM I?
I SEE NOTHING.
I FEEL NOTHING.
I SENSE NOTHING.
BUT...
I THINK I HAVE TO WAKE UP.
I'VE GOT TO GET UP AND DO SOMETHING.
SOMETHING...

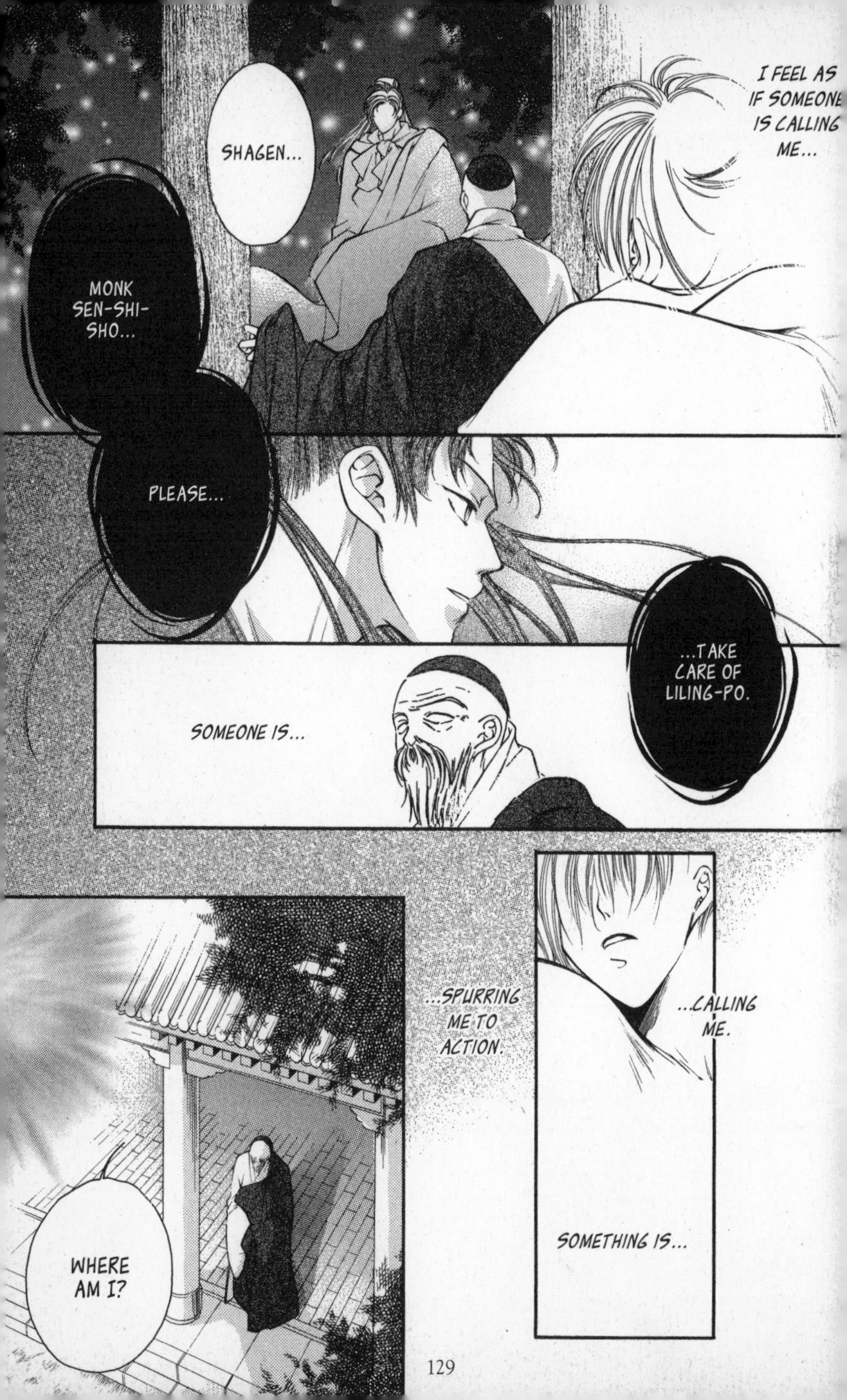
I FEEL AS IF SOMEONE IS CALLING ME...
SHAGEN...
MONK SEN-SHI-SHO...
PLEASE...
...TAKE CARE OF LILING-PO.
SOMEONE IS...
...CALLING ME.
SOMETHING IS...
...SPURRING ME TO ACTION.
WHERE AM I?

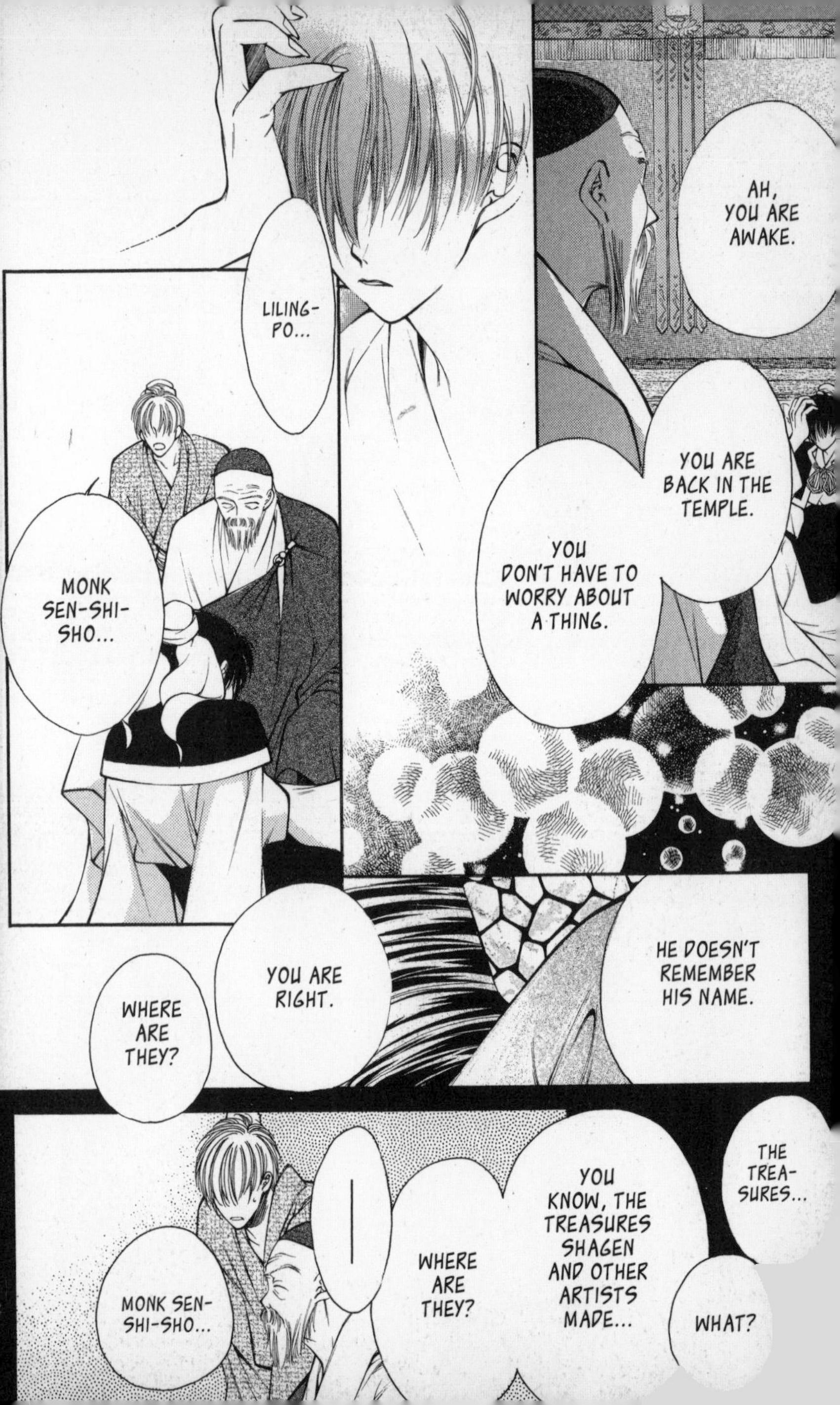
AH, YOU ARE AWAKE.
YOU ARE BACK IN THE TEMPLE.
YOU DON'T HAVE TO WORRY ABOUT A THING.
LILING-PO...
MONK SEN-SHI-SHO...
HE DOESN'T REMEMBER HIS NAME.
YOU ARE RIGHT.
WHERE ARE THEY?
THE TREA-SURES...
WHAT?
YOU KNOW, THE TREASURES SHAGEN AND OTHER ARTISTS MADE...
WHERE ARE THEY?
—
MONK SEN-SHI-SHO...

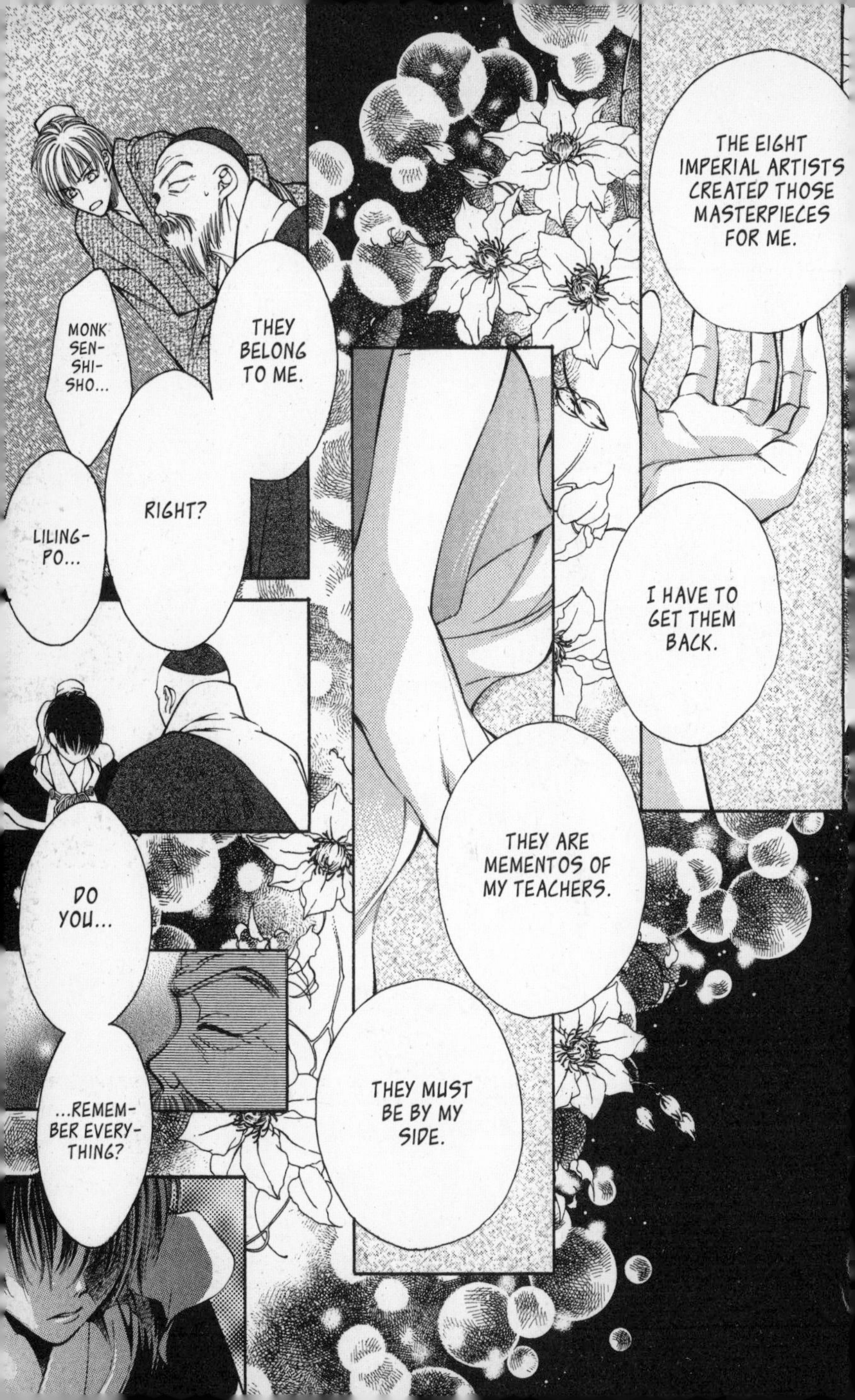
THE EIGHT IMPERIAL ARTISTS CREATED THOSE MASTERPIECES FOR ME.
I HAVE TO GET THEM BACK.
THEY ARE MEMENTOS OF MY TEACHERS.
THEY MUST BE BY MY SIDE.
THEY BELONG TO ME.
MONK SEN-SHI-SHO...
RIGHT?
LILING-PO...
DO YOU...
...REMEM-BER EVERY-THING?

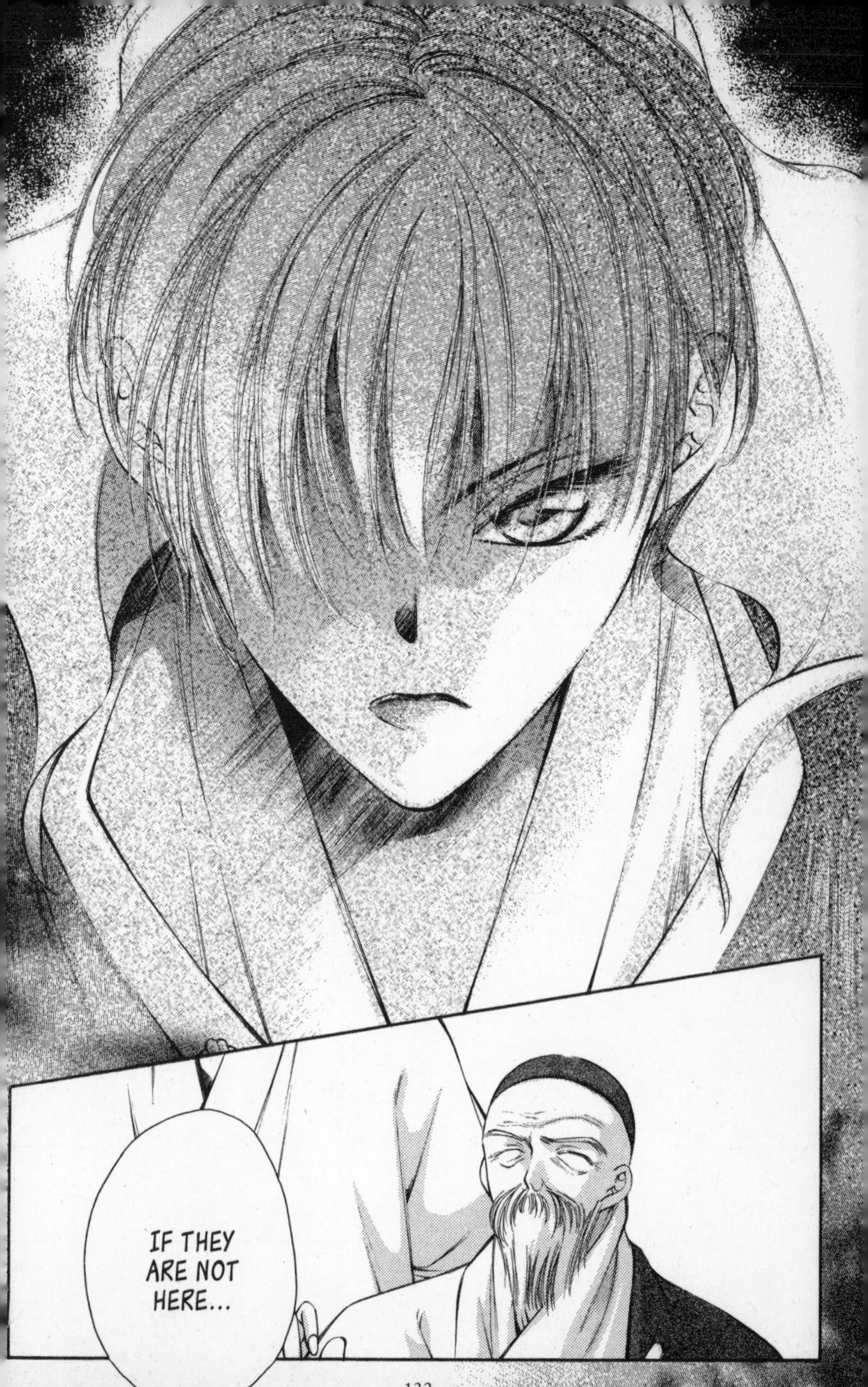
IF THEY ARE NOT HERE...

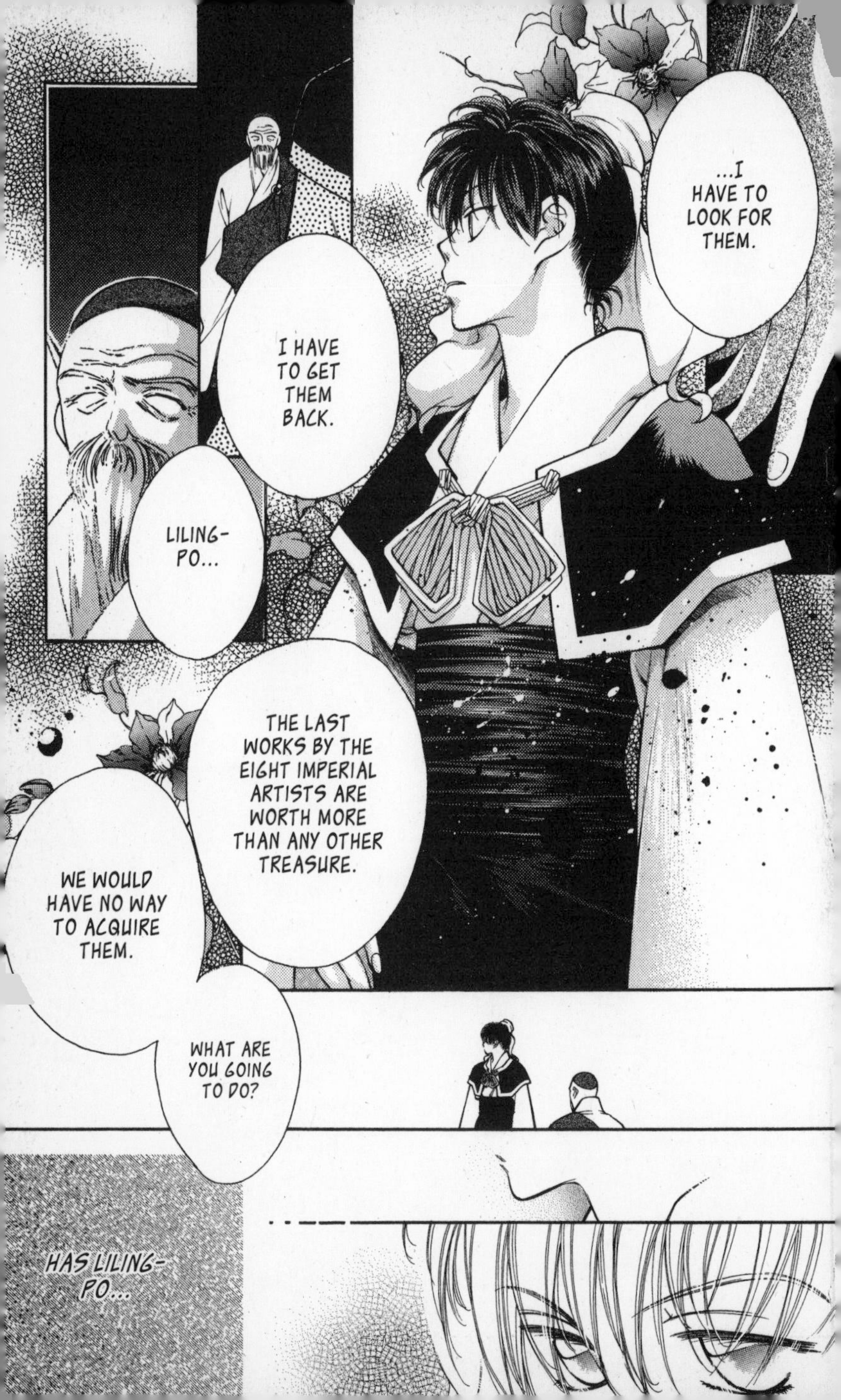
...I HAVE TO LOOK FOR THEM.
I HAVE TO GET THEM BACK.
LILING-PO...
THE LAST WORKS BY THE EIGHT IMPERIAL ARTISTS ARE WORTH MORE THAN ANY OTHER TREASURE.
WE WOULD HAVE NO WAY TO ACQUIRE THEM.
WHAT ARE YOU GOING TO DO?
- - ———
HAS LILING-PO...

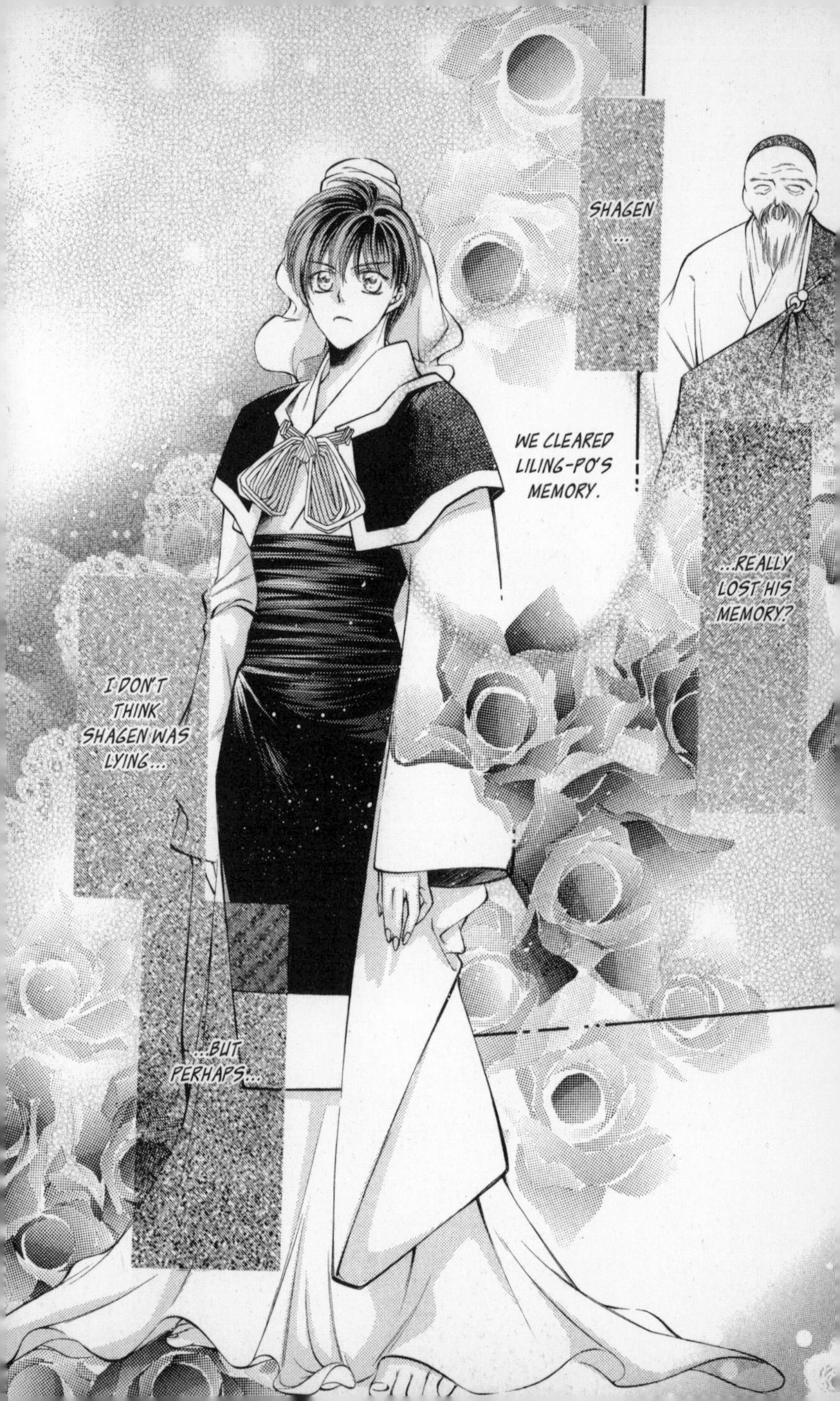
SHAGEN ...
WE CLEARED LILING-PO'S MEMORY.
...REALLY LOST HIS MEMORY?
I DON'T THINK SHAGEN WAS LYING...
...BUT PERHAPS...

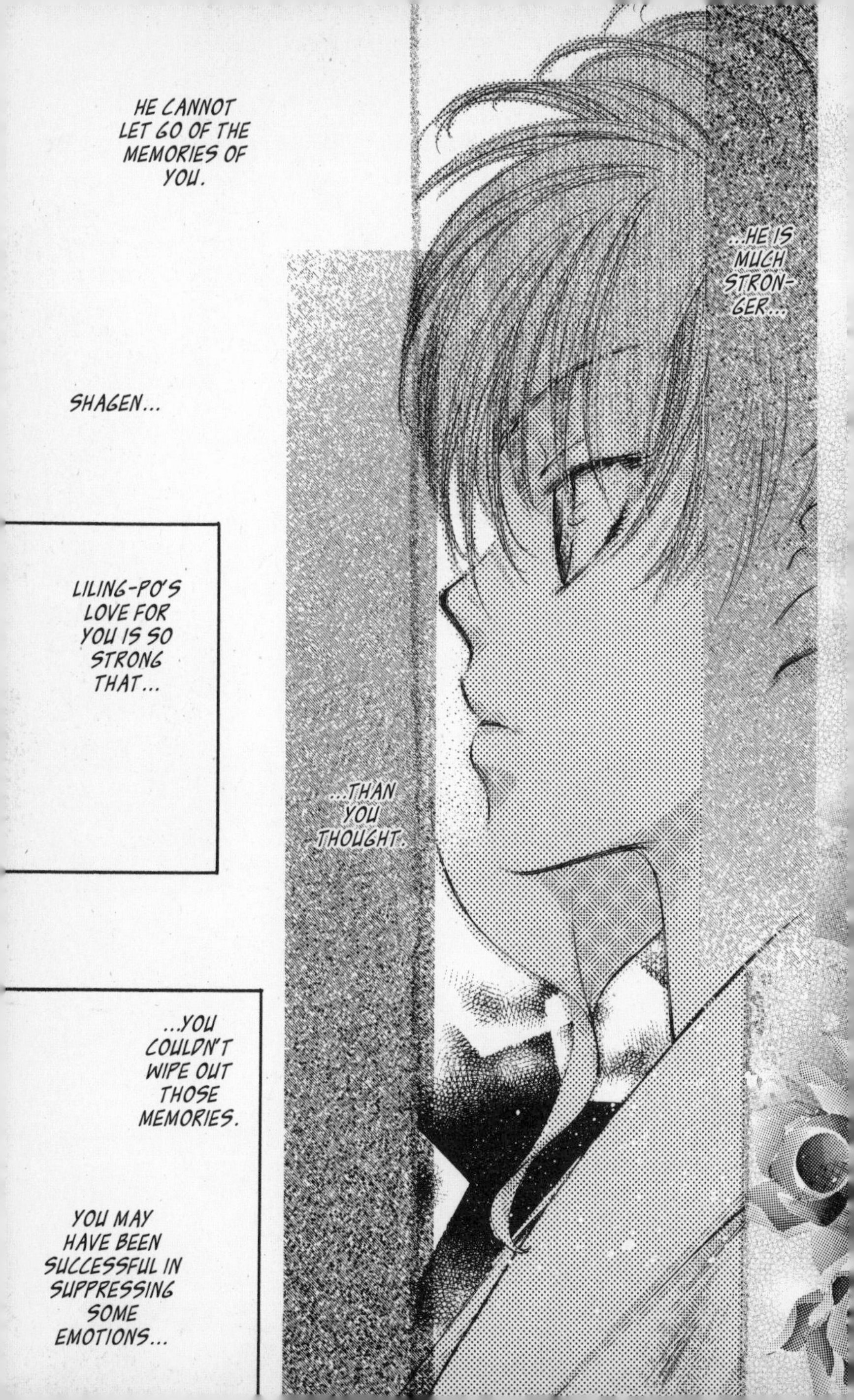
...HE IS MUCH STRONGER...
...THAN YOU THOUGHT.
HE CANNOT LET GO OF THE MEMORIES OF YOU.
SHAGEN...
LILING-PO'S LOVE FOR YOU IS SO STRONG THAT...
...YOU COULDN'T WIPE OUT THOSE MEMORIES.
YOU MAY HAVE BEEN SUCCESSFUL IN SUPPRESSING SOME EMOTIONS...

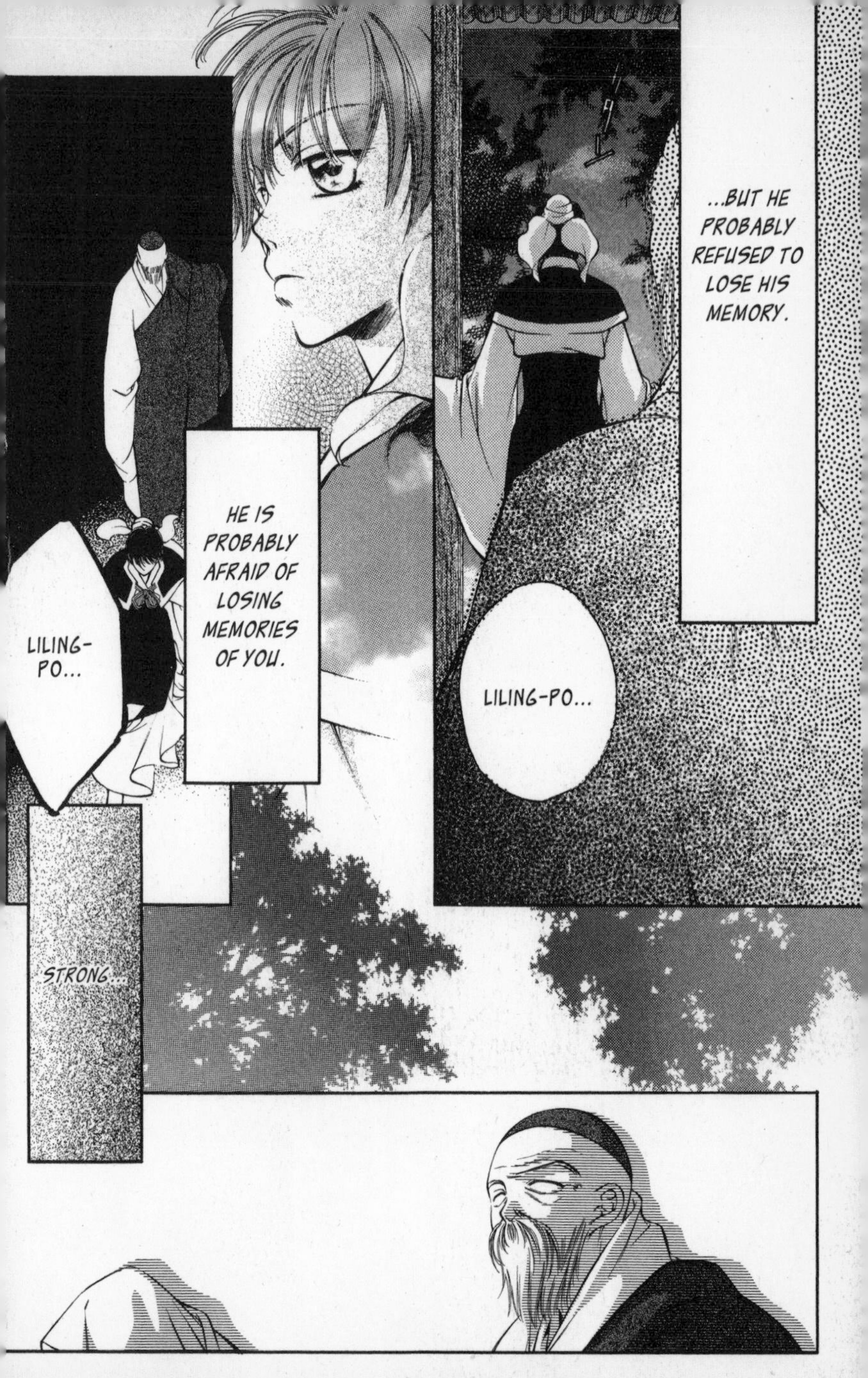
...BUT HE PROBABLY REFUSED TO LOSE HIS MEMORY.
LILING-PO...
HE IS PROBABLY AFRAID OF LOSING MEMORIES OF YOU.
LILING-PO...
STRONG...

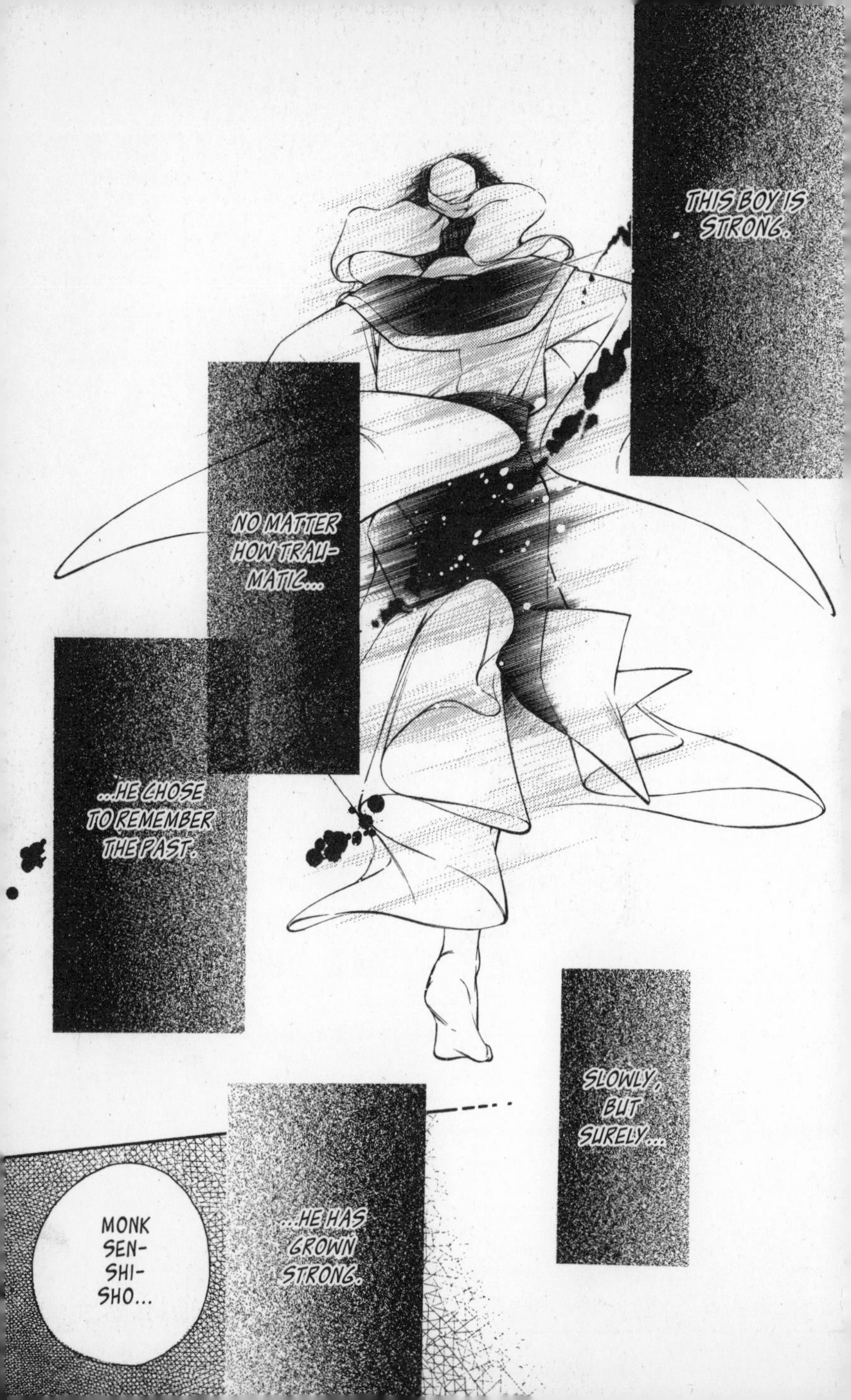
THIS BOY IS STRONG.
NO MATTER HOW TRAU-MATIC...
...HE CHOSE TO REMEMBER THE PAST.
SLOWLY, BUT SURELY...
...HE HAS GROWN STRONG.
MONK SEN-SHI-SHO...

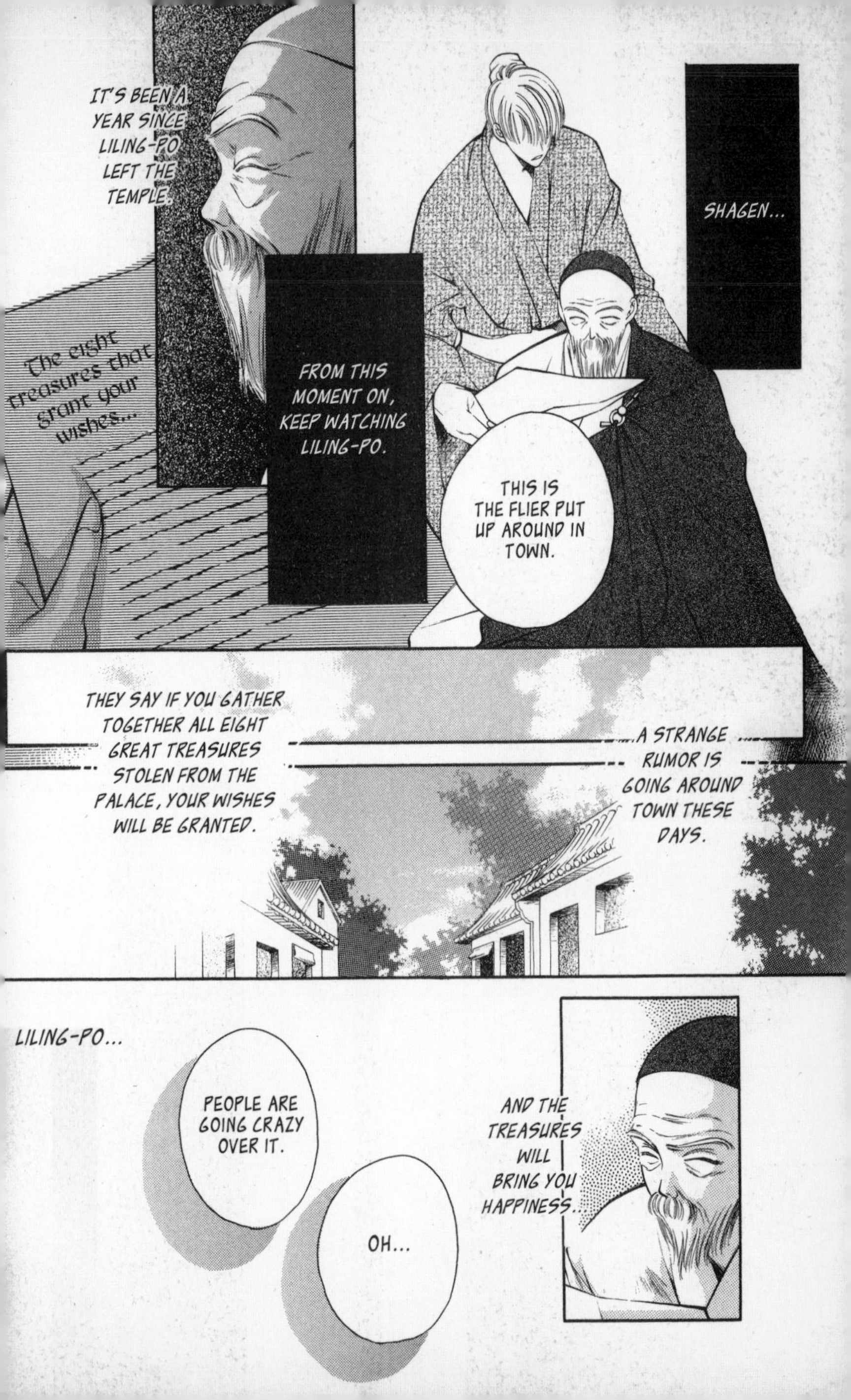

SHAGEN...
FROM THIS MOMENT ON, KEEP WATCHING LILING-PO.
THIS IS THE FLIER PUT UP AROUND IN TOWN.
IT'S BEEN A YEAR SINCE LILING-PO LEFT THE TEMPLE.
The eight treasures that grant your wishes...
A STRANGE RUMOR IS GOING AROUND TOWN THESE DAYS.
THEY SAY IF YOU GATHER TOGETHER ALL EIGHT GREAT TREASURES STOLEN FROM THE PALACE, YOUR WISHES WILL BE GRANTED.
AND THE TREASURES WILL BRING YOU HAPPINESS...
LILING-PO...
PEOPLE ARE GOING CRAZY OVER IT.
OH...

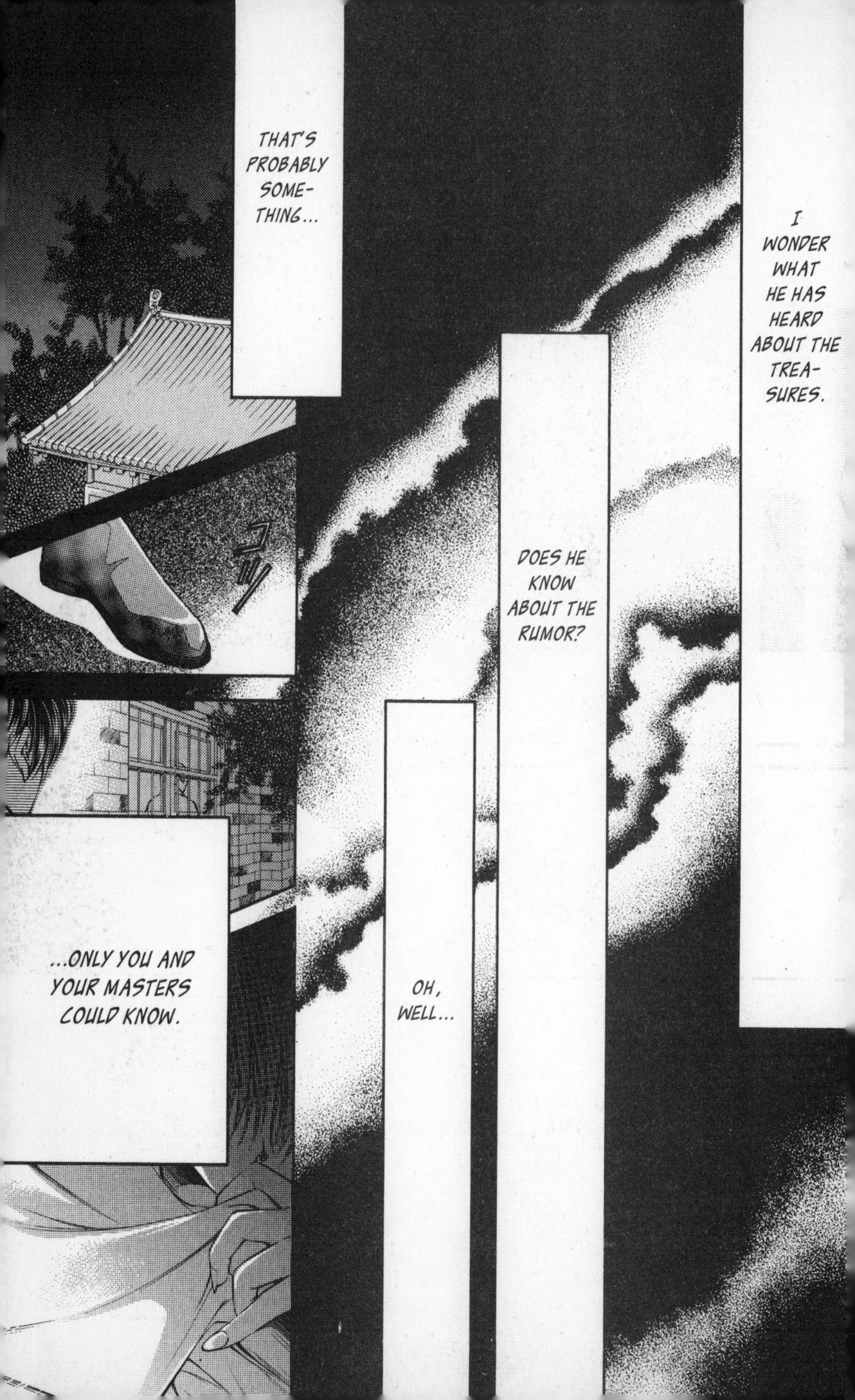
I WONDER WHAT HE HAS HEARD ABOUT THE TREASURES.
DOES HE KNOW ABOUT THE RUMOR?
OH, WELL...
THAT'S PROBABLY SOMETHING...
...ONLY YOU AND YOUR MASTERS COULD KNOW.

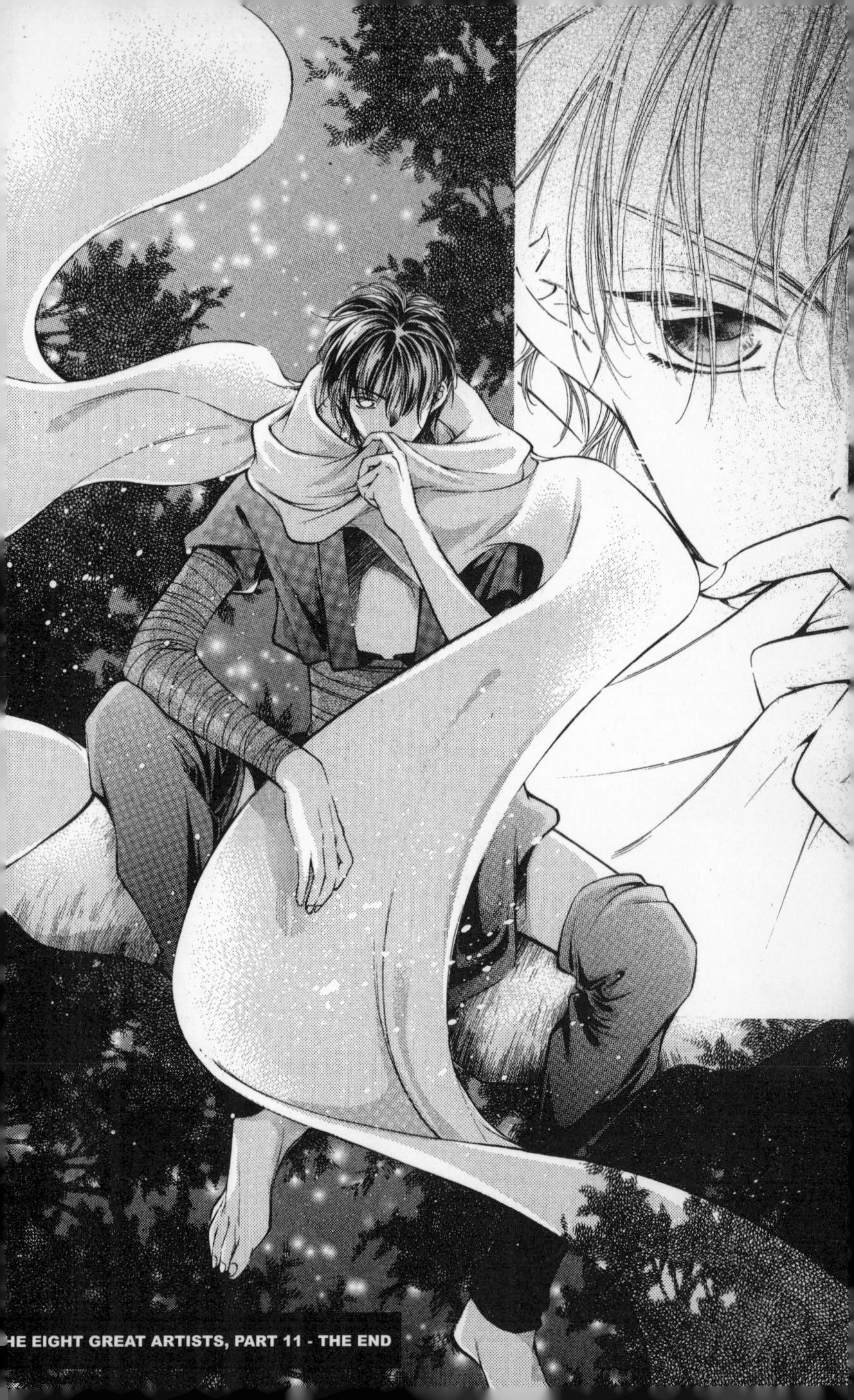
HE EIGHT GREAT ARTISTS, PART 11 - THE END

On watch...

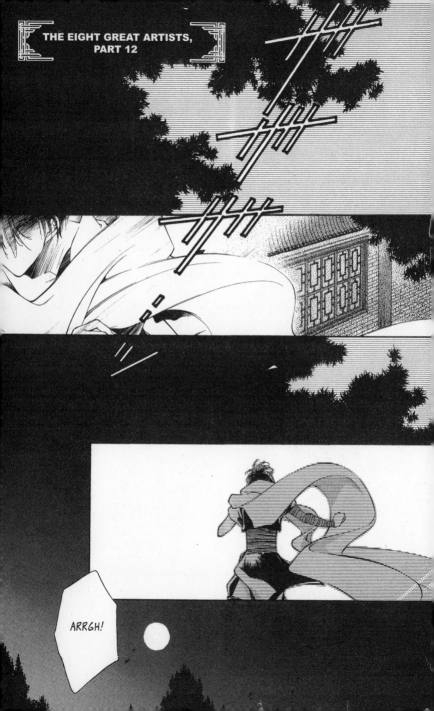

THE EIGHT GREAT ARTISTS, PART 12

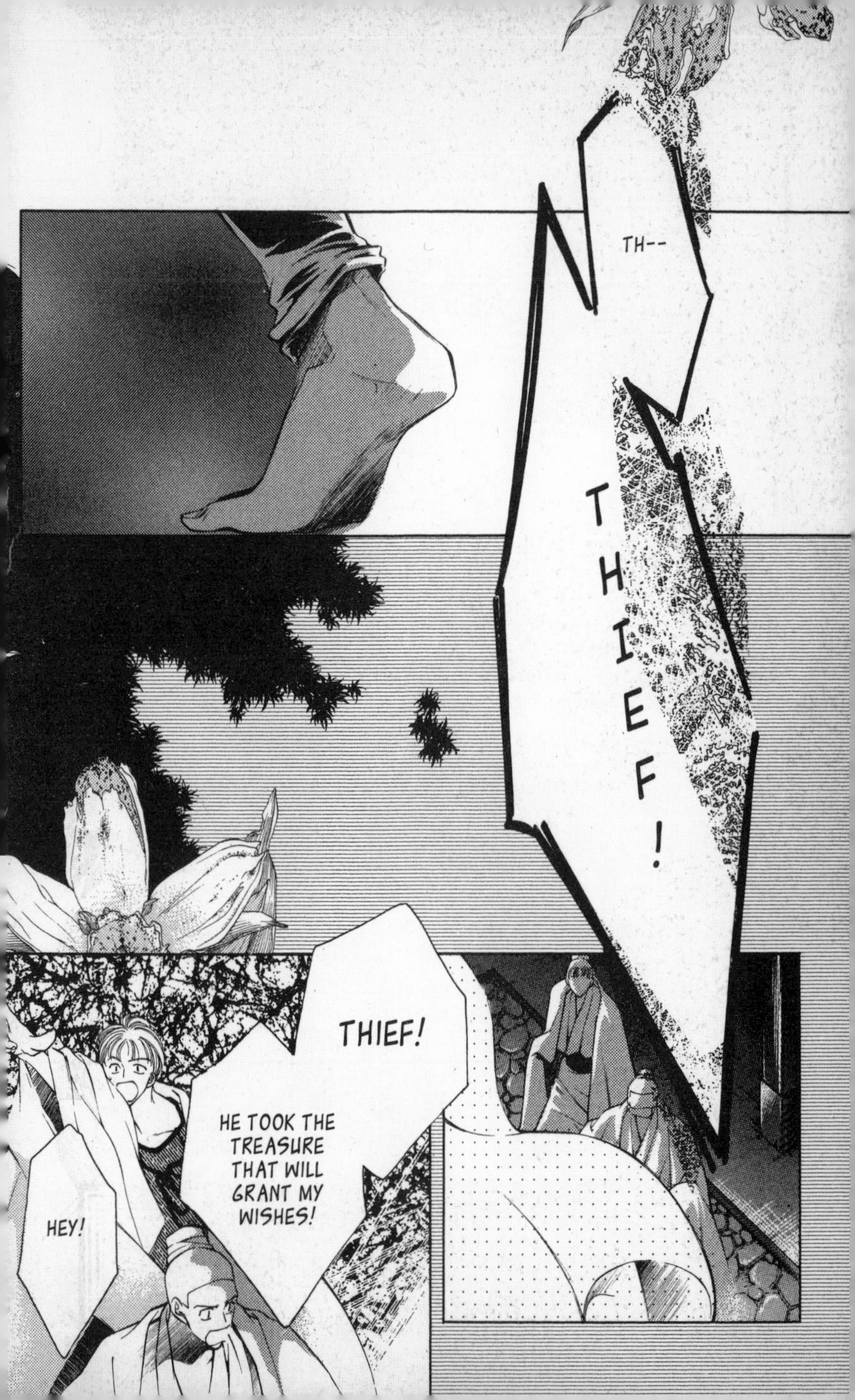
TH--
THIEF!
THIEF!
HE TOOK THE TREASURE THAT WILL GRANT MY WISHES!
HEY!

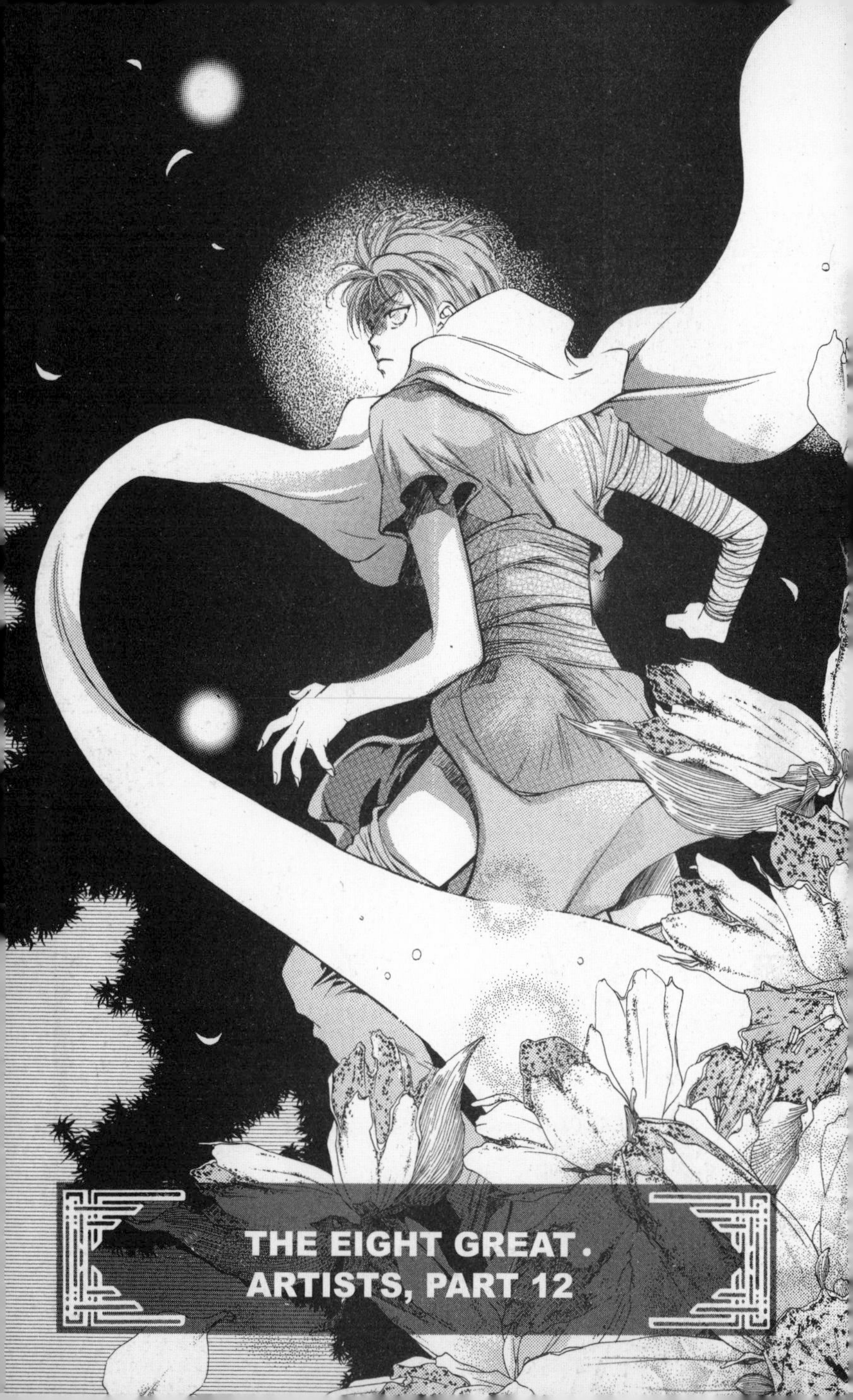
THE EIGHT GREAT .
ARTISTS, PART 12

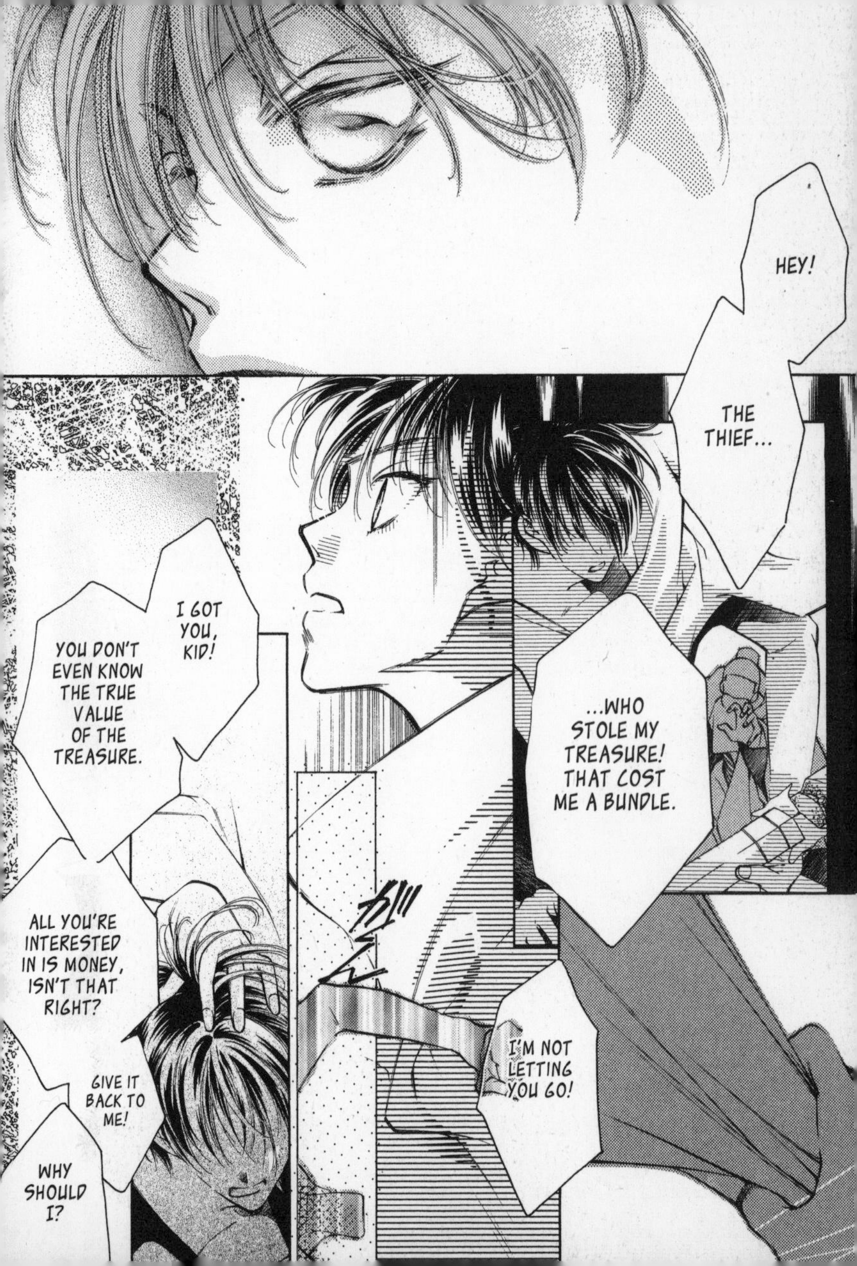
HEY!
THE THIEF...
...WHO STOLE MY TREASURE! THAT COST ME A BUNDLE.
I'M NOT LETTING YOU GO!
I GOT YOU, KID!
YOU DON'T EVEN KNOW THE TRUE VALUE OF THE TREASURE.
ALL YOU'RE INTERESTED IN IS MONEY, ISN'T THAT RIGHT?
GIVE IT BACK TO ME!
WHY SHOULD I?

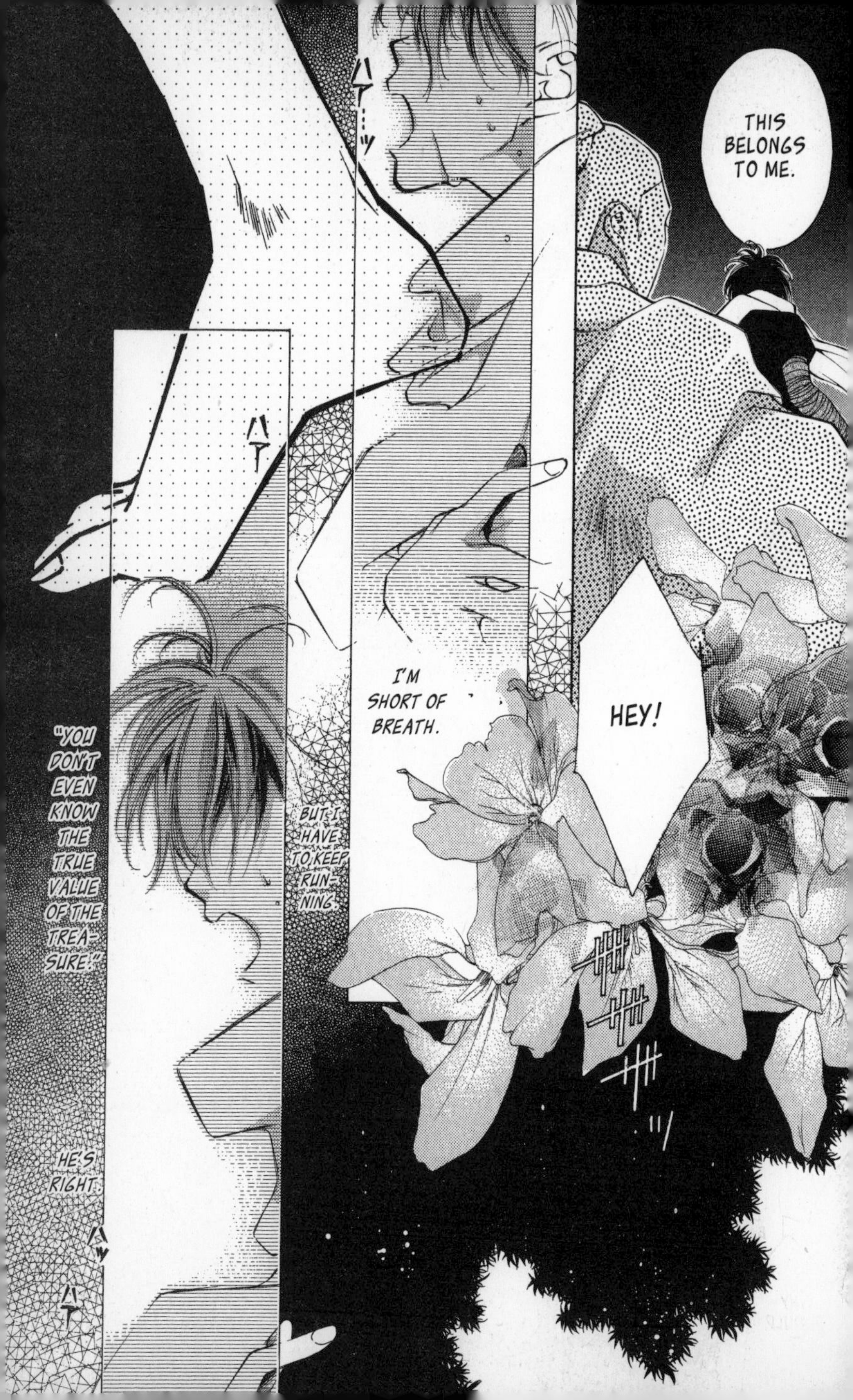
THIS BELONGS TO ME.
HEY!
I'M SHORT OF BREATH.
BUT I HAVE TO KEEP RUN-NING.
"YOU DON'T EVEN KNOW THE TRUE VALUE OF THE TREA-SURE."
HE'S RIGHT.

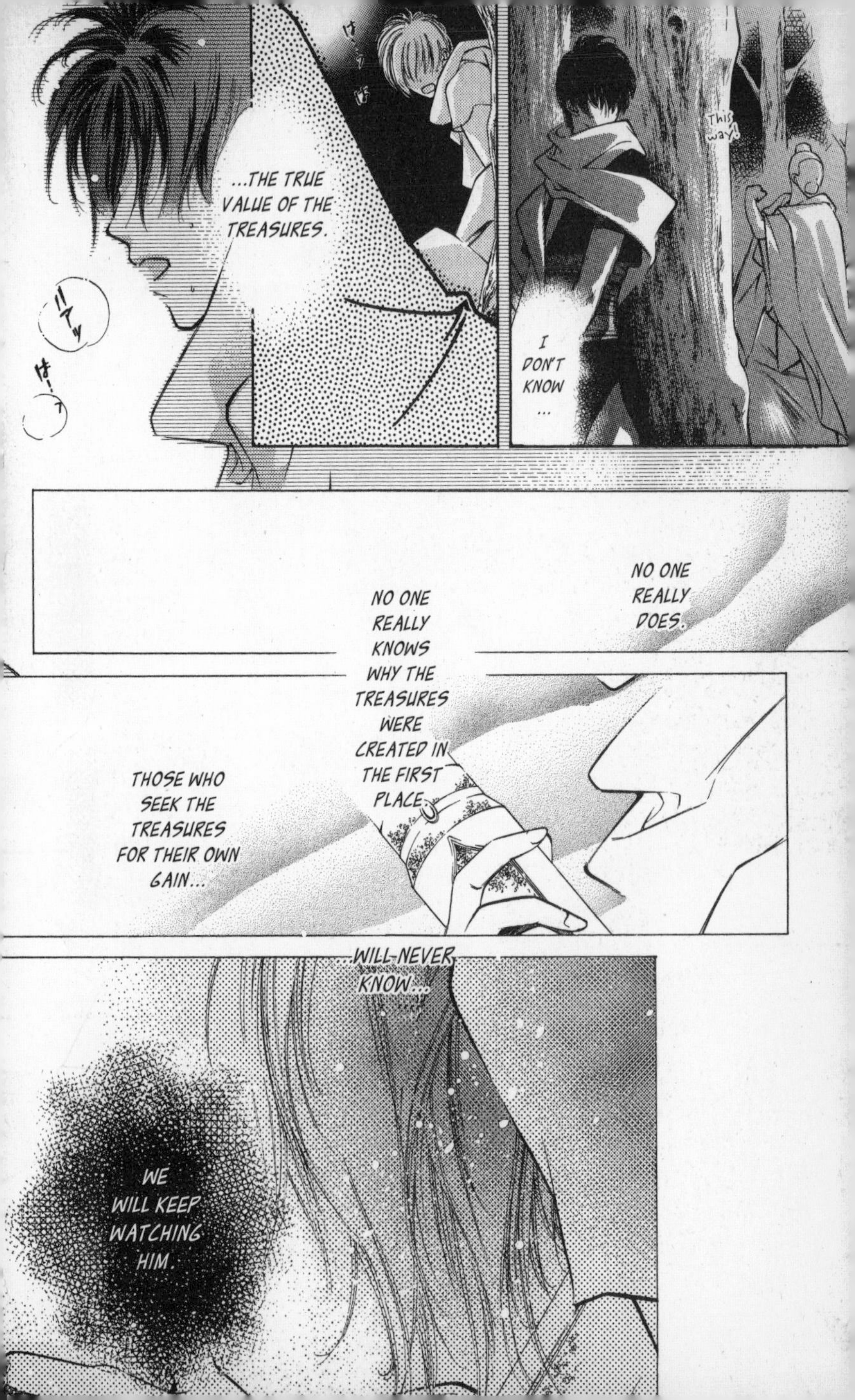

This way!
I DON'T KNOW...
...THE TRUE VALUE OF THE TREASURES.
NO ONE REALLY DOES.
NO ONE REALLY KNOWS WHY THE TREASURES WERE CREATED IN THE FIRST PLACE.
THOSE WHO SEEK THE TREASURES FOR THEIR OWN GAIN...
...WILL NEVER KNOW...
WE WILL KEEP WATCHING HIM.

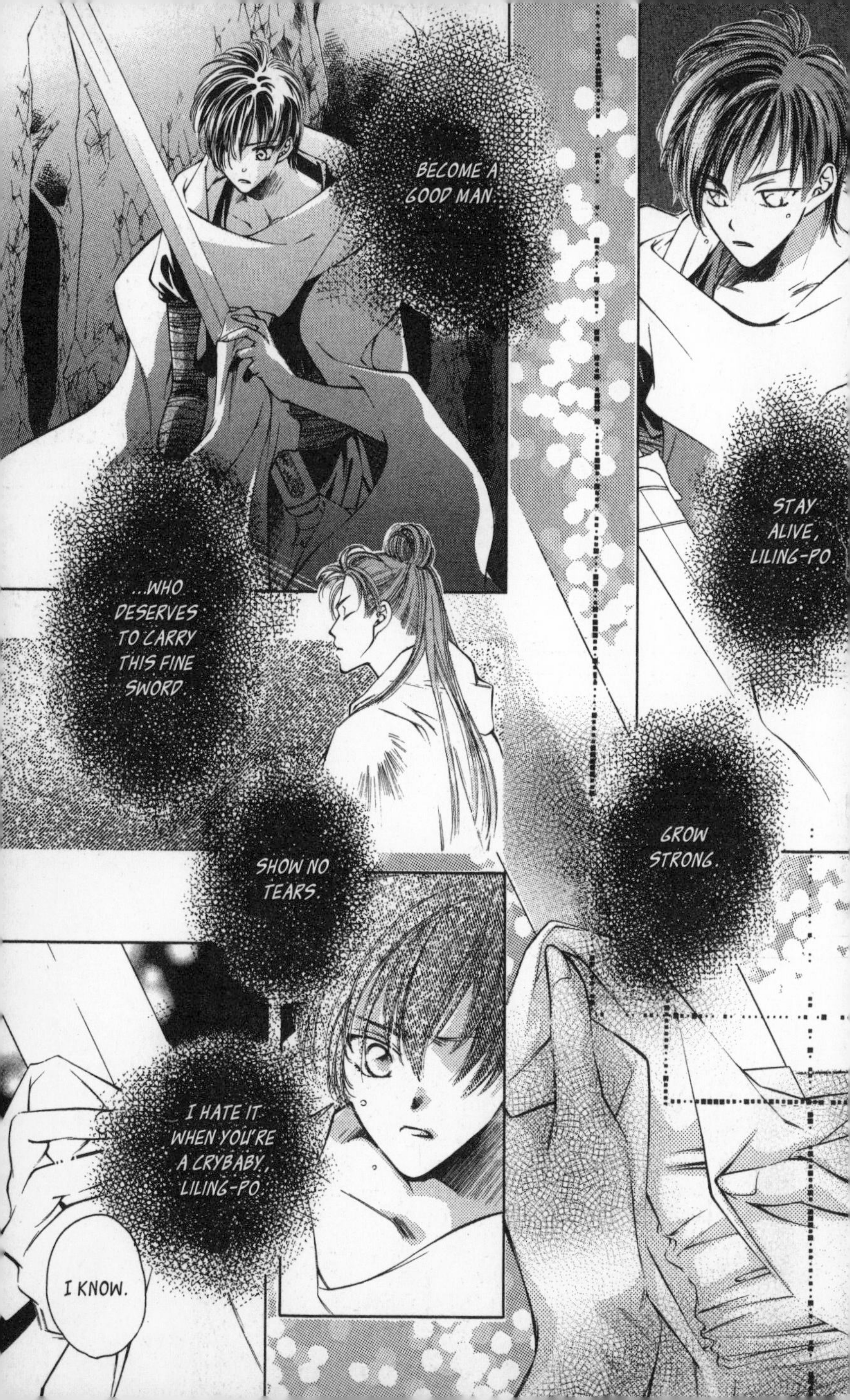
STAY ALIVE, LILING-PO.
BECOME A GOOD MAN...
...WHO DESERVES TO CARRY THIS FINE SWORD.
GROW STRONG.
SHOW NO TEARS.
I HATE IT WHEN YOU'RE A CRYBABY, LILING-PO.
I KNOW.

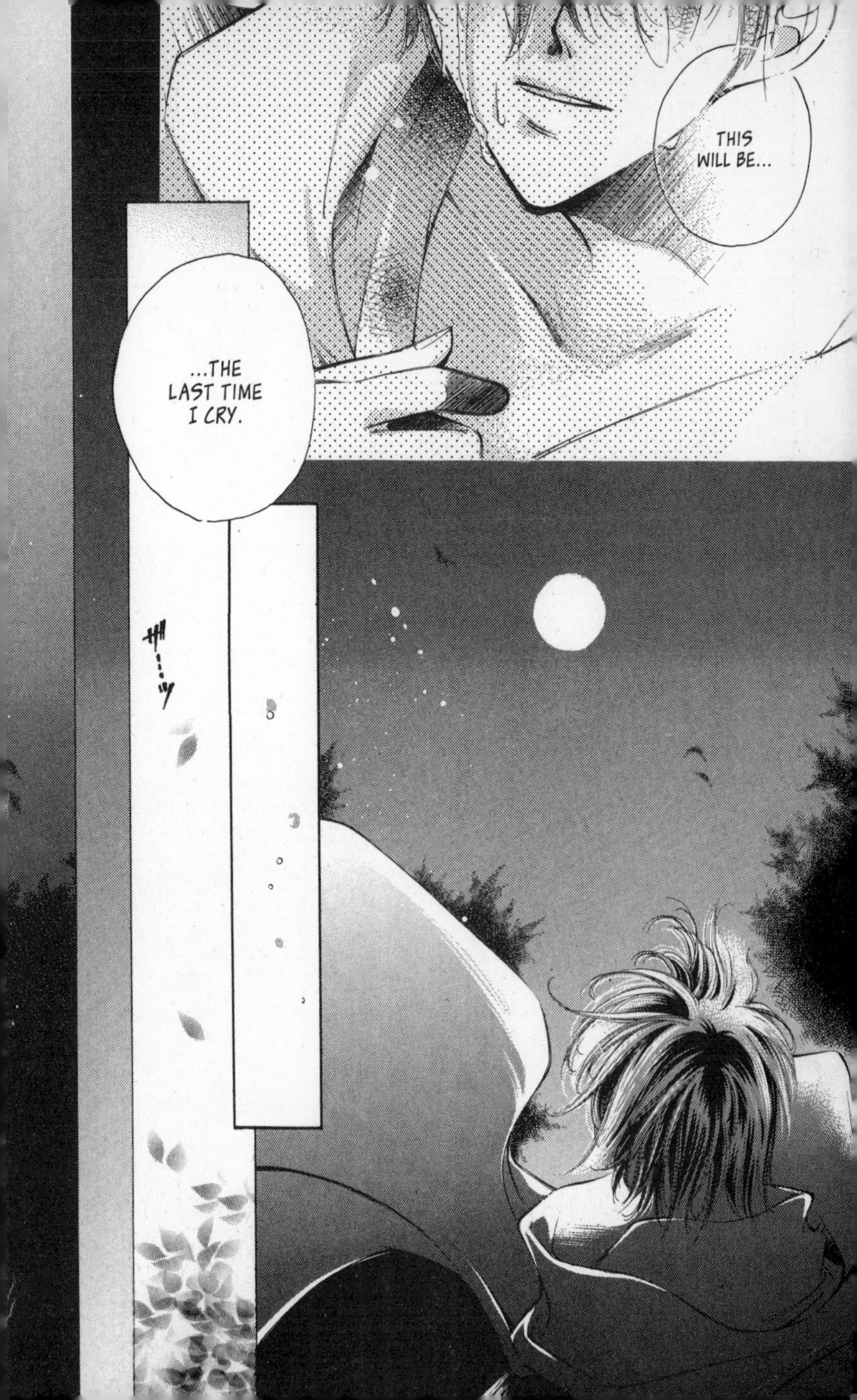
THIS WILL BE...
...THE LAST TIME I CRY.

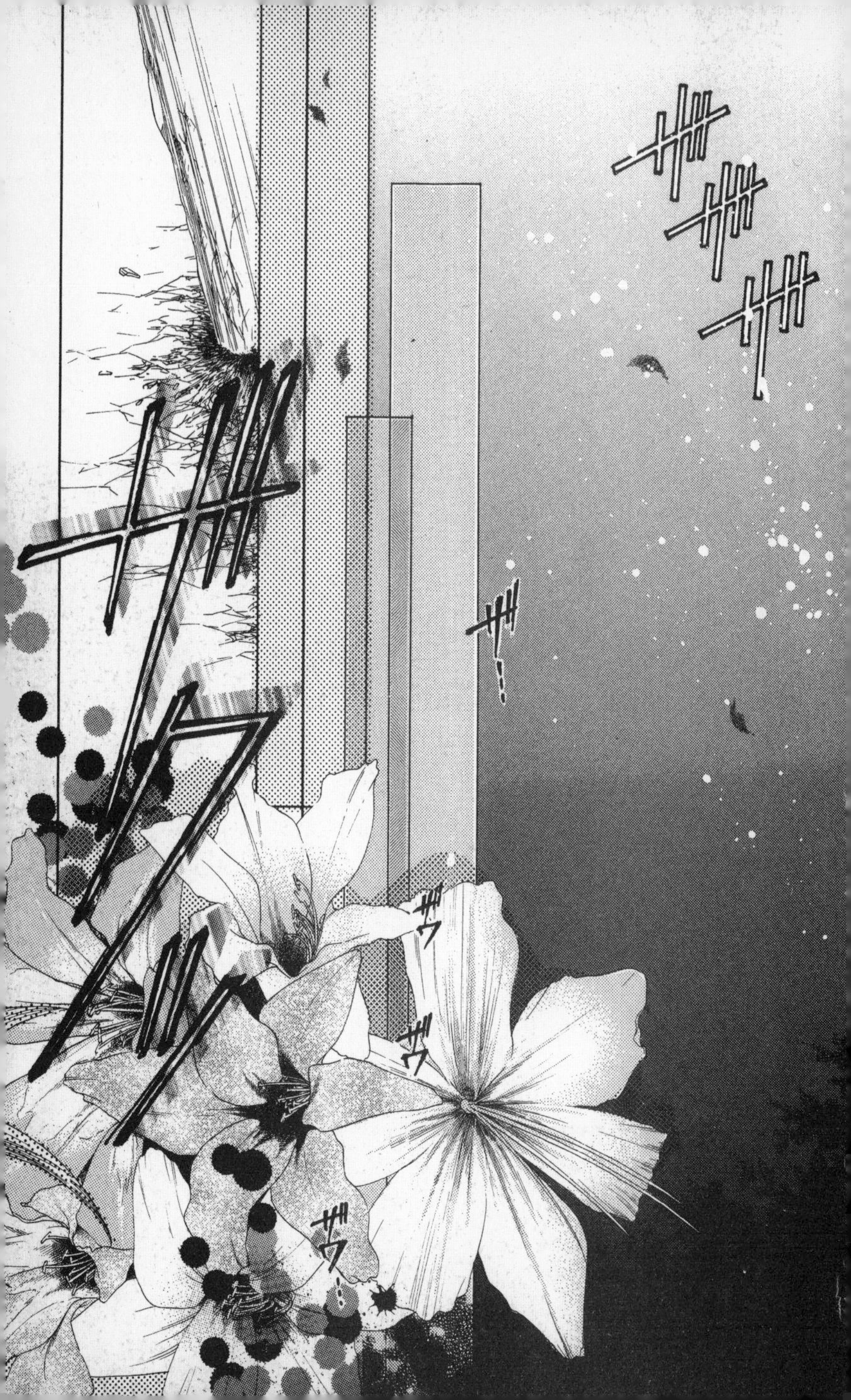

ザザザ
ザ…
ザワ
ザワ
ザワ…
ザクッ

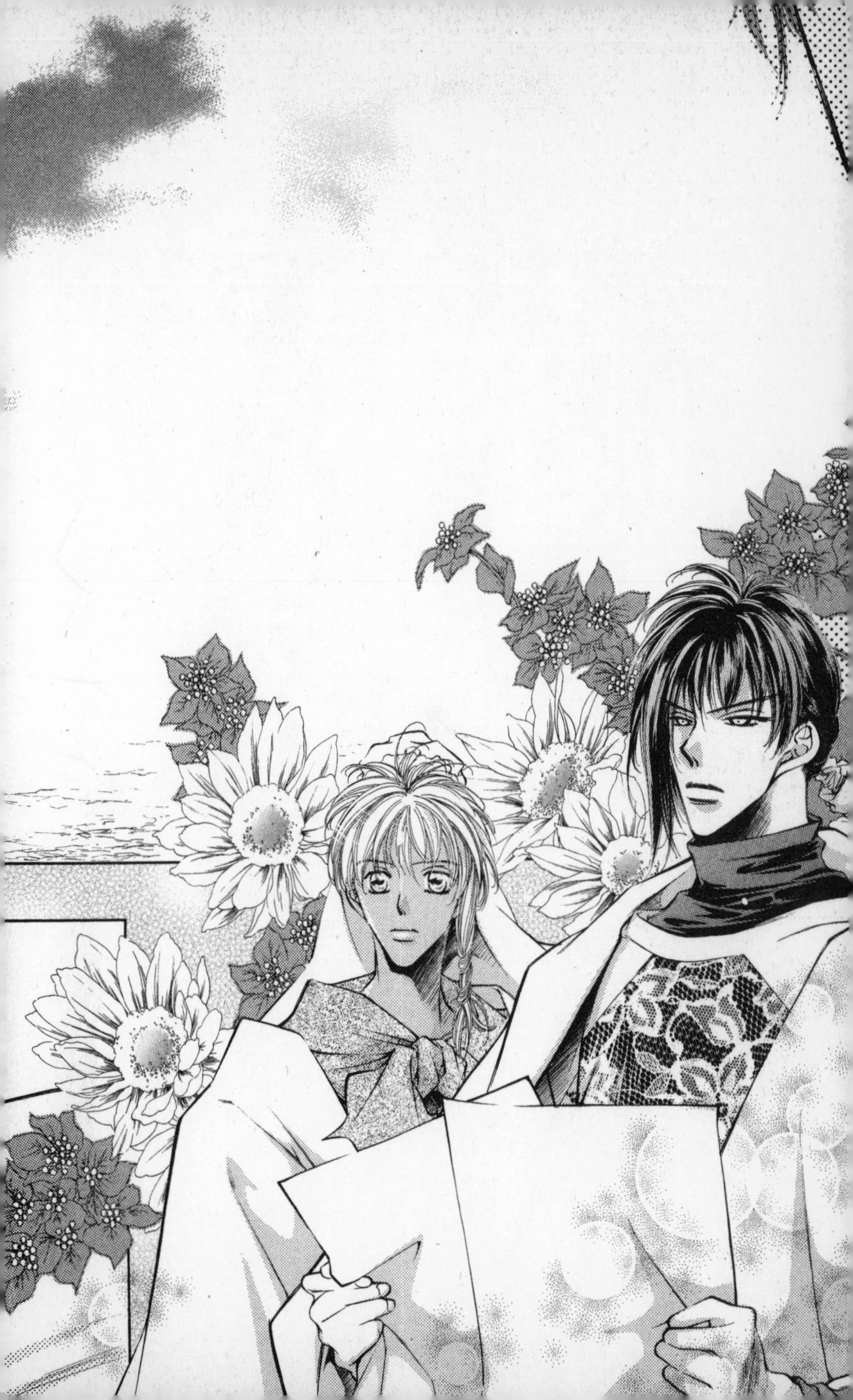

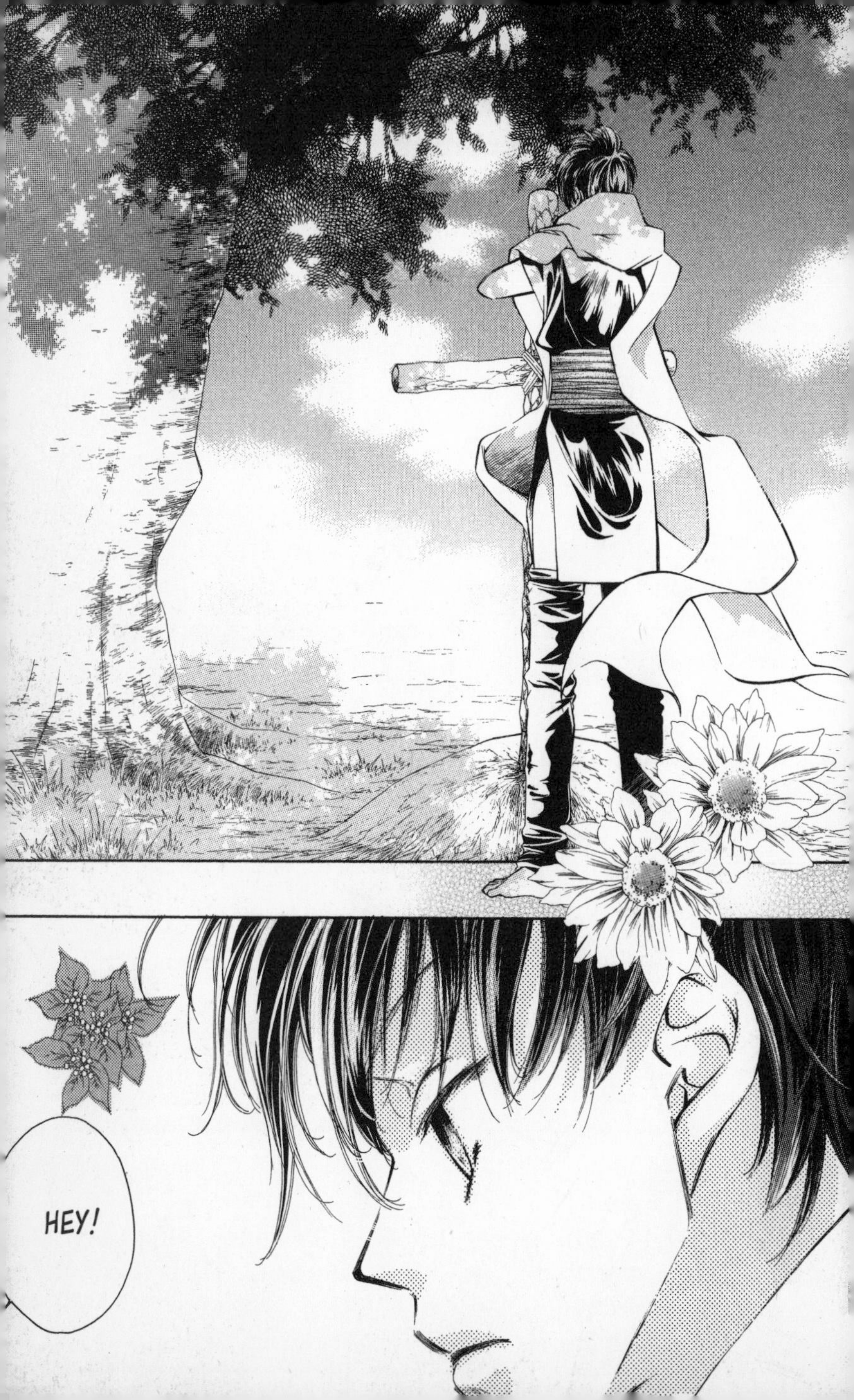
HEY!

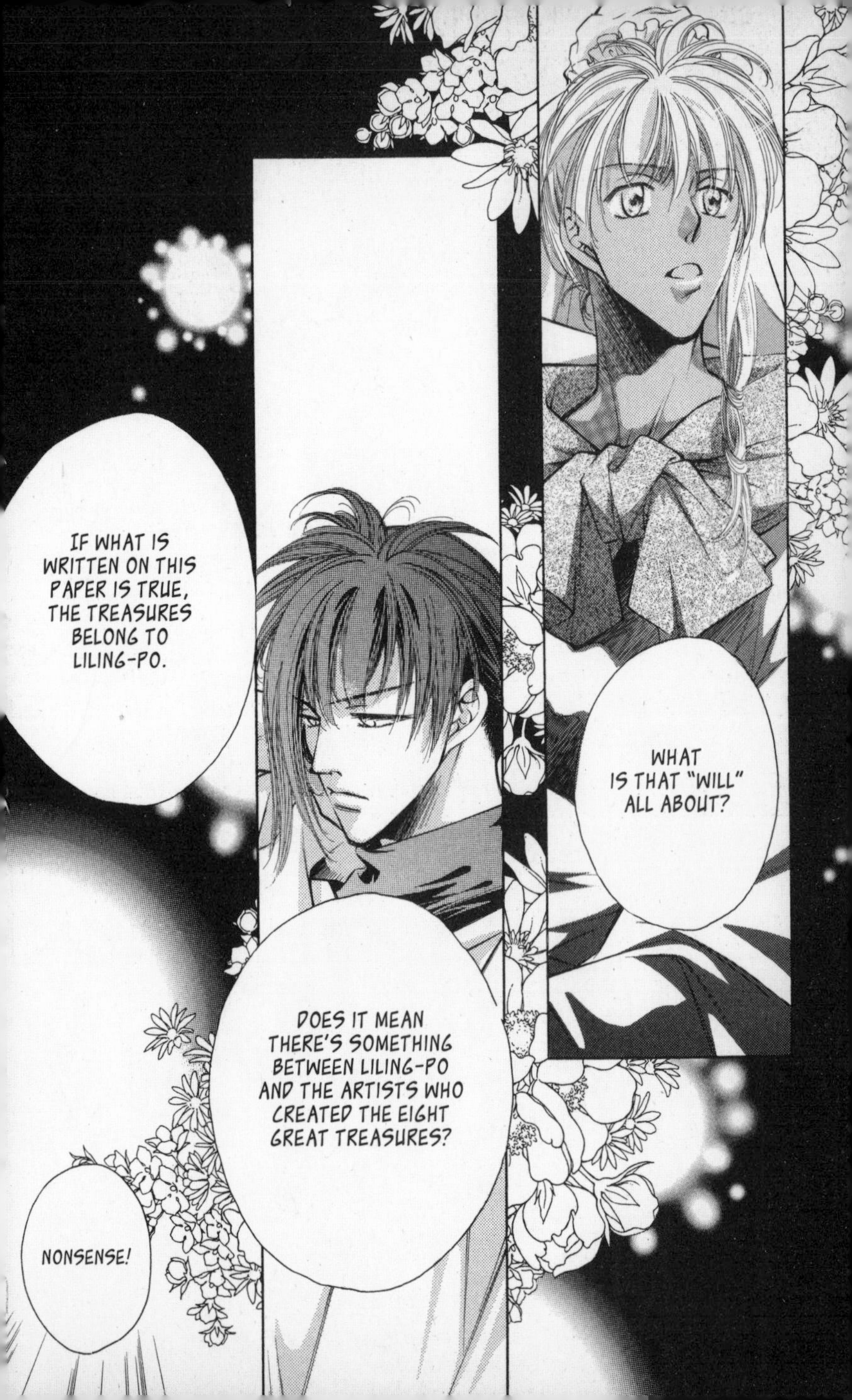
WHAT IS THAT "WILL" ALL ABOUT?
DOES IT MEAN THERE'S SOMETHING BETWEEN LILING-PO AND THE ARTISTS WHO CREATED THE EIGHT GREAT TREASURES?
IF WHAT IS WRITTEN ON THIS PAPER IS TRUE, THE TREASURES BELONG TO LILING-PO.
NONSENSE!

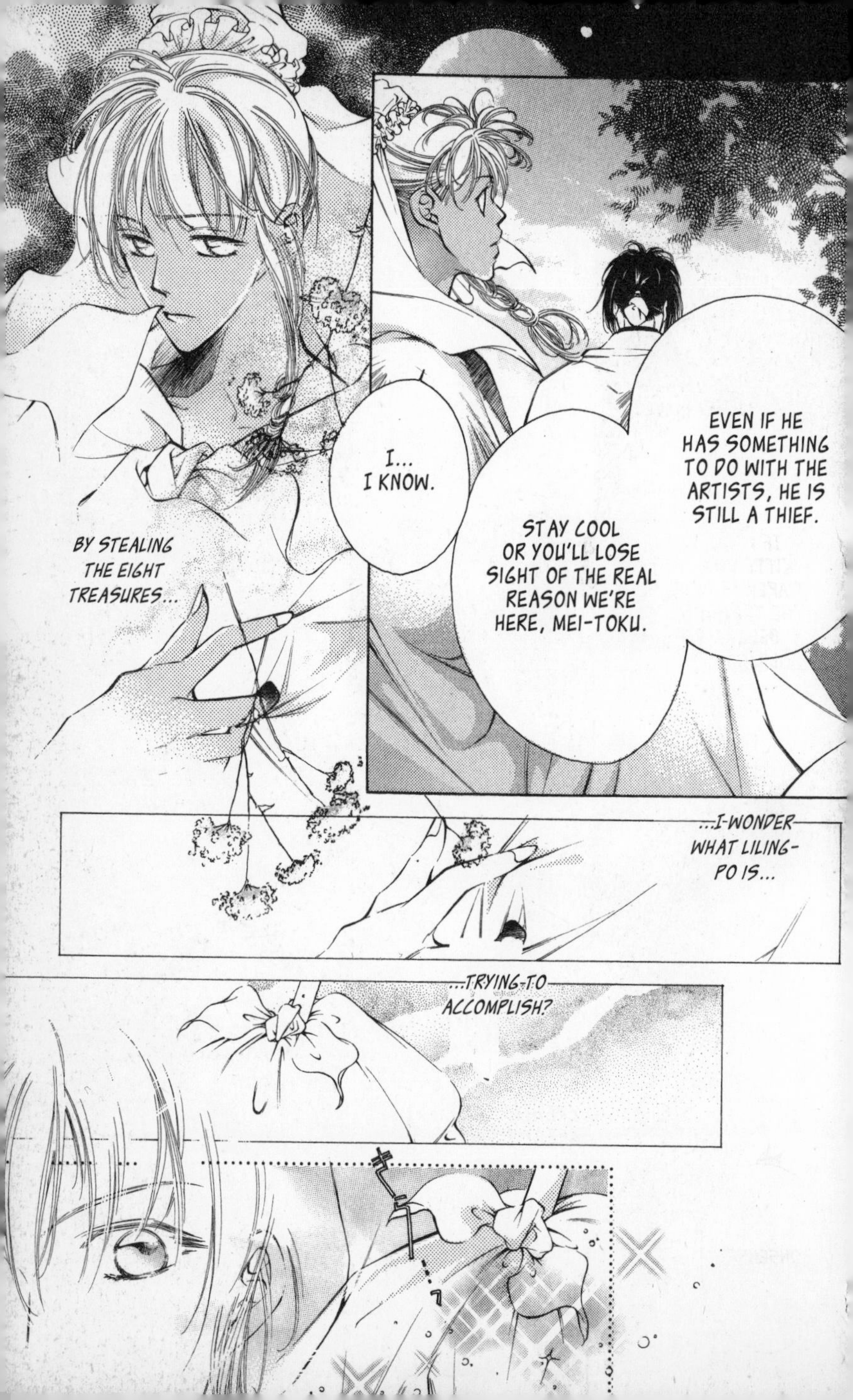
EVEN IF HE HAS SOMETHING TO DO WITH THE ARTISTS, HE IS STILL A THIEF.
STAY COOL OR YOU'LL LOSE SIGHT OF THE REAL REASON WE'RE HERE, MEI-TOKU.
I... I KNOW.
BY STEALING THE EIGHT TREASURES...
...I WONDER WHAT LILING-PO IS...
...TRYING TO ACCOMPLISH?

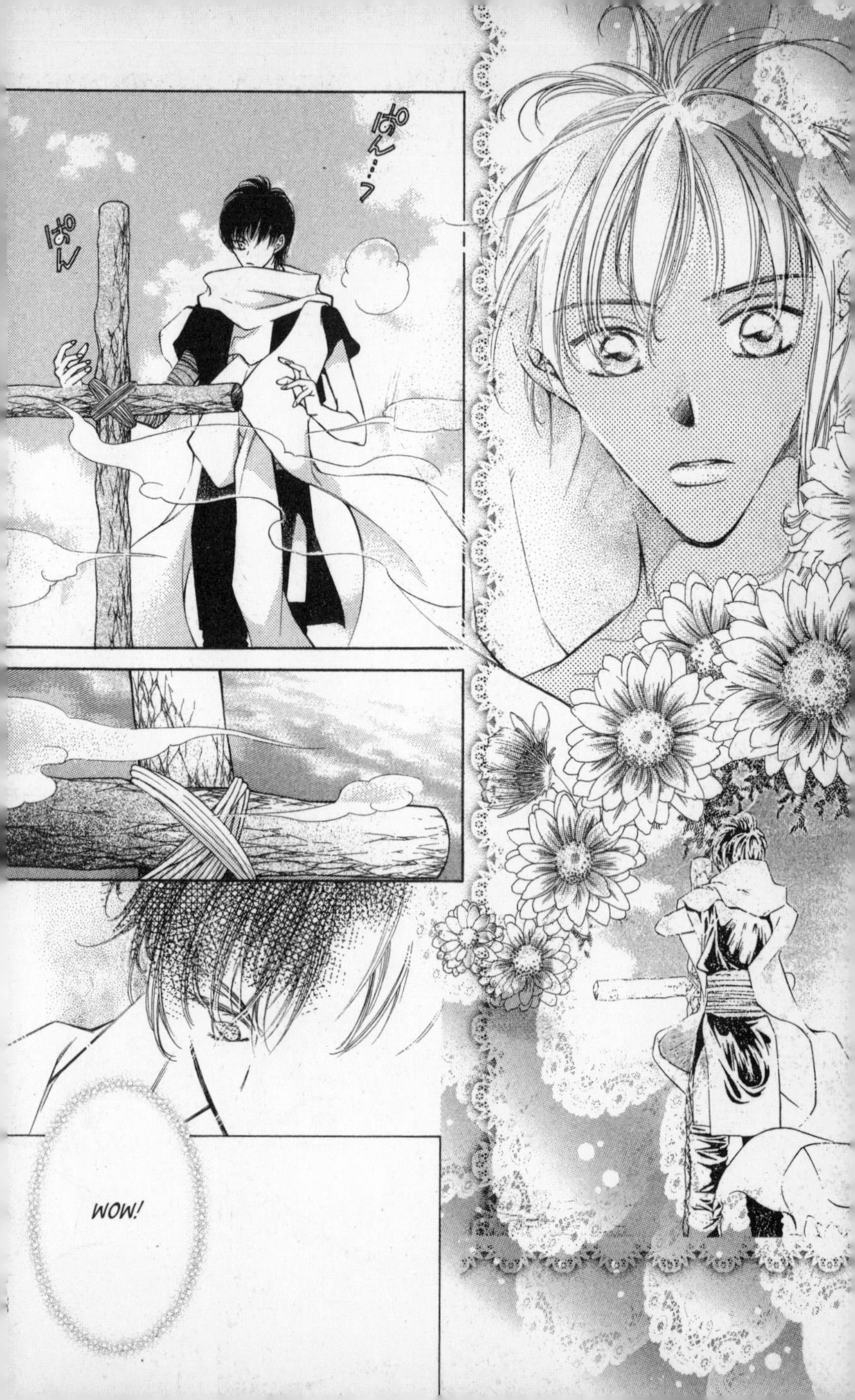

ぽぉん…っ
ぽぉん
WOW!

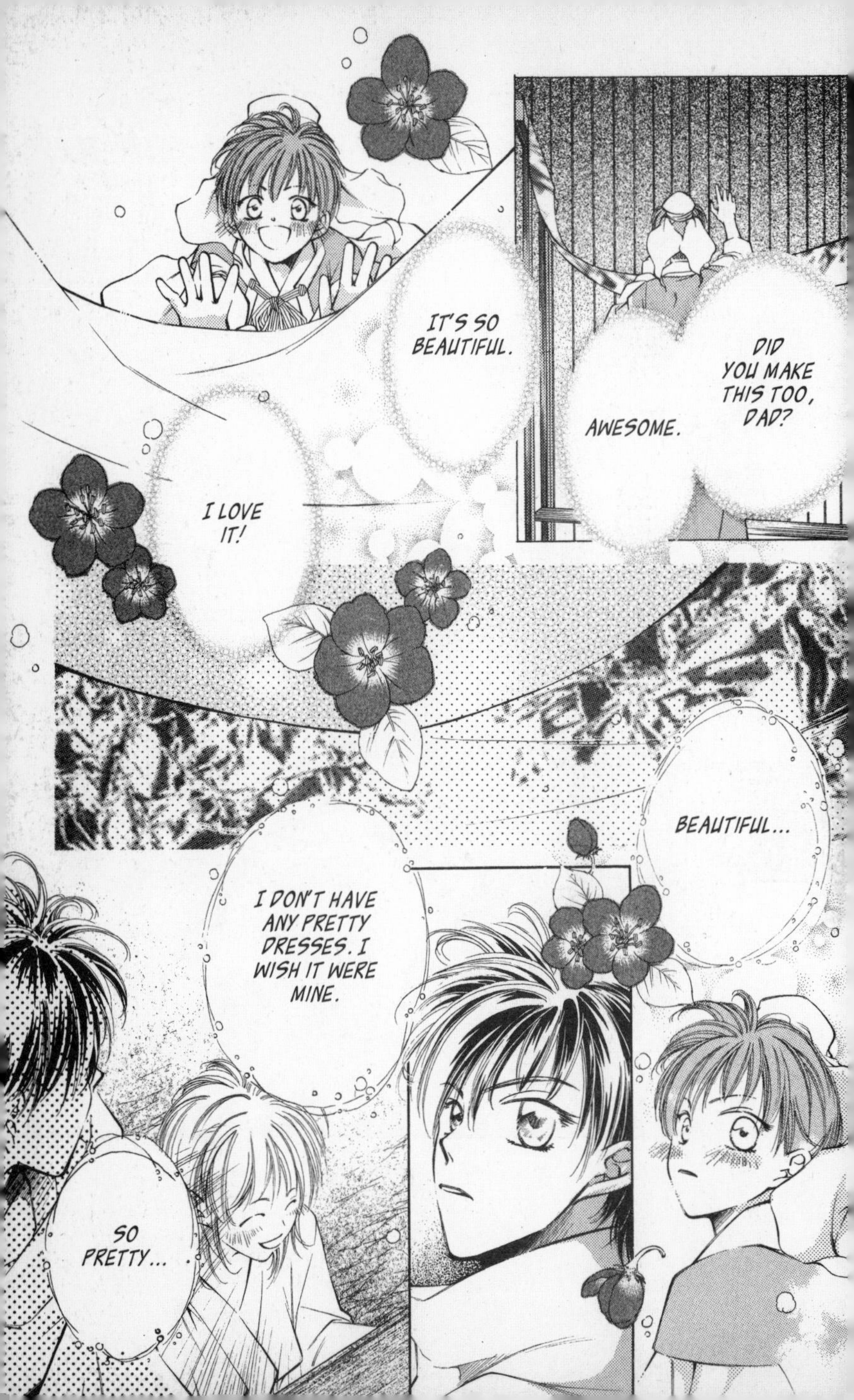
DID YOU MAKE THIS TOO, DAD?
AWESOME.
IT'S SO BEAUTIFUL.
I LOVE IT!
BEAUTIFUL...
I DON'T HAVE ANY PRETTY DRESSES. I WISH IT WERE MINE.
SO PRETTY...

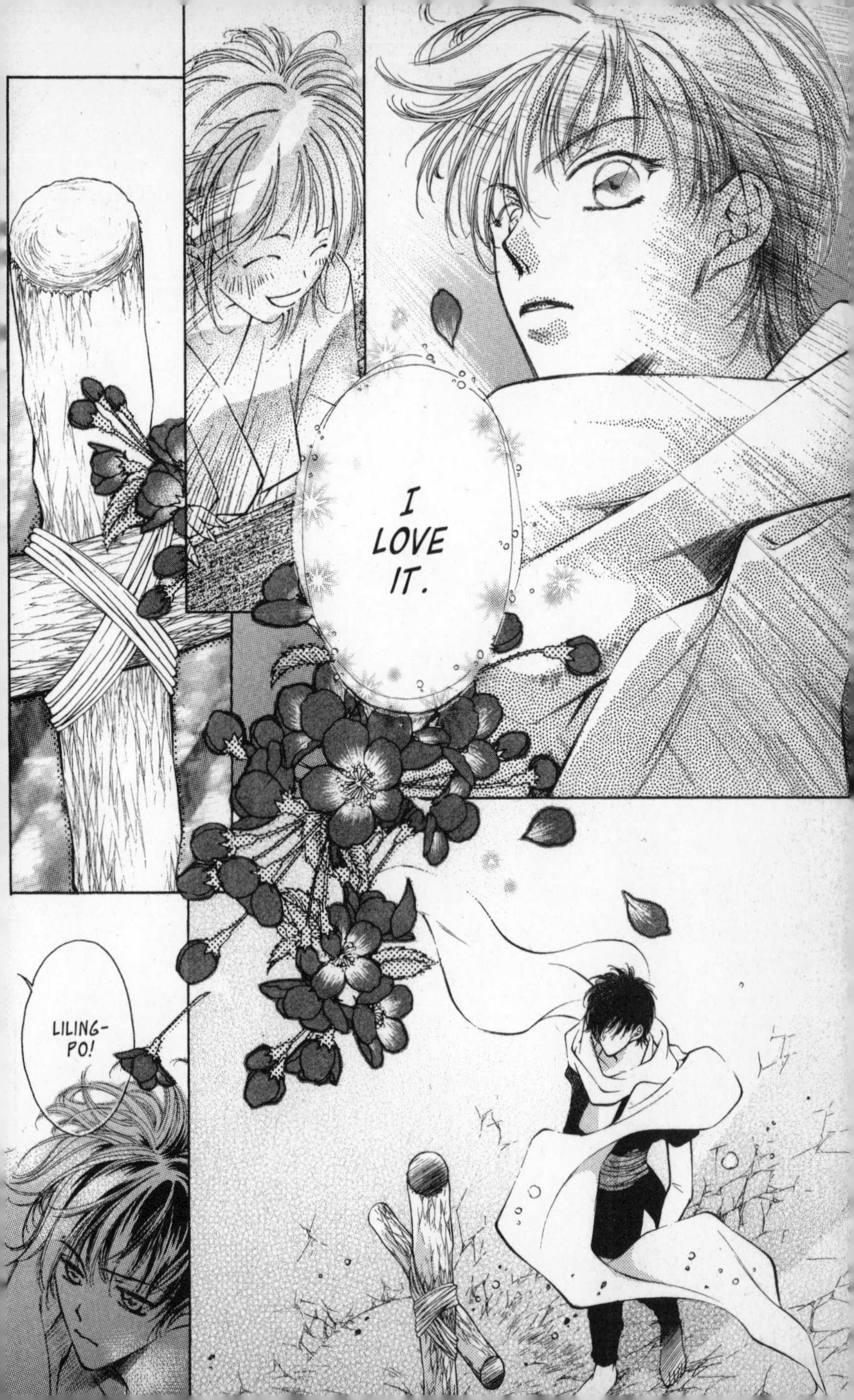
I LOVE IT.
LILING-PO!

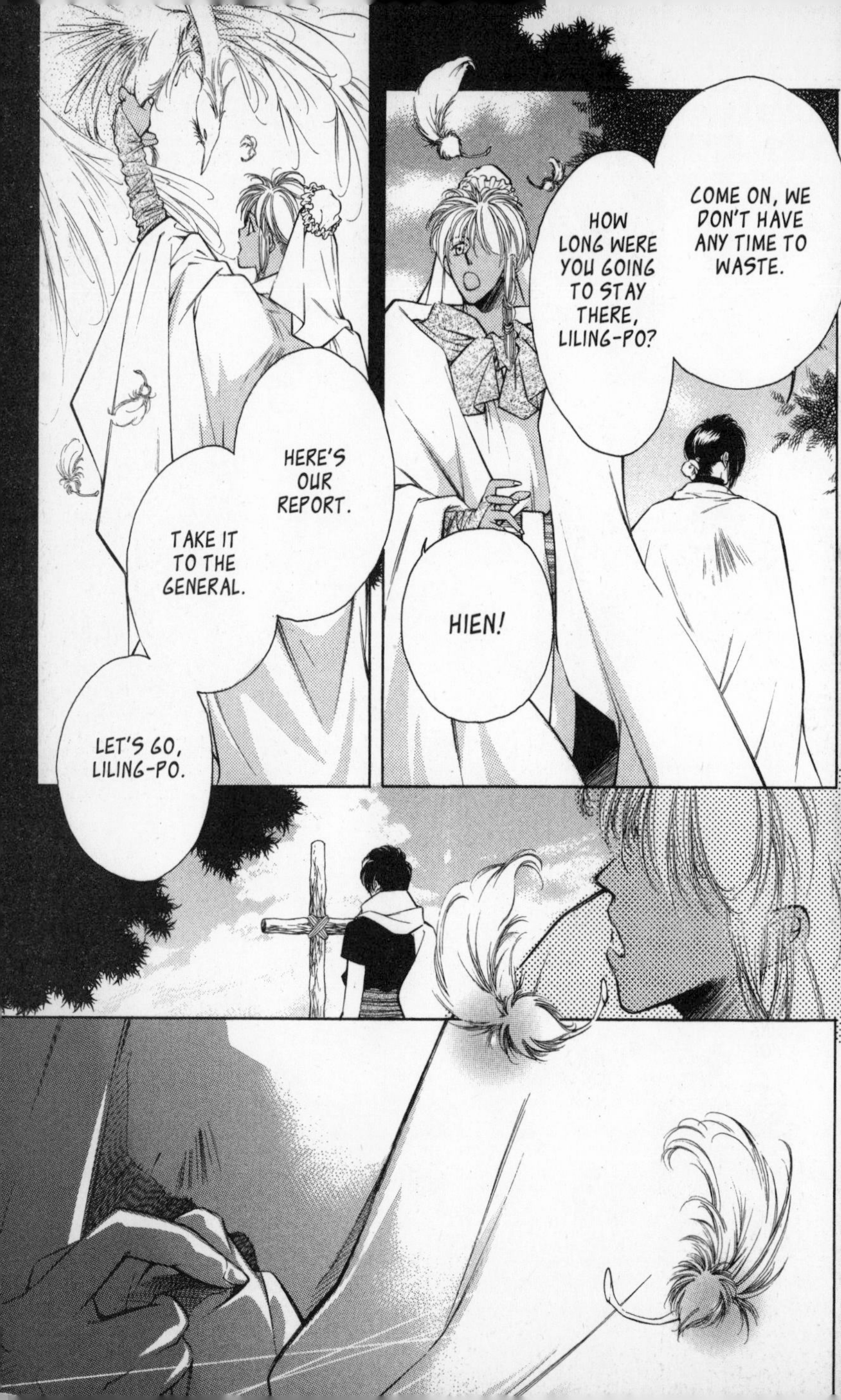
COME ON, WE DON'T HAVE ANY TIME TO WASTE.
HOW LONG WERE YOU GOING TO STAY THERE, LILING-PO?
HIEN!
HERE'S OUR REPORT.
TAKE IT TO THE GENERAL.
LET'S GO, LILING-PO.

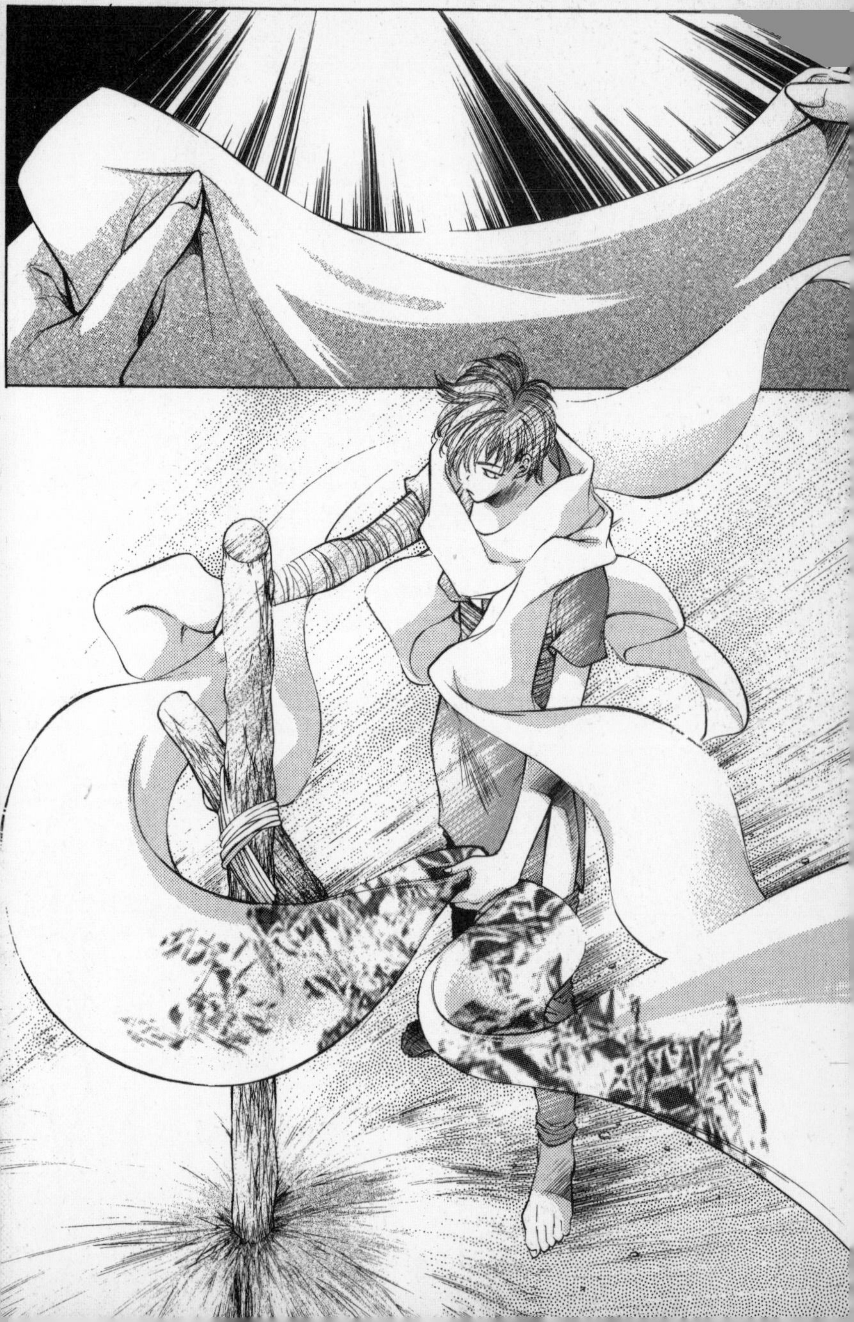

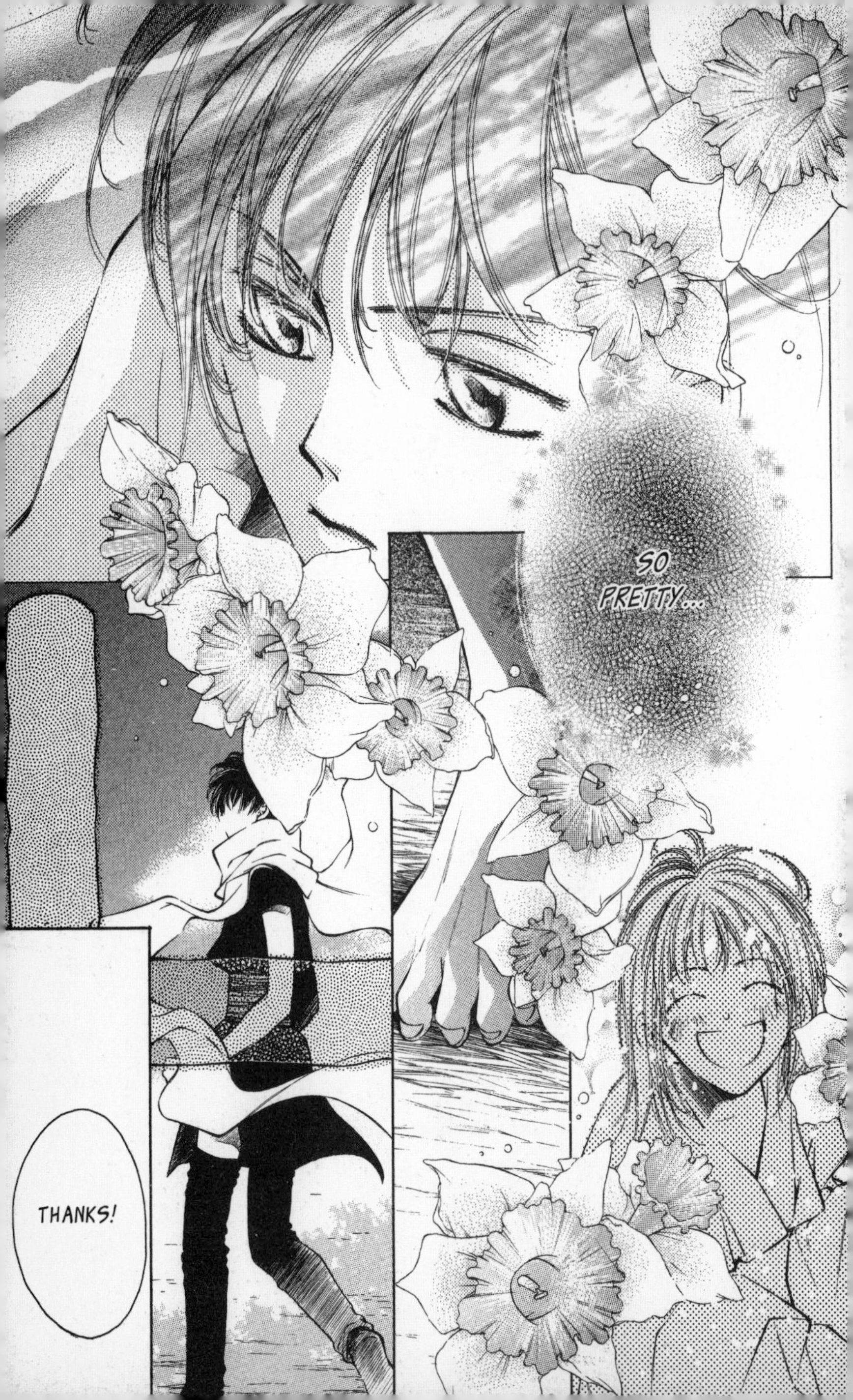
SO PRETTY...
THANKS!

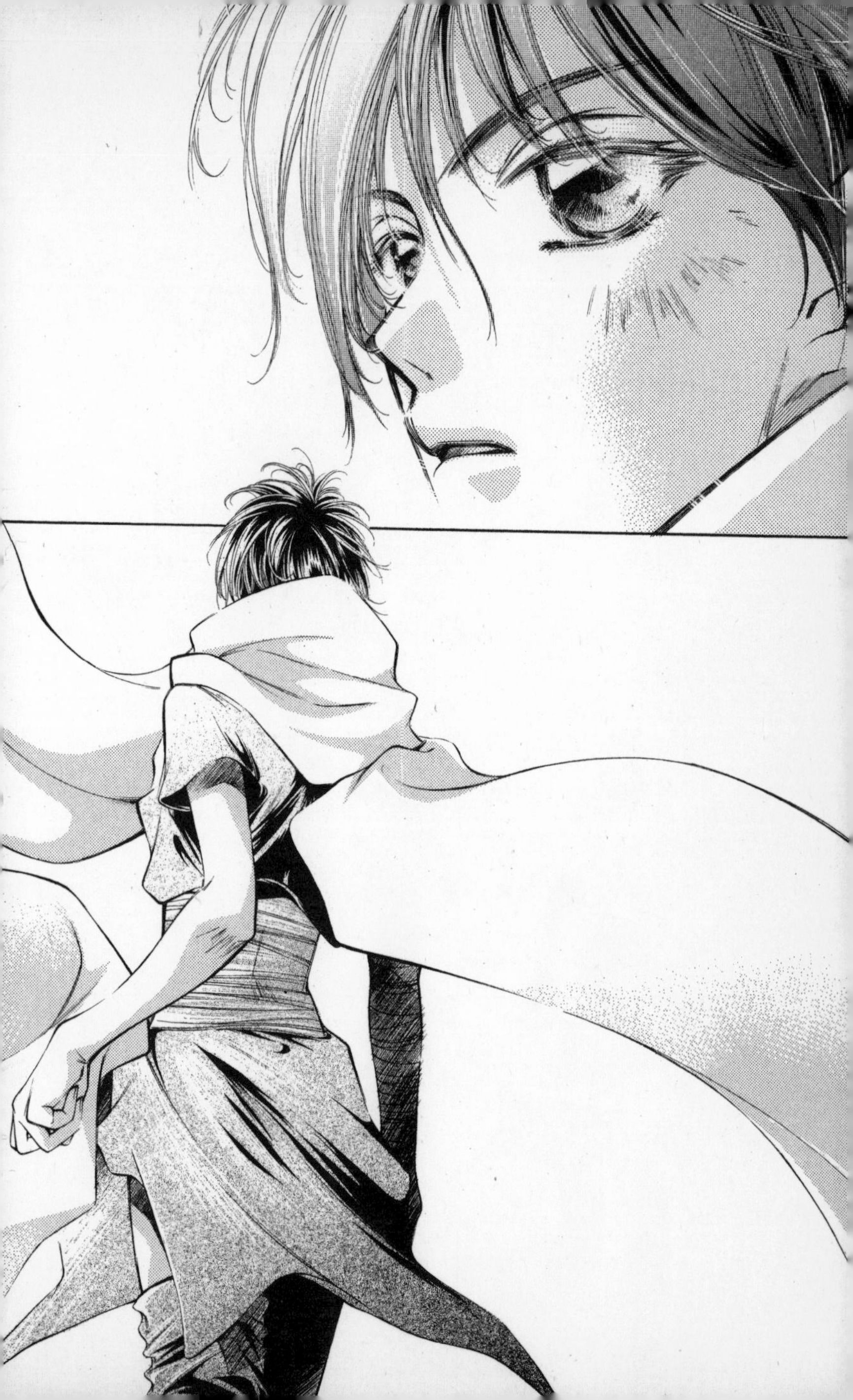

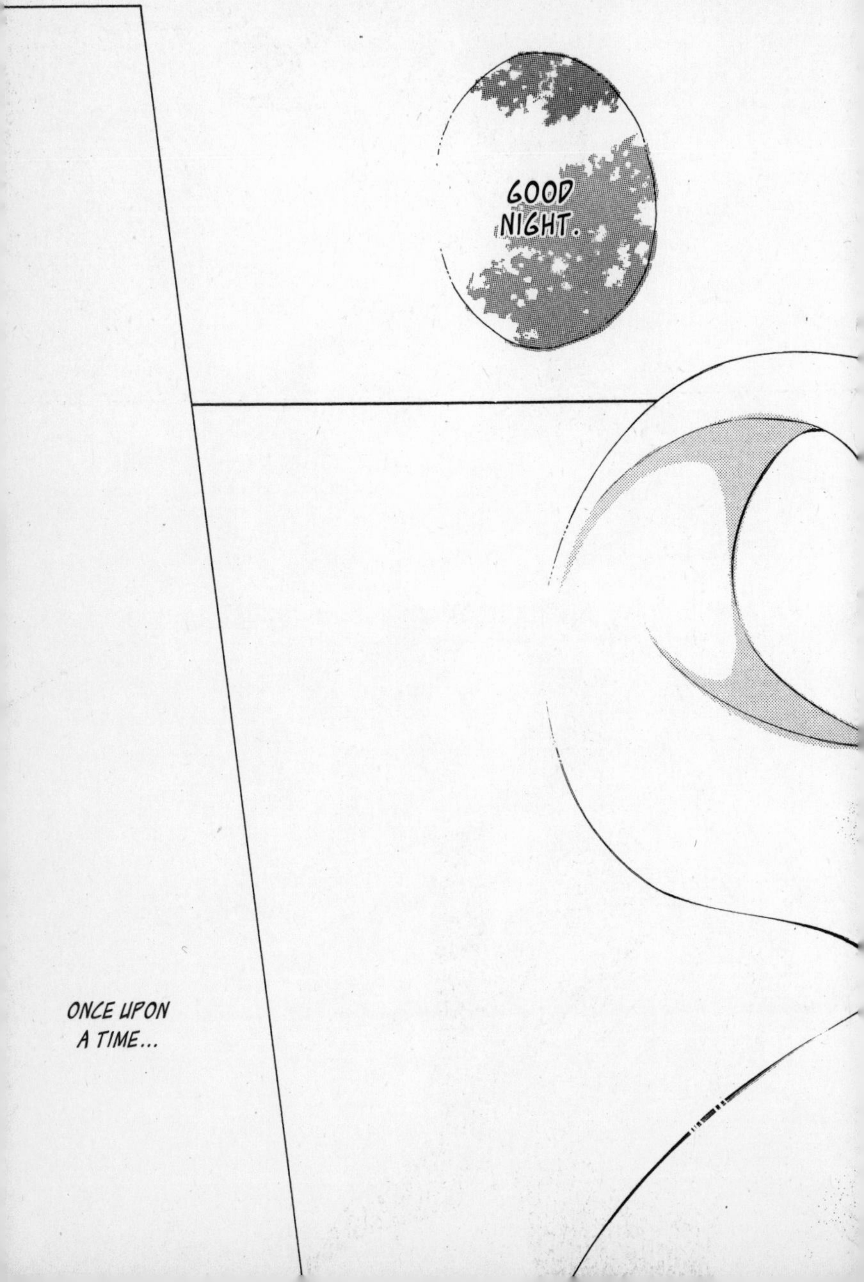
GOOD NIGHT.
ONCE UPON A TIME...

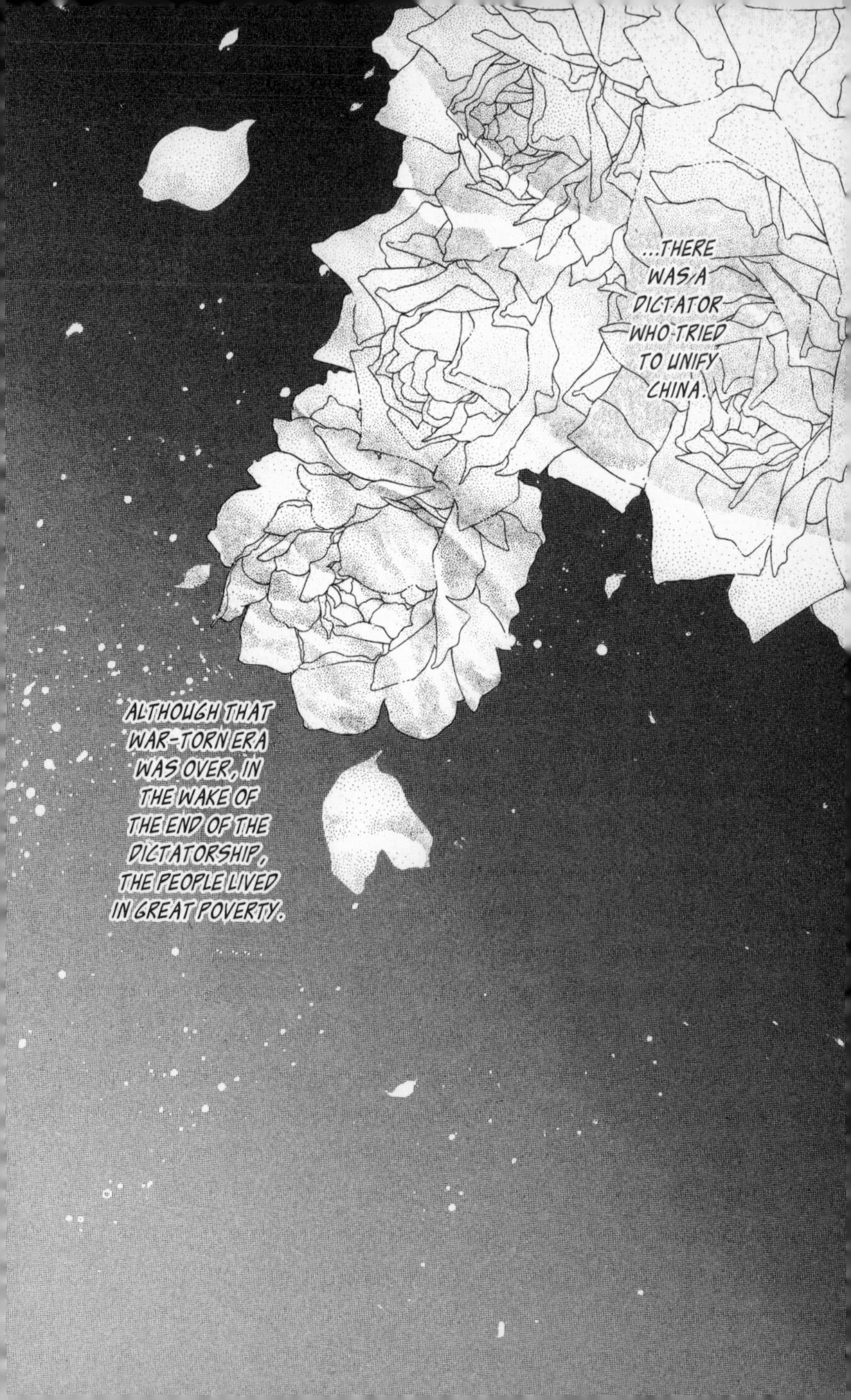
...THERE WAS A DICTATOR WHO TRIED TO UNIFY CHINA.
ALTHOUGH THAT WAR-TORN ERA WAS OVER, IN THE WAKE OF THE END OF THE DICTATORSHIP, THE PEOPLE LIVED IN GREAT POVERTY.

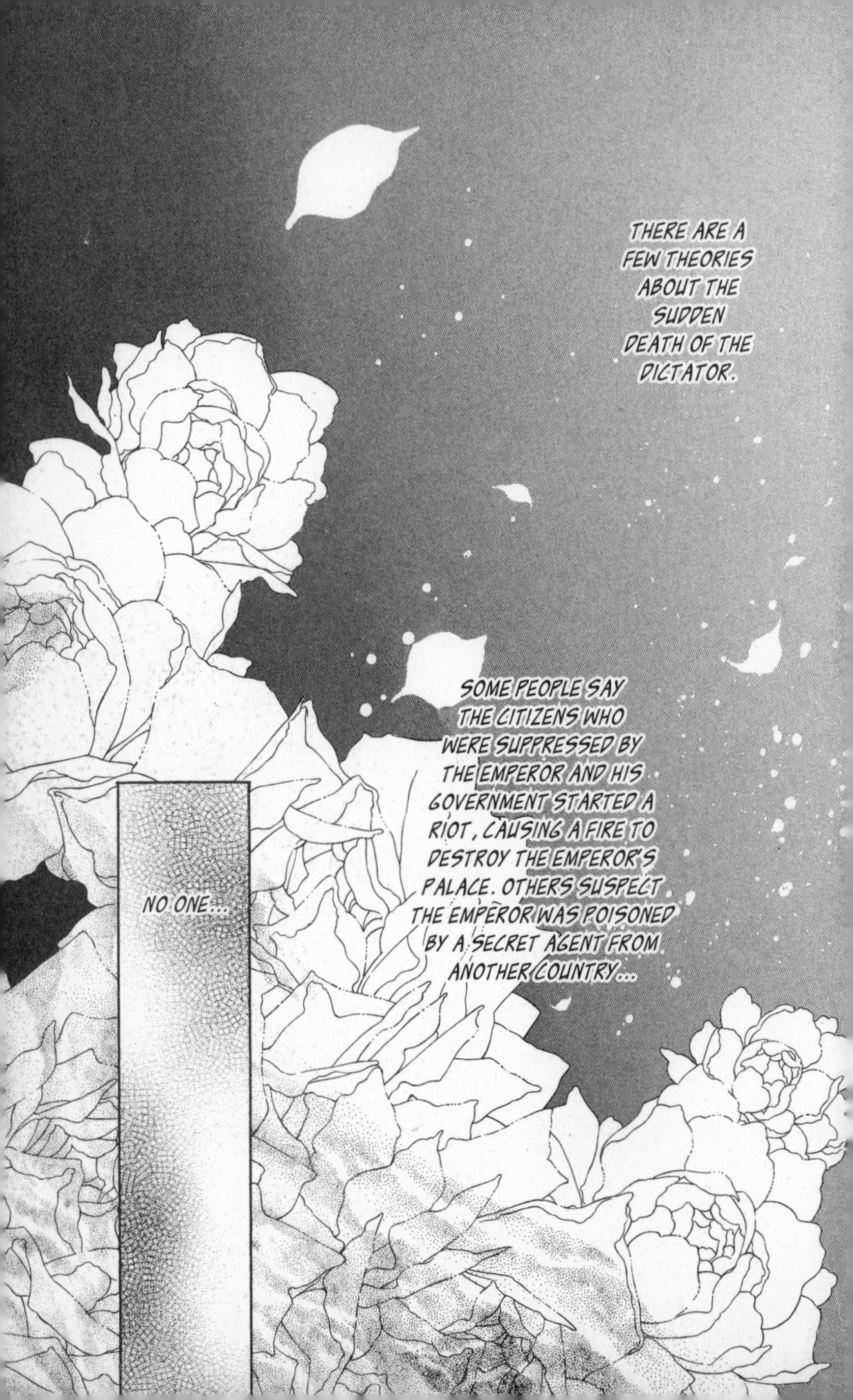
THERE ARE A FEW THEORIES ABOUT THE SUDDEN DEATH OF THE DICTATOR.
SOME PEOPLE SAY THE CITIZENS WHO WERE SUPPRESSED BY THE EMPEROR AND HIS GOVERNMENT STARTED A RIOT, CAUSING A FIRE TO DESTROY THE EMPEROR'S PALACE. OTHERS SUSPECT THE EMPEROR WAS POISONED BY A SECRET AGENT FROM ANOTHER COUNTRY...
NO ONE...

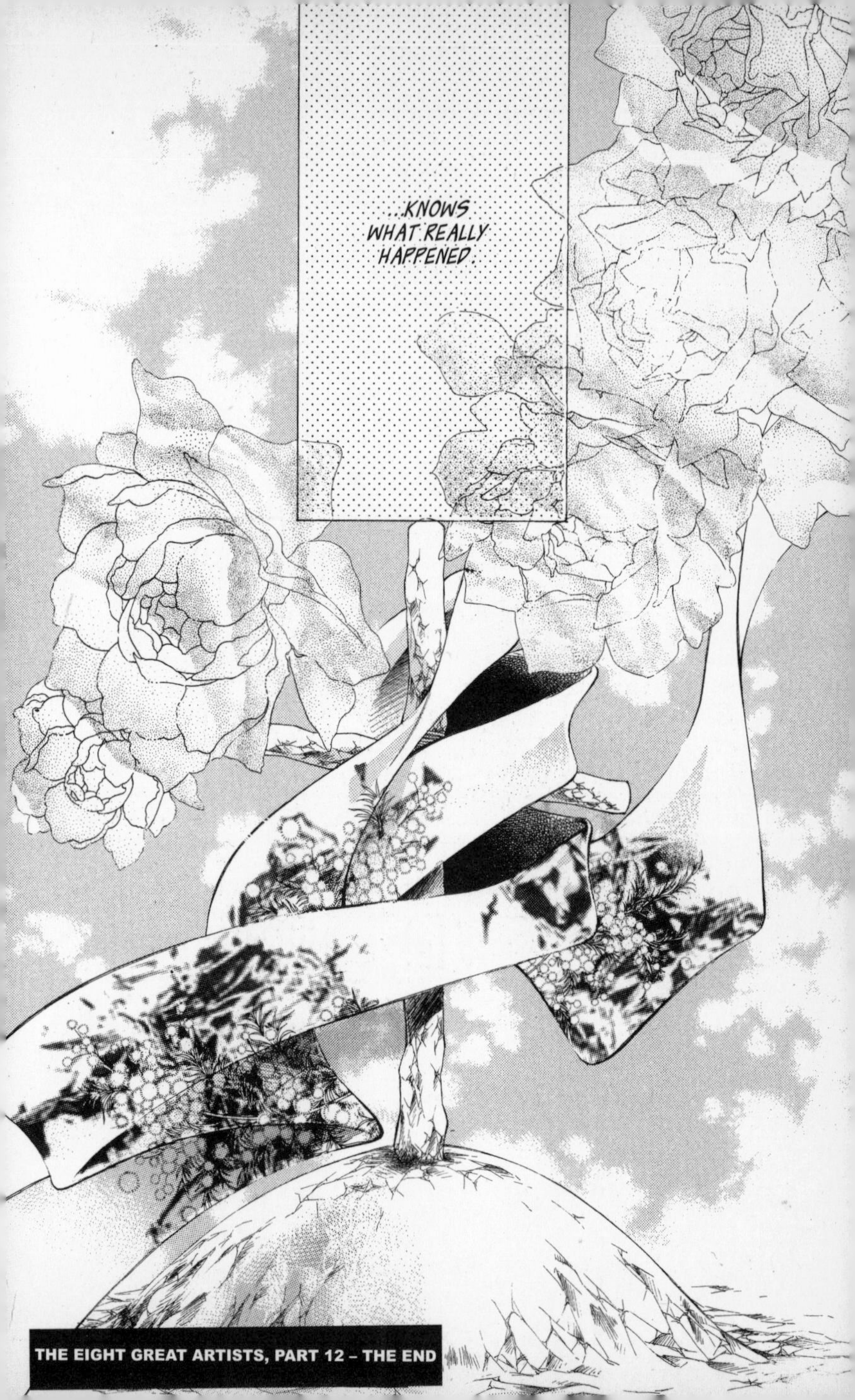
...KNOWS WHAT REALLY HAPPENED.
THE EIGHT GREAT ARTISTS, PART 12 – THE END

"Nihao"

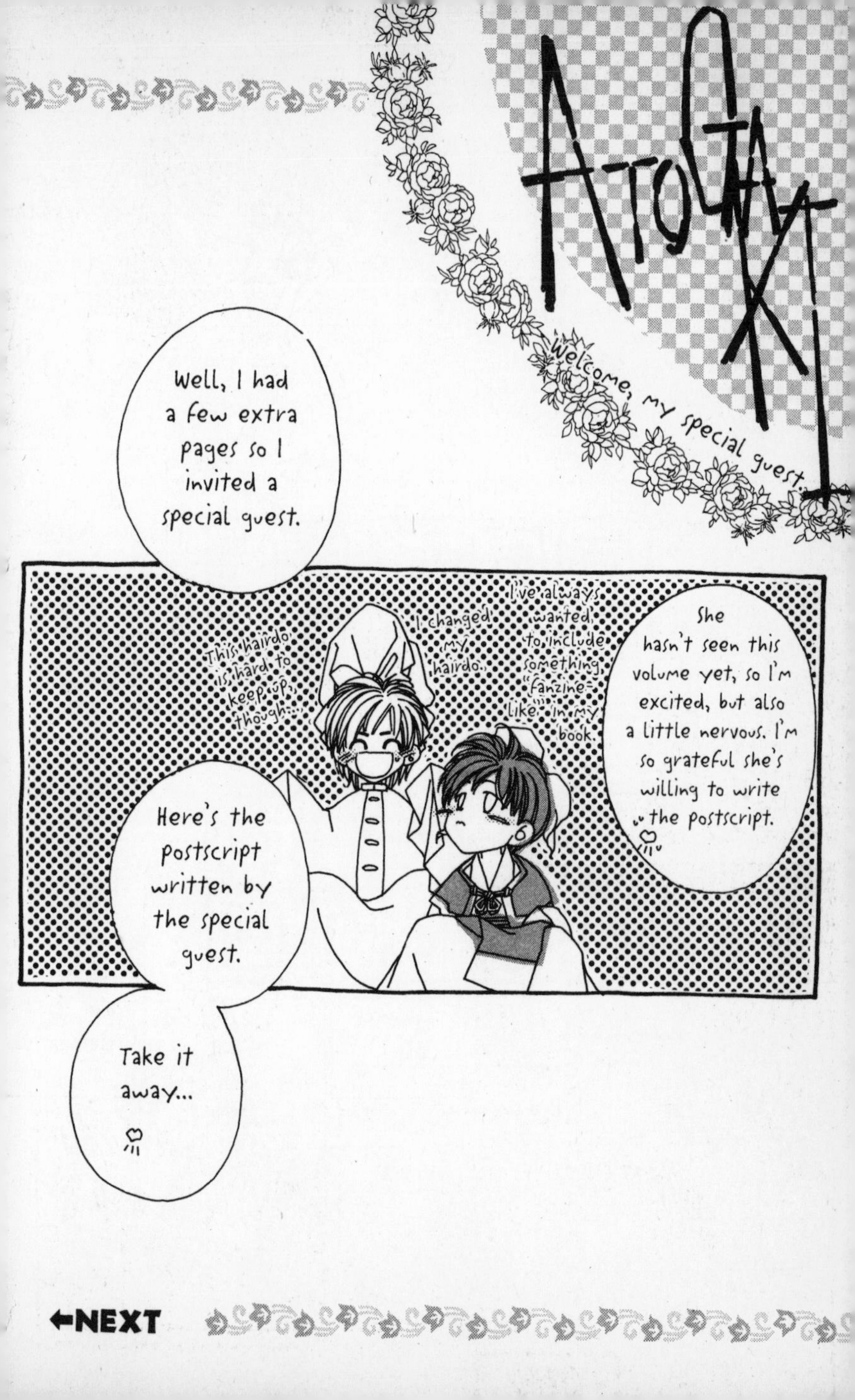
ATOGAKI
Welcome, my special guest.
Well, I had a few extra pages so I invited a special guest.
She hasn't seen this volume yet, so I'm excited, but also a little nervous. I'm so grateful she's willing to write the postscript.
I've always wanted to include something "fanzine-like" in my book.
I changed my hairdo.
This hairdo is hard to keep up, though...
Here's the postscript written by the special guest.
Take it away...
←NEXT

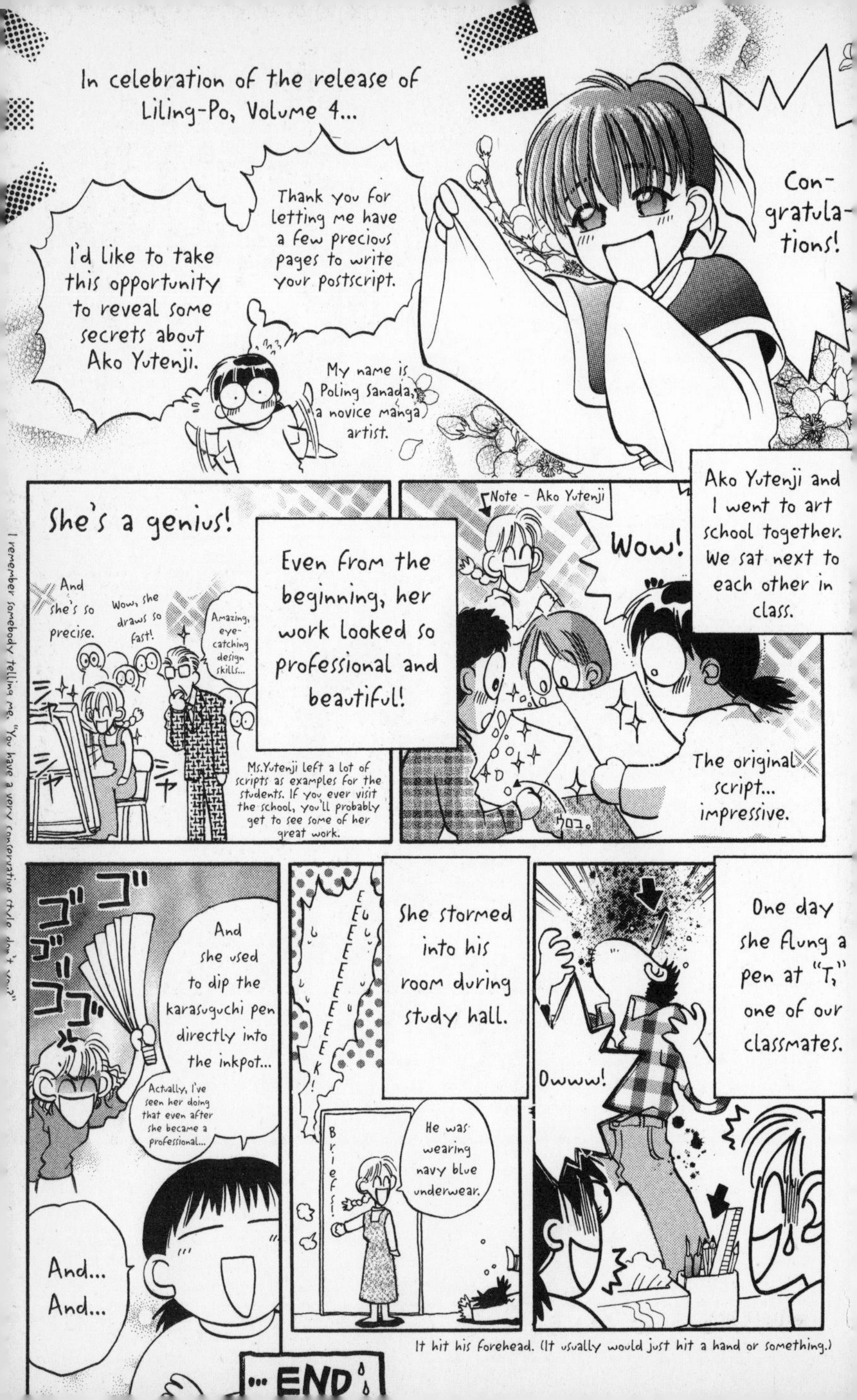
In celebration of the release of Liling-Po, Volume 4...
Con-gratula-tions!
Thank you for letting me have a few precious pages to write your postscript.
I'd like to take this opportunity to reveal some secrets about Ako Yutenji.
My name is Poling Sanada, a novice manga artist.
Ako Yutenji and I went to art school together. We sat next to each other in class.
Note - Ako Yutenji
Wow!
The original script... impressive.
Even from the beginning, her work looked so professional and beautiful!
She's a genius!
And she's so precise.
Wow, she draws so fast!
Amazing, eye-catching design skills...
Ms.Yutenji left a lot of scripts as examples for the students. If you ever visit the school, you'll probably get to see some of her great work.
One day she flung a pen at "T," one of our classmates.
Owww!
It hit his forehead. (It usually would just hit a hand or something.)
She stormed into his room during study hall.
EEEEEEEEEK!
Briefs!
He was wearing navy blue underwear.
And she used to dip the karasuguchi pen directly into the inkpot...
Actually, I've seen her doing that even after she became a professional...
And... And...
...END
I remember somebody telling me, "You have a very conservative style, don't you?"

Here comes the pest!

Mao Kirisaka

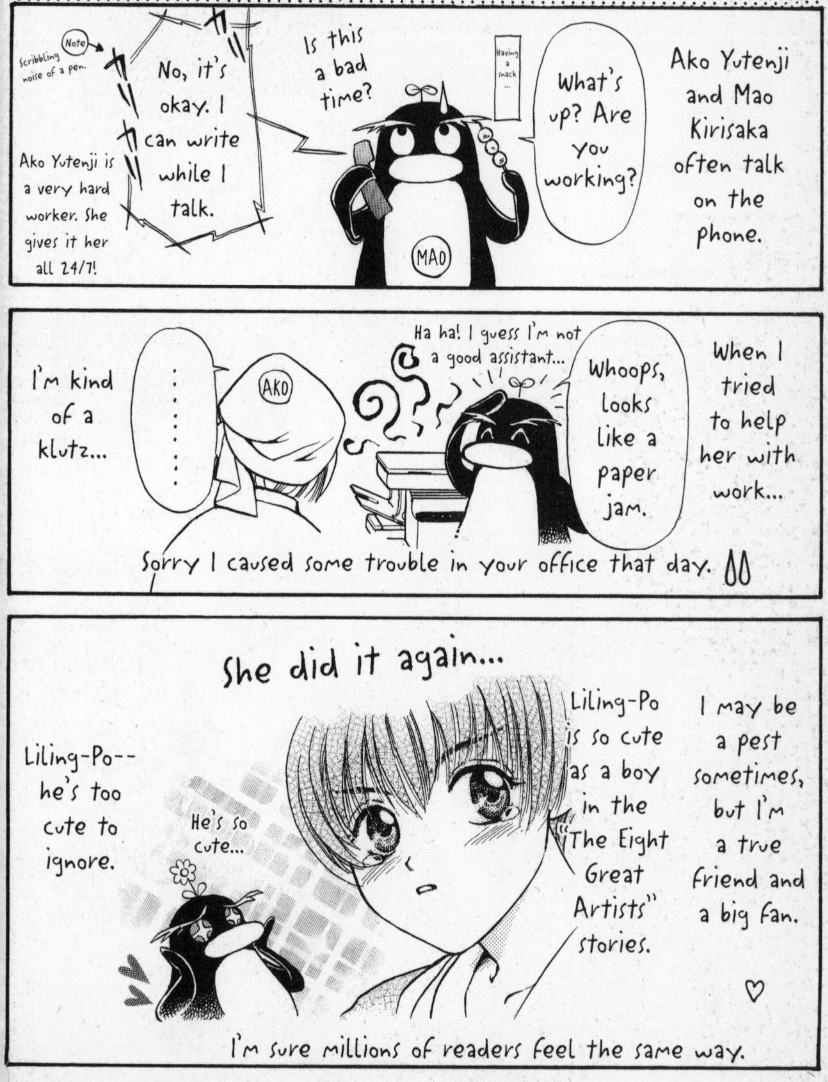
Ako Yutenji and Mao Kirisaka often talk on the phone.
Having a snack...
What's up? Are you working?
MAO
Is this a bad time?
No, it's okay. I can write while I talk.
Note
Scribbling noise of a pen.
Ako Yutenji is a very hard worker. She gives it her all 24/7!
When I tried to help her with work...
Whoops, looks like a paper jam.
Ha ha! I guess I'm not a good assistant...
AKO
......
I'm kind of a klutz...
Sorry I caused some trouble in your office that day.
She did it again...
I may be a pest sometimes, but I'm a true friend and a big fan.
Liling-Po is so cute as a boy in "The Eight Great Artists" stories.
He's so cute...
Liling-Po--he's too cute to ignore.
I'm sure millions of readers feel the same way.

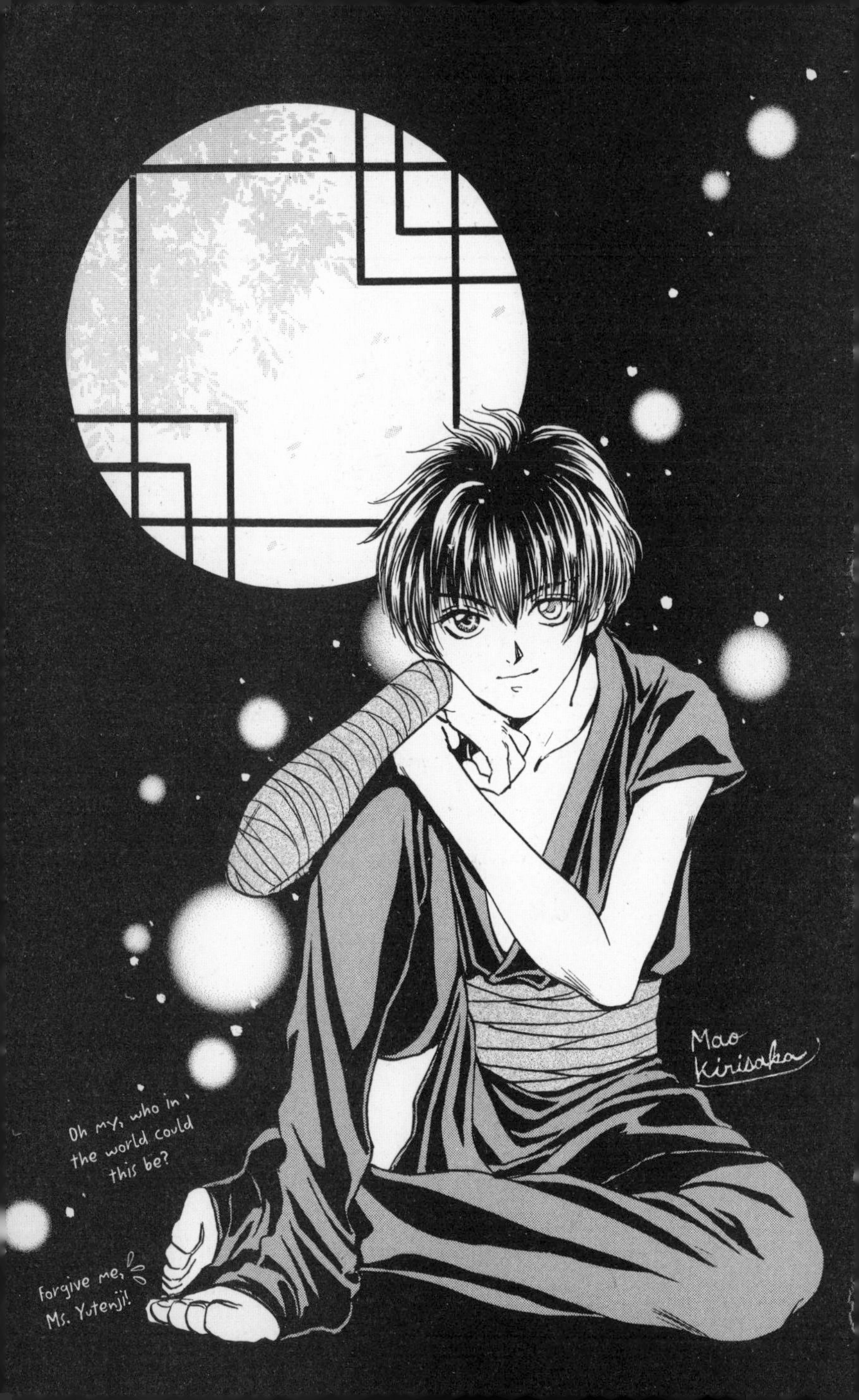
Mao Kirisaka
Oh my, who in the world could this be?
Forgive me, Ms. Yutenji!

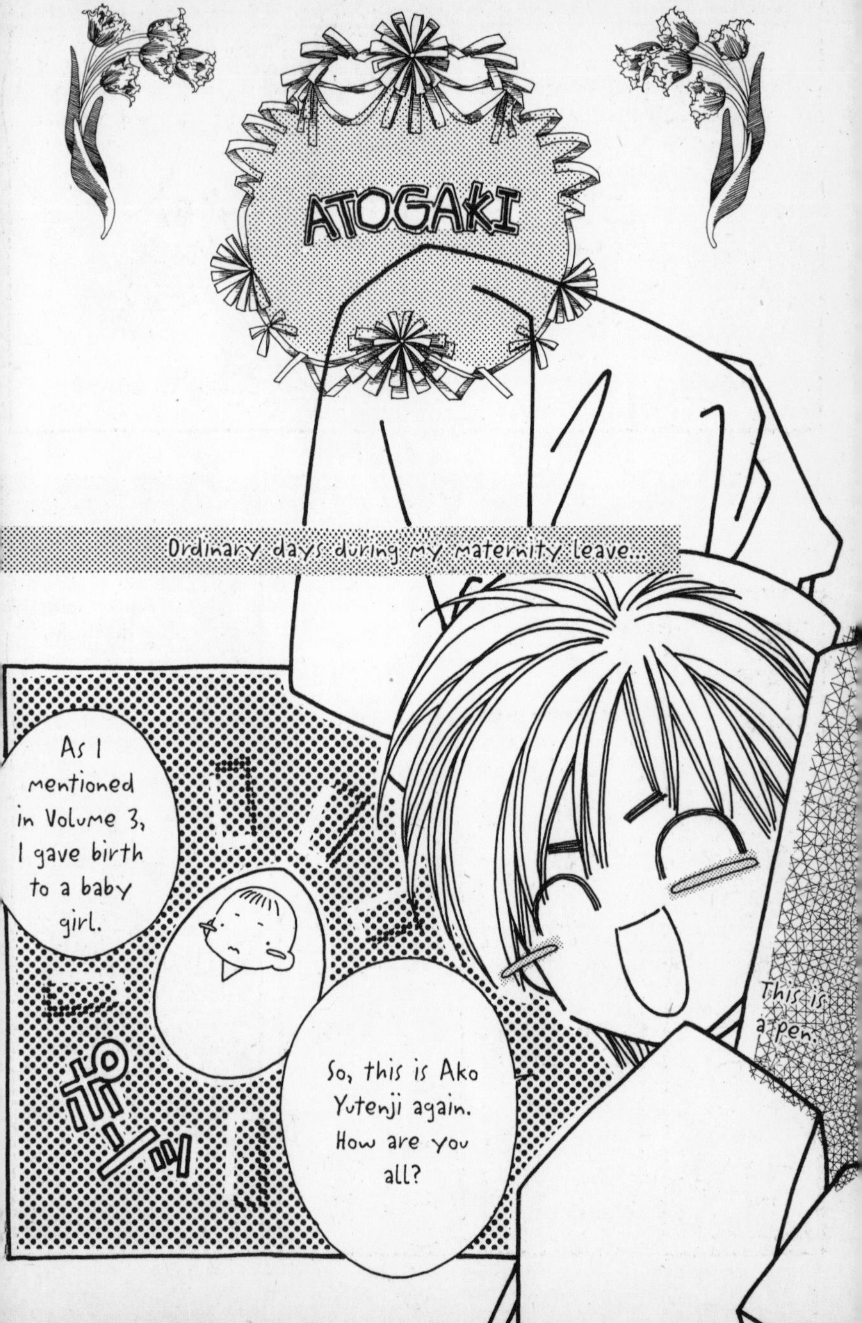
ATOGAKI
Ordinary days during my maternity leave...
So, this is Ako Yutenji again. How are you all?
As I mentioned in Volume 3, I gave birth to a baby girl.
This is a pen.

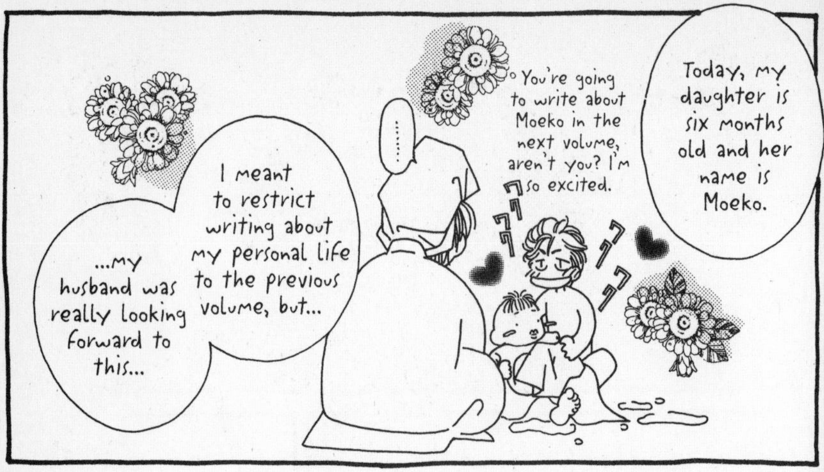
Today, my daughter is six months old and her name is Moeko.
You're going to write about Moeko in the next volume, aren't you? I'm so excited.
......
I meant to restrict writing about my personal life to the previous volume, but...
...my husband was really looking forward to this...

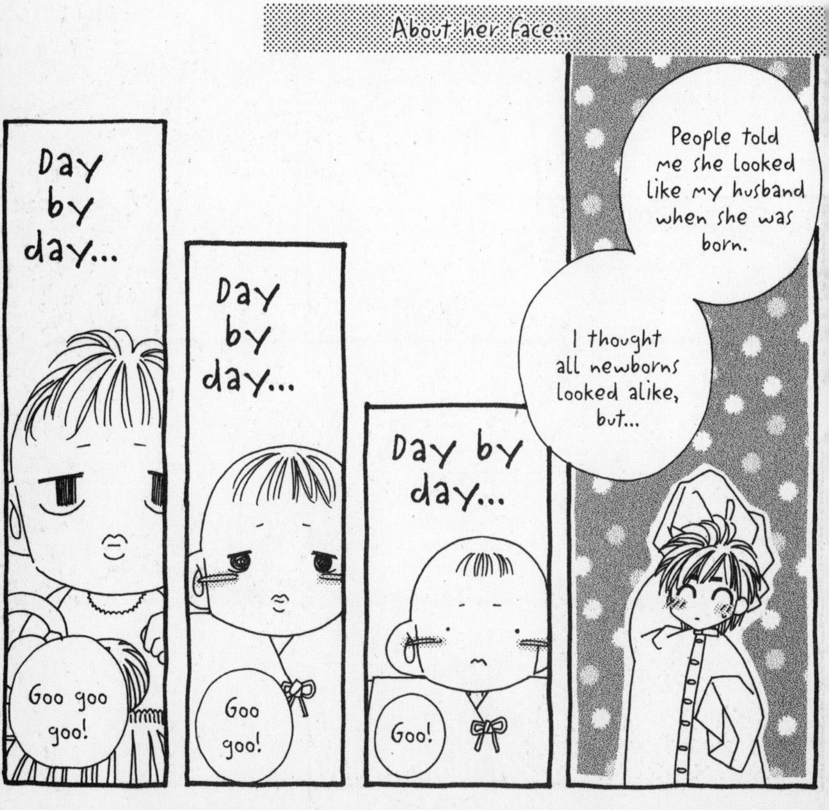
About her face...
People told me she looked like my husband when she was born.
I thought all newborns looked alike, but...
Day by day...
Goo!
Day by day...
Goo goo!
Day by day...
Goo goo goo!

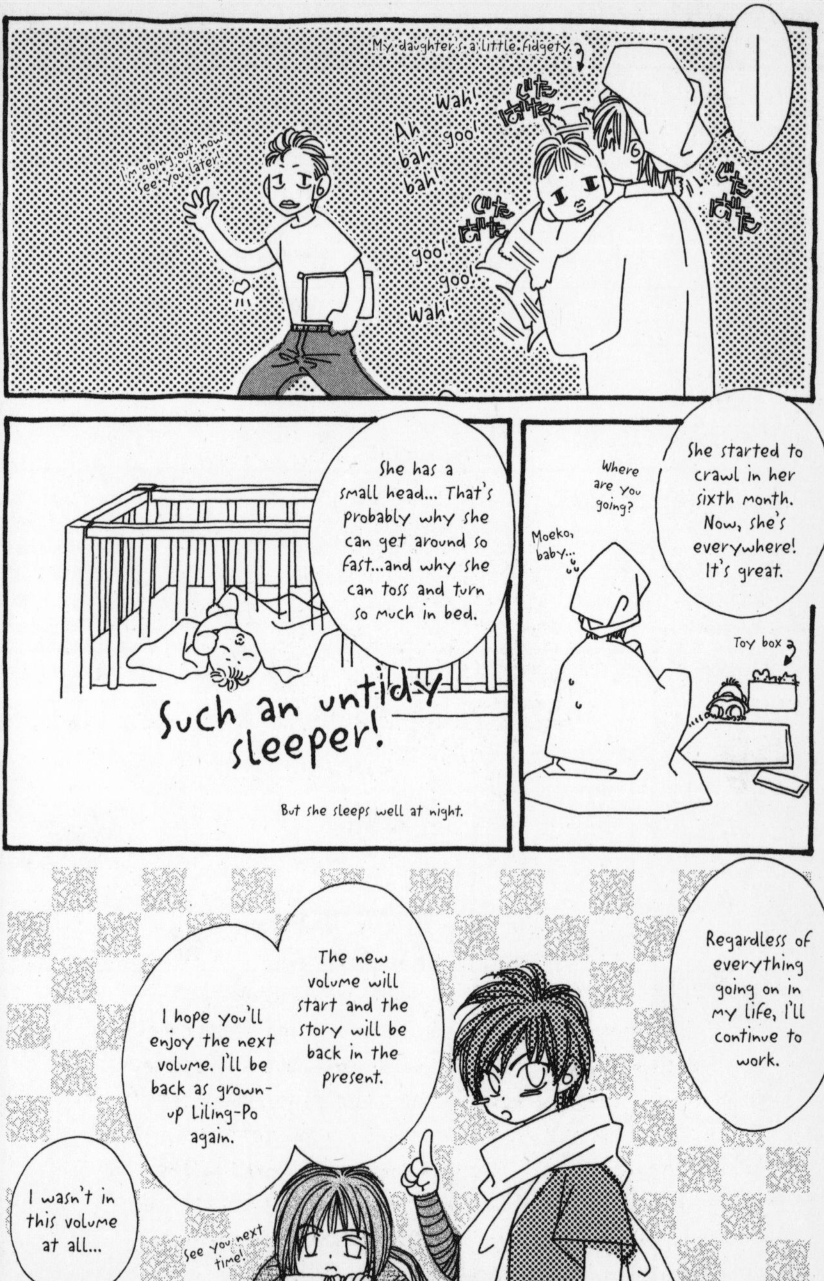

ぐたばた
My daughter's a little fidgety
ぐたばた
Wah! goo!
Ah bah bah!
ぐたばた
goo! goo! wah!
I'm going out now. See you later!
She started to crawl in her sixth month. Now, she's everywhere! It's great.
Where are you going?
Moeko, baby...
Toy box
She has a small head... That's probably why she can get around so fast...and why she can toss and turn so much in bed.
Such an untidy sleeper!
But she sleeps well at night.
Regardless of everything going on in my life, I'll continue to work.
The new volume will start and the story will be back in the present.
I hope you'll enjoy the next volume. I'll be back as grown-up Liling-Po again.
I wasn't in this volume at all...
See you next time!

Costume requests and single page
manga art ideas wanted!
Tell me if you have a character
in Liling-Po that you would like to see in specific
costumes. Also, let me know if you have any stories
you want me to write as single page manga art.
Send ideas by regular mail or in fan letters. I'm
planning to include the completed works in the
next postscript. You may not get exactly what you
want, but I'll do my best! I'm looking forward to
hearing from you all.

August, 1999 - Ako Yutenji

See you!

In the next volume of

LI LING ◆ PO

When Liling-Po and company
arrive at a mysterious village
where child labor is a common
practice, they meet a boy named
Kei-sho who claims that he has
one of the eight great treasures.
But everything isn't exactly as it
appears to be, and when Kei-sho's
treasure turns out to be a fake,
Liling-Po's journey may be taking
a turn for the worse...

that I'm not like other people...

BIZENGHAST

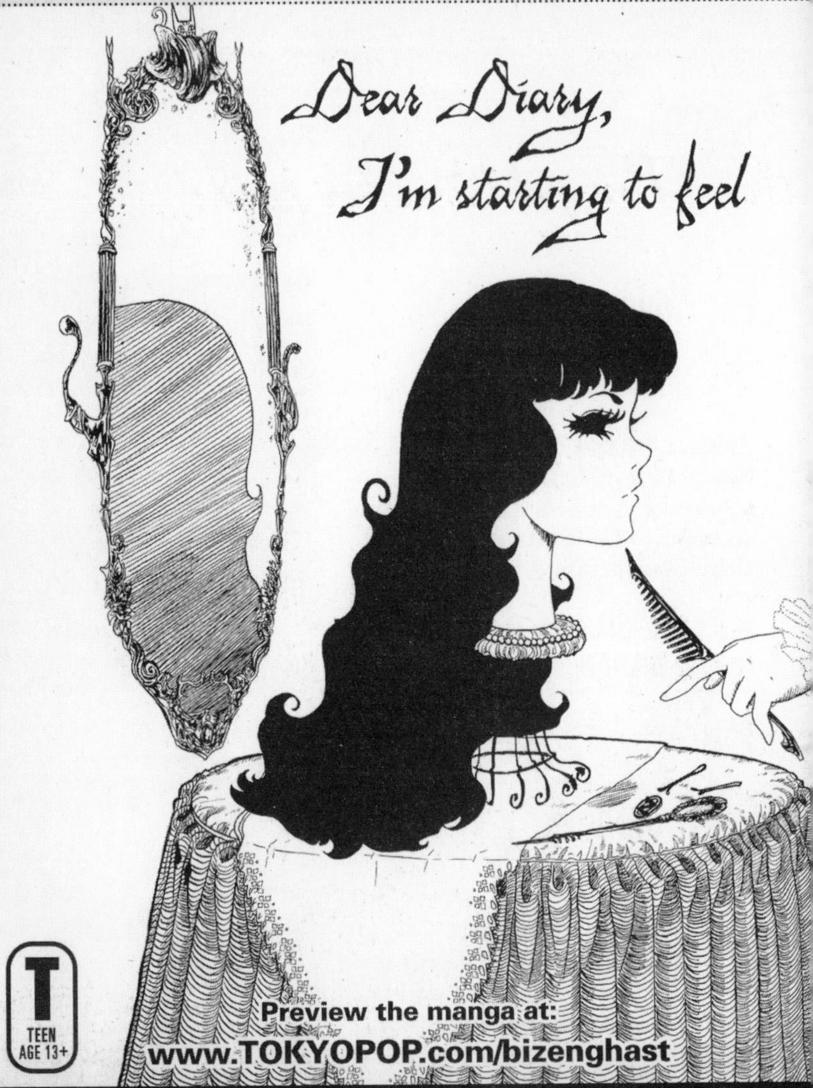
Dear Diary,
I'm starting to feel
TEEN
AGE 13+
Preview the manga at:
www.TOKYOPOP.com/bizenghast

When a young girl moves to the forgotten town of Bizenghast, she uncovers a terrifying collection of lost souls that leads her to the brink of insanity. One thing becomes painfully clear: The residents of Bizenghast are just dying to come home.

THIS FALL, TOKYOPOP CREATES A FRESH, NEW CHAPTER IN TEEN NOVELS...

For Adventurers...

Witches' Forest:
The Adventures of Duan Surk

By Mishio Fukazawa
Duan Surk is a 16-year-old Level 2 fighter who embarks on the quest of a lifetime—battling mythical creatures and outwitting evil sorceresses, all in an impossible rescue mission in the spooky Witches' Forest!

BASED ON THE FAMOUS
FORTUNE QUEST **WORLD**

For Dreamers...

Magic Moon

By Wolfgang and Heike Hohlbein
Kim enters the enigmatic realm of Magic Moon, where he battles unthinkable monsters and fantastical creatures—in order to unravel the secret that keeps his sister locked in a coma.

THE WORLDWIDE BESTSELLING FANTASY
THRILLOGY **ARRIVES IN THE U.S.!**

TOKYOPOP PRESENTS

POP FICTION

For Believers...

Scrapped Princess:
A Tale of Destiny

By Ichiro Sakaki

A dark prophecy reveals that the queen will give birth to a daughter who will usher in the Apocalypse. But despite all attempts to destroy the baby, the myth of the "Scrapped Princess" lingers on...

THE INSPIRATION FOR THE HIT ANIME AND MANGA SERIES!

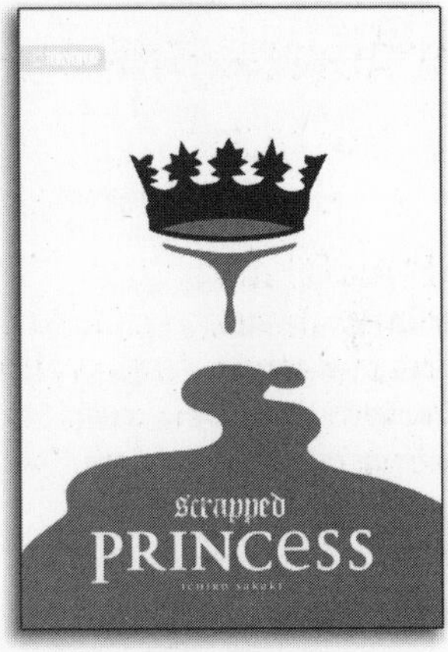
TOKYOPOP
Scrapped
PRINCESS
Ichiro Sakaki

For Thinkers...

Kino no Tabi:
Book One of The Beautiful World

By Keiichi Sigsawa

Kino roams the world on the back of Hermes, her unusual motorcycle, in a journey filled with happiness and pain, decadence and violence, and magic and loss.

THE SENSATIONAL BESTSELLER IN JAPAN HAS FINALLY ARRIVED!

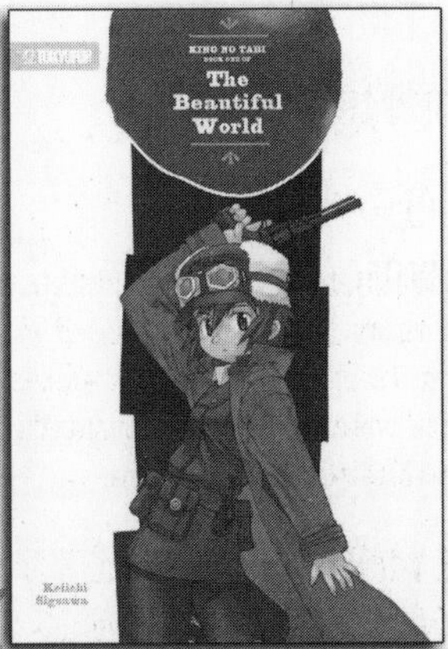
TOKYOPOP
KINO NO TABI
BOOK ONE OF
The Beautiful World
Keiichi Sigsawa

TOKYOPOP SHOP

STOP!

This is the back of the book.
You wouldn't want to spoil a great ending!

This book is printed "manga-style," in the authentic Japanese right-to-left format. Since none of the artwork has been flipped or altered, readers get to experience the story just as the creator intended. You've been asking for it, so TOKYOPOP® delivered: authentic, hot-off-the-press, and far more fun!

DIRECTIONS

If this is your first time reading manga-style, here's a quick guide to help you understand how it works.

It's easy... just start in the top right panel and follow the numbers. Have fun, and look for more 100% authentic manga from TOKYOPOP®!